LIVING HEAVEN HERE ON EARTH

Finding the Divinity Within You

notionpress
.com

LIVING HEAVEN HERE ON EARTH

Finding the Divinity Within You

ROBERT KHARSHIING

notionpress.com

Notion Press

Old No. 38, New No. 6

McNichols Road, Chetpet

Chennai - 600 031

First Published by Notion Press 2015

ISBN: 978-93-5206-309-3

Brief Note on the Author

Robert Kharshiing lives a simple life in an old cottage at the foothills of the Himalayas in the mountainous state called Meghalaya. As a Realized Soul, he spends most of his time now in silence, prayer and meditation. He served from 2002–2008 as a Member of Parliament in the Rajya Sabha, India's Upper House of Parliament, equivalent to the US Senate in the US or the House of Lords in the UK. Earlier to that, he served as a Member of the Legislative Assembly (MLA) in Meghalaya. He founded in 2002 the Grand Council of all the Tribal Kings, Rajahs and Chieftains in the State of Meghalaya and is its former Chairman. He hails from a longstanding and respected political family. Two uncles earlier before him were elected to India's Parliament. His Uncle, Hoover Hynniewta was a Member of Parliament in India's Lok Sabha (equivalent to the House of Representatives in the US or the House of Commons in the UK), while his late Uncle, Alexander Warjri served as an MP in India's Upper House of Parliament, Rajya Sabha.

Robert was the Co-Chairman, Indo-European Union Forum of Parliamentarians. He was an active member of the Indo-US Forum of Parliamentarians and visited the US a number of times with the Federation of Indian Chambers of Commerce and Industry (FICCI). He attended the Inaugural India-Yale Parliamentary Leadership Program at Yale University in a group of 10 Indian Members of Parliament. He visited Japan as part of an All-Party delegation with the Confederation of Indian Industry (CII). He also travelled to China on the invitation of the Chinese Communist Party. Kharshiing also served for many years in the Parliamentary Consultative Committee on Defense which is always headed by the Defence Minister of India.

His late father, Dr Martin Narayan Majaw was a Finance, Law and Revenue Minister in the State of Meghalaya and was a long time State Legislator. His late Mother, Edith Kharshiing was a lifelong co-worker with the late Mother Teresa. His parents helped Mother acquire land within the State of Meghalaya for the Sisters to set up homes for lepers and the poorest. His aunt, Sister Julia Narayan Majaw is a Catholic Nun currently serving the poorest in the Indian State of West Bengal near the Bangladesh border. Robert's relatives and family members live in the UK, Singapore, Canada, Armenia, France, Germany, USA, Russia, Australia and India.

Because millions of people in rural India are poor, and being deeply influenced by the teachings of Mahatma Gandhi and the example of Mother Teresa, he had consciously decided throughout his political life of 30 years to live a simple life, devoid of many material possessions. Robert does not own a car. He prefers to walk, take a bus or taxi and ride on the rickshaw like millions of ordinary Indians do. He feels this is his tiny contribution to preserving the environment and reduce pollution.

Mr. Kharshiing is a teetotaler. He does not drink or smoke. Besides his beloved parents and grandparents, he has been deeply influenced by the life, example and teachings of St. John Bosco and the Salesians of India, Lord Jesus and Mother Mary, Lord Buddha, Shri Nisargadatta Maharaj, Mother Teresa, Stanley Nichols Roy, Frank Buchman, Mahatma Gandhi, Captain John and Jeane Faber, many heroic friends in Moral Re-Armament which is now called Initiatives of Change, Dr. Vinod Mittal and his family in Mumbai and Anna Hazare.

After uncovering his Inner Self and finding the Kingdom of God within, his priorities changed. Though he continued in politics, his attention turned inwards more and more. Gradually withdrawing from public life, he increasingly found unspeakable joy in spending time in solitude and meditation.

Preface

My intention in writing this book is to lead you to your Source – the Kingdom of God within you. In finding that Source within yourself, you unearth Nirvana or Self Realization. The more time you spend with your Source, the more enlightened you become. The prophet Zoroaster spent 30 years in contemplation and solitude. I am not asking you to do the same. All I am doing is emphasizing how crucial finding your Real Self is in your life. All the problems that you may be having now are solved when you locate and reach Nothingness or the Void within. Since finding Realization, I feel that I am living Heaven here on earth. There is just continual joy and cheerfulness in my life. I deeply wish the same for you my brothers and sisters, mothers and fathers, those feeling alone, grandfathers and grandmothers, children and youngsters, rich and poor. You may belong to any faith, race, culture, colour or country. It does not matter. You may not even believe in any faith or religion. It does not matter. The One who created you loves you infinitely, more than any father would love his son or his daughter. The Eternal One, the Divine One is the best friend that you can ever have.

Search for the Divine within you by reading, praying often and by practising being silent, still and keeping an empty mind. After you have finished reading this book cover to cover, start again but much slower. Read a few lines or a paragraph and then pause. Think intensely and sincerely about the words in this book. What I am teaching is nothing new. It is as old as Eternity itself and yet ever new. No other subject that you will ever study in school, college or university can match the immensity of this subject. This subject is Life itself. If you master this subject, you will live forever happily. The great Masters and Teachers throughout history taught practically the same thing but using different words and languages suited to the times or period in which they lived. Find other spiritual books which inspire you. You need not stick to me or to this book. Not all will find this book appealing. It hardly matters. What is important is that you find the Joy of the Divinity within you. If not me, then for your own sake, look for some other teacher whom you can follow or read. Whoever you feel drawn to spiritually, follow that Master until you uncover the Secret of Happiness within you. Slowly you will go beyond any book or any Master, because your relationship with the Divine is yours alone. We are here just to guide you on the way. Ultimately, it is your journey. But my friends, never stop until you reach the Eternal Spring where you will never be thirsty again, where you will never be sad again, where you will never worry again and where you will find Happiness unending here on earth itself. I pray fervently that you my friends receive the greatest gift the Divine can give which is that you unearth the most fabulous treasure within your innermost self – your own Divinity.

Acknowledgement

I would like to express my heartfelt gratitude to my wife Nune Grigoryan who saw me through this book, who provided support, talked things over, read, wrote, offered comments and assisted in the editing, proofreading and design.

Contents

Blessings And Keys To Happiness For Everyone Throughout Time!! Seven Blessings And Seven Secret Keys To Happiness

1

Why Seven Blessings and Seven Secret Keys?

Seven is a sacred number. In Buddhism, Buddha is said to have walked 7 steps after his birth. In Hinduism, there are seven worlds in the universe, seven seas in the world and seven Rishis (seven saints) called sapta rishis. In the Bible, Genesis 1, the number 7 signifies 'Divine Perfection or a Divine Task fulfilled both physical and spiritual.' God's number is 7. We can say that the foundation of God's word is the number 7. There are about 860 references where 7 or 'sevenfold' and 'seventh' is used in the Bible. In Islam, the number of layers of the Earth is seven. The number of layers of Heaven is seven. In Japanese mythology, the Seven Lucky Gods mention the seven gods of good fortune. Among Native American Indians, in Cherokee cosmology, the number seven is of great importance. Just like the Khasi tribe of north-east India, the number seven represents the seven clans of the Cherokee Native Americans.

Here are **Seven Blessings** for each one of you wherever you are in the world:

- Be Blessed. Whoever reads this book with reverence daily even if just a few lines a day, may the Eternal bless in a special way. You take one step to uncover the Eternal within you; God will take a trillion steps towards you. So treasure and study this book. May you be faithful to the exercise of reading, of being silent, of being still and of being an Empty Mind everyday especially when it is not easy.
- Be Blessed. Those in great difficulty, sorrow and depression would receive plenty of joy and happiness as they begin reading this

book because hidden in this book are the secrets and riches of all faiths throughout history.

- Be Blessed. The Eternal was never born and will never die. May you and all future generations in your family be under the special care and protection of the Eternal One.
- Be Blessed. May all those who seek change in their lives find powerful transformation through the sacred teachings contained in this book. May the lessons learnt from all the great Masters and Teachers of history be beneficial to you and your loved ones. May your life never be the same again. May you find what you seek and may you become what you wish to become.
- Be Blessed. Listen to the 'Still Small Voice in your heart' and listen to God's whispers in your Silence. It was Mahatma Gandhi who said "The only tyrant I accept in this world is the 'still small voice' within me." Ask your Inner Voice for guidance and direction before taking any steps in your life, however small and insignificant. Then if you seek Divine Wisdom, advice and help, it shall be accurately and precisely given to you without fail.
- Be Blessed. There shall be no want and scarcity in the homes of those who follow the Eternal as taught in this book. May God take care of all your needs, spiritual and material. All the needs of those who obey and follow faithfully the sacred guidance from the ages contained in these pages will be taken care of. The Eternal Wisdom will help and assist all who seek advice.
- Be Blessed. Use the prayers for healing written in this book. Have faith and you shall be healed by the God who created everything in the Universe from Nothing. May you be cured and protected from all diseases and sicknesses. May every ailment leave you right now and may the Creator make you whole and healthy at this moment.

These are the Seven Secrets to live a very Happy Life:

1. Do not hurt anyone. Before you do or say anything in your life, ask yourself whether I am hurting anybody. If the answer is 'Yes', then don't do it. Never hurt anyone because it will come back to hurt you at some point. Avoid speaking ill against others. No one likes a gossiper. If you see something good in anyone, you can tell that person. But

if you see wrong in anyone, then be silent and instead look inwards at yourself to see where you can improve. Often we are sad and depressed because we roll over in our mind the grievances we have against others. Ignoring such negative thoughts will give you much peace and calm. Love also means not hurting others. Take special care of your loved ones. It is easy to love friends whom you do not live with. It is not easy to love your own family with whom you live daily. Familiarity breeds contempt. Therefore, show great affection for your father, mother, brother, sister, grandfather, grandmother, wife, husband, children and anyone who lives with you. Ignore their mistakes. Everyone makes mistakes. God always loves you. You must show the same love to your dearest ones.

2. Everyday practice being alone Silent and Still. You can start with 20 minutes in the morning and 20 minutes before going to bed. The moment you get up, wish God or the Eternal 'Good morning.' Be positive and avoid getting into arguments or getting angry. It is good to begin well in the morning. As you go on in life, you will realize that you enjoy more and more these moments of silence in solitude. And you will increase their frequency during the day. Just as your body hungers for food every now and then, your soul will hunger for these times of quiet.
3. Be loyal and faithful to God. No matter what, be consistent in your practice of Silence. Even if you are distracted, it doesn't matter. Remember that you went to school every day many years even when you did not feel like it.
4. Pray often and keep praying till your requests are granted. Make sure that what you ask for is genuine and good.

   Jesus taught in Matthew 7:7-11 "Ask, and it shall be given you; seek, and ye shall find; knock, and it shall be opened unto you: For every one that asketh receiveth; and he that seeketh findeth; and to him that knocketh it shall be opened. Or what man is there of you, whom if his son ask bread, will he give him a stone? Or if he ask a fish, will he give him a serpent?

   If ye then, being evil, know how to give good gifts unto your children, how much more shall your Father which is in heaven give good things to them that ask him?" King James Version

Jesus also taught us to be persistent. Read Luke 11:5-13 'And he said to them: "Which of you will have a friend and will go to him in the middle of the night, and will say to him: 'Friend, lend me three loaves, because a friend of mine has arrived from a journey to me, and I do not have anything to set before him.' And from within, he would answer by saying: 'Do not disturb me. The door is closed now, and my children and I are in bed. I cannot get up and give it to you.'

Yet if he will persevere in knocking, I tell you that, even though he would not get up and give it to him because he is a friend, yet due to his continued insistence, he will get up and give him whatever he needs.' – The Sacred Bible Catholic (Public Domain).

Make sure that what you ask for is genuine and good.

5. Be thankful always. To practice gratefulness, make a list of things that you need to be grateful for and say 'Thank you God' for each one of them. You will be pleasantly surprised at the many things you asked for in prayer but forgot to remember and thank God after you received them. Remember there are Three Magical Words – 'Please, Sorry and Thank you'
6. Be honest. You can buy a new mobile, a new car or a new house but you cannot buy a new reputation. So wherever you are, be honest. Whether you work in a company or as a farmer, work to the best and highest of your ability. If others are dishonest, don't follow their example. You set the highest standards of honesty and integrity.
7. Be humble. Look at our Mother Earth. It supports all of us and the whole of life. Yet it is so humble that it allows us to trample on it, walk on it without complaining. When we build huge tall skyscrapers and all sorts of construction on mother earth, it just bears the heavy burden without a word of complaint. Be humble enough to say 'Sorry' when you make mistakes in life. It requires great courage to say 'Sorry'. It is easier to lie and cover-up. But you can only improve your character if you learn to say 'Sorry'. Leaders who say sorry do not lower their dignity. It only enhances the respect that people have for them. The common man has lots of compassion and forgiveness. They expect their leaders to say sorry when they make mistakes. Yes, it is not easy. It is tough. Are you tough enough? Do not make a halfhearted apology. If you say sorry, do it with all the sincerity of your heart. People can easily see through when you are not genuine.

Oneness 2

Question: Why is Oneness so important? What happens when our mind is empty, when it is blank and when we are totally one with God?

Answer: Oneness with all around us is at the heart of everything. It is the fruit of Self Realization. Oneness is the essence of Divinity. Oneness is another word for Love. Oneness overcomes anger, fear and hatred. In fact, Oneness conquers death itself. When we are one with God, we are one with ourselves and the whole Universe. Oneness is found in the Void or Emptiness or Nothingness. It is a strange contradiction that we find Everything by becoming Nothing. We find Divinity by being Empty. We discover the best Treasure when we discard all things to be the Void. Empty yourself and become ALL.

To reach the Oneness within you, daily practise silence, stillness and emptiness of mind. As you focus yourself and remain in that silence and state of Emptiness, you will find that after some time, deep breathing begins naturally, right down to the core. What is amazing is that without any effort on your part, you find that your whole body begins to breathe in and out very deeply by itself. We become full of joy and filled with utter peace of mind. There are no evil thoughts against anybody because the mind is empty. In this state, I am not hurting anybody. There are absolutely no worries. You become calm and tranquil with no feelings. There is just a sense of contentment. All your nerves, veins, tissues and the whole body relaxes. Miracles occur around you. Important things are done and completed just like that. Things happen in your favour. Angels help you through people who come into your life at the right moment. All your needs including financial are taken care of. Your character and personality transforms itself for the better without any effort from your side. Life gets better and better. You are able to help others around you.

One takes right decisions. You feel as if there are twenty thousand or thirty thousand angels protecting you at all times. Life becomes full of beautiful unexpected surprises. Your dreams come true one by one. You feel free. You can live anywhere and travel anywhere. Trust me, it is the best life on earth. Being one with God is like being one with the President of the Universe. You feel one with the whole of Creation. You can do all things. Oneness has no beginning and no end. It is just unending, eternal joy. The moment you are empty, God fills you with his presence and his blessings. It is the greatest feeling on earth.

Be one with the trees, be one with the earth, be one with the animals, be one with the forests, be one with the grass, be one with the plants, be one with the insects, be one with the mountains, be one with the hills, be one with the streams, be one with the rain, be one with the waterfalls, be one with the sea, be one with the ocean, be one with the fishes, be one with the glaciers, be one with the Arctic and Antarctic regions, be one with all mankind, be one with the stars, be one with the galaxies, be one with the moon, be one with the exalted Masters who lived before you and be one with the Divine.

A story about Oneness:

Once upon a time, a seeker of Truth asks an Enlightened Master, 'Teacher, who are you? Are you an American? Are you English? Are you Japanese? Are you Chinese? Are you German? Are you Russian? Are you an Indian? Are you French? Are you Korean? When I look at you in your appearance and attire, I cannot make out who you are. You could be anybody. Why do you remain silent to this question? Why don't you answer me? Are you the reincarnation of the Lord Buddha? Are you the Lord Jesus? Are you Lord Krishna? Or are you the reincarnation of Swami Vivekananda? Are you a Christian monk? Are you a Hindu monk? Are you a Buddhist monk? Or are you a Muslim mystic saint? Please answer me.

The Master replies "Let me tell you a story. A man stands on the shores of the Atlantic Ocean and asks the ocean "Who are you? Many rivers flow into you. I wish to identify myself with just one river. Are you the Connecticut River? Are you the Delaware River? Are you the Hudson River? Are you the Mississippi River? Are you the Rio Grande?" The ocean keeps silent initially but seeing the man's persistence, replies "I am none of the above and yet I am all of the above." Unsatisfied the man then went to the shores of the Pacific Ocean and called out "Tell me which river are you? I want to journey on and link myself with just one river. Are you the Sacramento River? Are you the Columbia River? Are you the River Hood? Are you the River Klamath? Like the Atlantic Ocean, the Pacific Ocean then replied "No, I am none of them. Yet, I am all of them." So it is I tell you that "I am none of what you think me to be and yet I am all of what you think me to be. I am not any of them but I embrace all of them. Just as the rivers that you have named, after reaching the ocean, lose their identity and become one with the ocean, so have I become one with all creation. I am the sky and not just the clouds. I am the mountain and not just the snow. I am the tree and not just the leaves. I am the Universe and not just one star. I am Eternity and not just 90 years of your life."

Nothing can match the beauty of that Emptiness, of being one with that Oneness. No words can describe the Joy and Happiness. It is indescribable. It is beyond words and thoughts. That Oneness is the Greatest Love. Temporary and fickle human love pales in comparison to that Eternal Love. That Oneness is the Greatest Pleasure. Human pleasure is fleeting and full of pain. But divine love is untold bliss, joy, free and never ending. You never get tired of it. Once you have experienced that Eternal Love, you feel like experiencing it again and again. You feel hungry spiritually when you are away from it for a long time. You always yearn for that Eternal Love. All human love is but the tiniest reflection of Eternal Love. That is why they say that Hell is actually being far away from God.

ONENESS – ETERNAL:

1. Pray for Oneness, to live the Eternal, to walk as the Eternal. O Thou One with me as I am one with Thee, I ask Thee for more & more Oneness with Thee until your Thoughts become my thoughts, your Actions become my actions. I ask Thee that I walk as the Eternal and live as the Eternal.
2. Pledge yourself to walk as the Eternal, to work full time with the Eternal.

   Great Intelligent One, my Creator, we pledge ourselves to work full time with Thee & to walk on this Earth as the Eternal. Please take care of us.

Who is God? 3

The Character of the Supreme One - The many Qualities of God: All Power, Creator, Empty, Eternal, Formless, indescribable Beauty, Invisible, Life & Healing, Peace & Calm, Silent, Still, unbelievable Bliss, super Intelligence, Unknown, Pure Love, Light & Darkness, Source of all Energy, deepest Compassion, all Pervasive, Omni-present, as Pure and Innocent as a new born child, never born, never will die, Kindness and Gentleness, all-Knowing, Unheard, Unknown, Unseen, Oneness, Real, True, Untold Wisdom, Unbelievable Joy and Happiness, Fantastic Wealth, Just Being, Awareness, Consciousness, Goodness, One finds God in emptiness, The Void, Harmony. He is childlike, Absolute Purity at all times; He has no beginning and no end, Timeless and Ageless, present here and everywhere.

May I humbly suggest that you spend time to ponder and think about each one of the above Attributes of God. I cannot emphasize enough how important this is. It is the most important task in your life. **Nothing else matters as much as this, that you daily think about and study the nature of God.** It will change your life. When you study God, you fall in love with the Divine Person. God then comes after you in a way. You will feel Divine love envelop you and every aspect of your life. Your life becomes magical bliss. What I have attempted to describe through these writings is nothing because The Eternal is beyond all description. You have to experience yourself the unbelievable warmth, love, joy and happiness that fills and surrounds anyone who searches to understand the nature of God.

Silence is the language of the Eternal Lord. You will hear God in silence. In utter and deep silence, one can hear the creative vibration of God's sound. It is the most beautiful language. From silence emerges the greatest music, the most inspiring words and the most wonderful sounds of nature. God gave man two ears and just one mouth, but we speak much more than we listen. It's time we speak more than we listen. God speaks to us in the silence of our heart. He whispers to us without uttering a word. If we listen, He can teach us such unbelievable Wisdom. The best time to be silent is very early morning or at night. Try to be alone if possible. Switch off your TV, mobile and radio. If you are on your own, then close the door, so that no one disturbs your privacy. If you are a company, try having a silent room where any of your staff can go to recollect themselves. You will find productivity of your company improving dramatically. Mother Teresa taught us "God is the friend of silence. See how nature - trees, flowers, grass- grows in silence; see the stars, the moon and the sun, how they move in silence... We need silence to be able to touch souls."

"God writes the gospel not in the Bible alone, but on trees and flowers and clouds and stars." - Martin Luther (10 November 1483 – 18 February 1546)

"Listen, O heavens, to what I am saying. Let the earth hear the words of my mouth. Let my doctrine accumulate like the rain. Let my eloquence form like the dew, like a mist upon the plants, and like water droplets upon the grass." - Deuteronomy 32:1-2

"Believe an expert: you will find something far greater in the woods than in books. Trees and stones will teach you that which you cannot learn from the masters." - St. Bernard of Clairvaux (1090-1153), renowned French abbot and author.

Stillness is the fastest movement. Nothing can match the speed of stillness. The moment you are completely still, instantaneously, much faster than a fraction of a second, you reach the presence of the Eternal. Much more can be accomplished by stillness than by mindless activity. Try it and you will be pleasantly surprised. Stillness is the speed of God. He completes everything in stillness.

Emptiness is the Source of all things. When one sees the Void, the Emptiness, the Vacuum, the Blankness, one sees the awesome face of the Eternal.

Every day set aside time to be silent, to be still, to think about God, to listen to your innermost thoughts.

Just as the mobile or laptop or computer had an inventor or manufacturer, the human body had a Maker. God created us. We need to discover our Maker and Creator. That is the most important task of our lives. Nothing is as important. To learn about God is the greatest school, college, Institute or University that one can attend. Why is this important? Because studying at this University will benefit and last us forever, for all Eternity and not for just this human lifespan of 80 to 120 years. How do we attend this school or University? We study in this Divine University by spending time in silence. Just as we have specific hours when we attend school or college; we need to spend time daily in silence and stillness. Why? Because just as a teacher or professor teaches us using a particular language that we understand, God teaches us using His language. What is God's language? God's language is silence. In utter silence of both mind and lips, God teaches us without us even being aware of absorbing Eternal Teaching. We just have to be silent and still every day for Divine Wisdom to gradually flood our being. We will be amazed at the changes that take place in our thinking, our behaviour and our habits. We will be transformed without any effort on our part. Many old bad habits will just fall away and disappear over time. All we have to do is be disciplined, persistent and consistent in setting aside regular time every day to be Silent & Still. How long should be set aside each day for Silence? As long as possible. You will find that you slowly enjoy it so much that you slip into silence at every available time. You can begin at practising Silence first thing in the morning after washing your face, then again a bit later when you feel less groggy. You should spend some time in Silence before going to bed. Then throughout the day, you can slip into silence and stillness wherever you are. Try doing that while waiting for a bus or taxi, in the toilet, in the office, at school or at work. It will calm and de-stress you. It will help you work better, plan better, study better and be much more peaceful and happier. A human body without Silence and Stillness is like a torch without a battery – dead with no light and no use to anybody.

You have found the Kingdom of God when you love all of God's children no matter what their religion or colour or background. In Matthew 6:33, Jesus said "But seek ye first the kingdom of God, and his righteousness; and all these things shall be added unto you."

You have found Self Realization/Samadhi when you practise what the Bhagavad Gita teaches

'This Inner Realization is the Sovereign of sciences, the noble secret, the unrivalled cleanser, the real meaning of the path of righteousness. It is the direct awareness of truth—the eternal illumination, extremely blissful to carry out' - The Bhagavad Gita Chapter 9, Verse 2

Divine Consciousness is the knowing—in body, mind, and soul—that we are one with the Eternal - that we are not merely near it at all times, but that God's Oneness is our Oneness - that we are just as much a part of Him now as we ever will be.

All we have to do is improve our Awareness.

You have found Nirvana, a state of supreme liberation when you follow what Buddha said 'The wise achieve the highest blessing, nirvana."

You will go to Paradise when you obey what Muhammad taught 'You will not go into paradise until you have belief. And you will not achieve your belief until you love one another.'

You are one with the Eternal as the Eternal is one with you.

Jesus told us in John 15:4-7 "Abide in me, and I in you. Just as the branch is not able to bear fruit of itself, unless it abides in the vine, so also are you unable, unless you abide in me.

I am the vine; you are the branches. Whoever abides in me, and I in him, bears much fruit. For without me, you are able to do nothing.

If anyone does not abide in me, he will be cast away, like a branch, and he will wither, and they will gather him and cast him into the fire, and he burns.

If you abide in me, and my words abide in you, then you may ask for whatever you will, and it shall be done for you.' - Sacred Bible Catholic

In Matthew 6:19-20, Jesus teaches 'Do not choose to store up for yourselves treasures on earth: where rust and moth consume, and where thieves break in and steal.

Instead, store up for yourselves treasures in heaven: where neither rust nor moth consumes, and where thieves do not break in and steal.'

The Upanishads (Hindu spiritual texts) written about 800–200 BC -

"The one God, hidden in 'all things,
All-pervading, the Inner Soul of all things,
The Overseer of deeds, in all things abiding,
The witness, the Sole Thinker, devoid of all qualities,
The One Controller of the inactive many,
Who makes the one seed manifold—
The wise who perceive Him as standing in one's self
They, - and no others, have eternal happiness."
– Upanishads, Indian Inner and Mystic Teaching (about 800–200 BC)

Is there hope for me? 4

Qs. I am deep in sin. How can God love me?

Ans: God never condemns, he never judges. Have you ever heard in history that God ever came down himself to scold anybody? No, never. No matter how grievous the sin, he has not come down himself to condemn anyone. Jesus said in Luke 6:37: 'Judge not, and ye shall not be judged: condemn not, and ye shall not be condemned: forgive, and ye shall be forgiven.' King James Version

Do you remember the story of the woman caught in adultery? In John 8:1-11, 'Jesus went unto the mount of Olives.

And early in the morning he came again into the temple, and all the people came unto him; and he sat down, and taught them.

And the scribes and Pharisees brought unto him a woman taken in adultery; and when they had set her in the midst,

They say unto him, Master, this woman was taken in adultery, in the very act.

Now Moses in the law commanded us, that such should be stoned: but what sayest thou?

This they said, tempting him, that they might have to accuse him. But Jesus stooped down, and with his finger wrote on the ground, as though he heard them not.

So when they continued asking him, he lifted up himself, and said unto them, He that is without sin among you, let him first cast a stone at her.

And again he stooped down, and wrote on the ground.

And they which heard it, being convicted by their own conscience, went out one by one, beginning at the eldest, even unto the last: and Jesus was left alone, and the woman standing in the midst.

When Jesus had lifted up himself, and saw none but the woman, he said unto her, Woman, where are those thine accusers? Hath no man condemned thee?

She said, No man, Lord. And Jesus said unto her, Neither do I condemn thee: go, and sin no more.' King James Version

God gives rain to everybody, the sinner and the saint. He makes the Sun shine on everybody. No matter how great and how numerous your wrongdoings and sins, God still loves you. In Mark 2:15-20, 'And it happened that, as he sat at table in his house, many tax collectors and sinners sat at table together with Jesus and his disciples. For those who followed him were many.

And the scribes and the Pharisees, seeing that he ate with tax collectors and sinners, said to his disciples, "Why does your Teacher eat and drink with tax collectors and sinners?"

Jesus, having heard this, said to them: "The healthy have no need of a doctor, but those who have maladies do. For I came not to call the just, but sinners." Sacred Bible Catholic Public Domain

His love is as infinite as the Universe. His love has no beginning and no end. All you have to do is say sorry and get up.

Qs. What if I keep falling? I have tried to give up this bad habit many times but each time have failed.

Ans: Never give up. Keep saying sorry and keep starting again. After every dark cloudy day, there is the beautiful sunny day. Ignore how many times you have fallen. Instead focus on Being Daily Silent and Still. Your faults will then drop away to your utter amazement. In the end, you will win. If you start the practice of Emptying your mind, of being silent and being totally still every day, you will be surprised to find that your bad habits and weaknesses disappear by themselves one by one. This does not happen suddenly (although it could) but over a period of time. What is amazing is that without any effort from you, these failings just leave your life and you become a better person provided you faithfully and loyally keep Silent and Still often and daily. You don't even need to struggle. Your sins just fall away. You discover to your wonder that you are no longer in their grip. You are free from them.

Qs. "I am very busy. I have no time."

Ans: Well, all the more reason then for you to practise Silence and Stillness. Do you not eat every day? Do you not eat many times during the day? I do not know what you eat. But perhaps you have bed tea, breakfast, lunch, afternoon tea and dinner. Maybe, snacks too, during the day. If for the body which will last only 80-100 years you have time to feed many times during the day, how much more should you not feed the Soul which will last forever, which has never been born and will never die. That is why we are taught that the Soul is immortal. One day when you are constantly Aware and Conscious of your Eternal Being every moment of the day, then sin will have totally gone from your life. You will live as the Eternal – Walk as the Eternal. You will constantly see a bright light in your life at all times. You will experience Heaven or Paradise here on earth itself. Your life will be full of joy and happiness. Sheer bliss will fill you. Sorrow and depression, fear and hatred, stress and anxiety will leave you completely. You will always have a big smile lighting up you face. People will even ask "Why are you laughing all the time? Why are you always smiling?" It is because *Oneness with the Divine* has become your natural state and the smiling face just happens naturally without you being even conscious of it. Remember it took you a whole year of 365 days just to pass Class 1 in school. It took you many years to pass Class 10. It took you many more years to pass whatever further education you have done. For what? Just to study about our planet – its history, its sciences, its geography etc. Well, there are billions of planets out there about which we know nothing. There are billions of galaxies, stars, comets, asteroids and moons. There is Dark Matter about which we know almost nothing. Yes. Zip. Zero. Our knowledge is just a fraction of the vast knowledge of the Universe. So if we are prepared to spend years for such limited knowledge, how much more effort and time should we not put into Eternal Knowledge and Wisdom which spans the Universe. This Goodness and Transformation which comes to us in Silence and Stillness is the Highest Form of Education. Nothing even comes close to it. It is the Wisdom of the Ages. It is Timeless. It reveals the Greatest Secrets. It is the Greatest Job on earth serving the Most Majestic Boss. God is the Highest President or King that ever was and ever will be. Being with the Eternal is the best work that you can do. You become part of the Divine Royal Family. It is the most fantastic Teaching.

The Chinese Master Lao Tzu (580-500 B.C.) was a renowned philosopher of ancient China. He founded Taoism and wrote the famous Tao Te Ching, a classic Chinese treatise. Lao Tzu taught us "To the mind that is still, the whole universe surrenders." Swami Vivekananda, revered Indian monk and teacher (12 January 1863 – 4 July 1902) born in Kolkata, said:

"The greatest men in the world have passed away unknown. Silently they live and silently they pass away; and in time their thoughts find expression in Buddhas or Christs, and it is these latter that become known to us.

Better be ready to live in rags with Christ than to live in palaces without him.

It is impossible to find God outside of ourselves. We are the greatest temple.

The happiest moments we will ever know, are when we entirely forget ourselves." - Swami Vivekananda (12 January 1863 – 4 July 1902)

"Alone let him constantly meditate in solitude on that which is salutary for his soul, for he who meditates in solitude attains supreme bliss". - Guru Nanak, (Saturday 15 April 1469 - Monday 22 September, 1539), the holy founder of the Sikhs

"Thou has a thousand eyes and yet not one eye; Thou host a thousand forms and yet not one form." - Guru Nanak (1469 - 1539)

"He who is harmony with Nature hits the mark without effort and apprehends the truth without thinking."

- Confucius, eminent Chinese philosopher

"To put the world in order, we must first put the nation in order; to put the nation in order, we must put the family in order; to put the family in order, we must cultivate our personal life; and to cultivate our personal life, we must first set our hearts right."

- Confucius

"First there must be order and harmony within your own heart. Only then can there be peace and harmony in the world."

- Confucius

"Creating the world, God has made it a place to practice spirituality."

- Guru Granth Sahib (1035), the sacred Holy Book of the Sikh faith.

As St Augustine (13 November 354 AD – 28 August 430 AD) famously expressed in his Confessions "You have made us for yourself, O Lord, and our heart is restless until it rests in you." (The Confessions of Saint Augustine). Augustine born in present day Algeria, Africa lived a life of wickedness. His mother Saint Monica prayed and prayed for him to change. Before he reformed his life, his favourite prayer was "O God, make me pure, but not now." He ultimately changed his life and became one of the greatest theologians.

After his change, he prayed thus: "Great art thou, O Lord, and greatly to be praised; great is thy power, and infinite is thy wisdom... And man desires to praise thee, for he is a part of thy creation; he bears his mortality about with him and carries the evidence of his sin and the proof that thou dost resist the proud. Still he desires to praise thee, this man who is only a small part of thy creation. Thou hast prompted him, that he should delight to praise thee, for thou hast made us for thyself and restless is our heart until it comes to rest in thee. Grant me, O Lord, to know and understand whether first to invoke thee or to praise thee; whether first to know thee or call upon thee. But who can invoke thee, knowing thee not? For he who knows thee not may invoke thee as another than thou art. It may be that we should invoke thee in order that we may come to know thee. But "how shall they call on him in whom they have not believed? Or how shall they believe without a preacher?" Now, "they shall praise the Lord who seek him," for "those who seek shall find him," and, finding him, shall praise him. I will seek thee, O Lord, and call upon thee. I call upon thee, O Lord, in my faith which thou hast given me, which thou hast inspired in me through the humanity of thy Son, and through the ministry of thy preacher.

CHAPTER II

2. And how shall I call upon my God–my God and my Lord? For when I call on him I ask him to come into me. And what place is there in me into which my God can come? How could God, the God who made both heaven and earth, come into me? Is there anything in me, O Lord my God, that can contain thee? Do even the heaven and the earth, which thou hast made, and in which thou didst make me, contain thee? Is it possible that, since without thee nothing would be which does exist, thou didst make it so that whatever exists has some capacity to receive thee? Why, then, do I ask thee to come into me, since I also am and could not be if thou wert not in me? For I am not, after all, in hell–and yet thou art there too, for "if I go down into hell, thou art there." Therefore I would not exist–I would simply not be at all–unless I exist in thee, from whom and by whom and in whom all things are. Even so, Lord; even so. Where do I call thee to, when I am already in thee? Or from whence wouldst thou come into me? Where, beyond heaven and earth, could I go that there my God might come to me–he who hath said, "I fill heaven and earth"?

CHAPTER III

3. Since, then, thou dost fill the heaven and earth, do they contain thee? Or, dost thou fill and overflow them, because they cannot contain thee? And where dost thou pour out what remains of thee after heaven and earth are full? Or, indeed, is there no need that thou, who dost contain all things, shouldst be contained by any, since those things which thou dost fill thou fillest by containing them? For the vessels which thou dost fill do not confine thee, since even if they were broken, thou wouldst not be poured out. And, when thou art poured out on us, thou art not thereby brought down; rather, we are uplifted. Thou art not scattered; rather, thou dost gather us together. But when thou dost fill all things, dost thou fill them with thy whole being? Or, since not even all things together could contain thee altogether, does any one thing contain a single part, and do all things contain that same part at the same time? Do singulars contain thee singly? Do greater things contain more of thee, and smaller things less? Or, is it not rather that thou art wholly present everywhere, yet in such a way that nothing contains thee wholly?

CHAPTER IV

4. What, therefore, is my God? What, I ask, but the Lord God? "For who is Lord but the Lord himself, or who is God besides our God?" Most high, most excellent, most potent, most omnipotent; most merciful and most just; most secret and most truly present; most beautiful and most strong; stable, yet not supported; unchangeable, yet changing all

things; never new, never old; making all things new, yet bringing old age upon the proud, and they know it not; always working, ever at rest; gathering, yet needing nothing; sustaining, pervading, and protecting; creating, nourishing, and developing; seeking, and yet possessing all things. Thou dost love, but without passion; art jealous, yet free from care; dost repent without remorse; art angry, yet remainest serene. Thou changest thy ways, leaving thy plans unchanged; thou recoverest what thou hast never really lost. Thou art never in need but still thou dost rejoice at thy gains; art never greedy, yet demandest dividends. Men pay more than is required so that thou dost become a debtor; yet who can possess anything at all which is not already thine? Thou owest men nothing, yet payest out to them as if in debt to thy creature, and when thou dost cancel debts thou losest nothing thereby. Yet, O my God, my life, my holy Joy, what is this that I have said? What can any man say when he speaks of thee? But woe to them that keep silence—since even those who say most are dumb.

CHAPTER V

5. Who shall bring me to rest in thee? Who will send thee into my heart so to overwhelm it that my sins shall be blotted out and I may embrace thee, my only good? What art thou to me? Have mercy that I may speak. What am I to thee that thou shouldst command me to love thee, and if I do it not, art angry and threatenest vast misery? Is it, then, a trifling sorrow not to love thee? It is not so to me. Tell me, by thy mercy, O Lord, my God, what thou art to me. "Say to my soul, I am your salvation." So speak that I may hear. Behold, the ears of my heart are before thee, O Lord; open them and "say to my soul, I am your salvation." I will hasten after that voice, and I will lay hold upon thee. Hide not thy face from me. Even if I die, let me see thy face lest I die.

The house of my soul is too narrow for thee to come in to me; let it be enlarged by thee. It is in ruins; do thou restore it. There is much about it which must offend thy eyes; I confess and know it. But who will cleanse it? Or, to whom shall I cry but to thee? "Cleanse thou me from my secret faults," O Lord, "and keep back thy servant from strange sins." "I believe, and therefore do I speak." But thou, O Lord, thou knowest. Have I not confessed my transgressions unto thee, O my God; and hast thou not put away the iniquity of my heart? I do not contend in judgment with thee, who art truth itself; and I would not deceive myself, lest my iniquity lie even to itself. I do not, therefore, contend in judgment with thee, for "if thou, Lord, shouldst mark iniquities, O Lord, who shall stand?"

Augustine also said:

"O Holy Spirit, descend plentifully into my heart. Enlighten the dark corners of this neglected dwelling and scatter there Thy cheerful beams. God loves each of us as if there were only one of us. The world is a book and those who do not travel read only one page. We make ourselves a ladder out of our vices if we trample the vices themselves underfoot. Find out how much God has given you and from it take what you need; the remainder is needed by others.

Faith is to believe what you do not see; the reward of this faith is to see what you believe. It was pride that changed angels into devils; it is humility that makes men as angels. What does love look like? It has the hands to help others. It has the feet to hasten to the poor and needy. It has eyes to see misery and want. It has the ears to hear the sighs and sorrows of men. That is what love looks like.

Pray as though everything depended on God. Work as though everything depended on you. If we live good lives, the times are also good. As we are, such are the times. If you believe what you like in the gospels, and reject what you don't like, it is not the gospel you believe, but yourself.

Since you cannot do good to all, you are to pay special attention to those who, by the accidents of time, or place, or circumstances, are brought into closer connection with you. Indeed, man wishes to be happy even when he so lives as to make happiness impossible."

- St Augustine (354 AD – 430 AD)

How do I Change? 5

Qs. Ok. I wish to change my life. But how do I begin?

Ans: Well, get down on your knees or stand with folded hands alone in your room or wherever you are. Focus your mind on God's presence and then pray for change. If you are a Buddhist, you can pray using Buddhist prayers, if you are a Christian, pray using Christian prayers, if you are a Muslim, pray to Allah. Whatever be your faith, use the prayers of your faith. God loves and forgives and transforms all whether you are a Jew or a Buddhist or a Sikh or a follower of the Shinto religion or a Parsi or a Jain or a Catholic or an atheist. It does not matter. The Eternal created you. He cares for each one of his Creation. If you wish you can say the following prayer: "Eternal Father and God, you created me out of nothing. I am deeply sorry for the way I have been living. I am sorry for hurting you, hurting other human beings, hurting my loved ones and hurting myself. I wish to change here and now. I need your help. I know that it will not be easy. But I am willing to begin and will not give up whether I fall again or not. Help me to be silent and be still with you every day as often as I can. I know that if I just BE with you daily, you will work the transformation in my life without any effort from my side. Give me the strength to say 'No' when I am tempted. May I be aware of who I am – One with You as You are One with me. Thank you."

Qs: Why is the above prayer so long?

Ans: Well, how long do you talk to your friends on your mobile? Here you are talking to the greatest friend that you will ever have – One who will never ever betray you. After you finish saying the prayer, pause in silence for a few minutes. Try to stand still with an Empty Mind.

> This is very important. There are over 7 billion people right now on our planet. This will distinguish your prayer from so many millions storming heaven all of whom want something or the other from God.

Sri Ramakrishna Paramahamsa, a holy 19th century mystic of India (1836 - 1886) teaches 'By constantly repeating, "I am free, I am free", a man verily becomes free. On the other hand, by constantly repeating, "I am bound, I am bound", he certainly becomes bound to worldliness. The fool who says only, "I am a sinner, I am a sinner", verily drowns himself in worldliness. One should rather say: "I have chanted the name of God. How can I be a sinner? How can I be bound? - Sri Ramakrishna, a Hindu saint and reformer (1836 – 1886)

Seeker: I find it very difficult to practise silence and stillness...

Answer: Yes, I know. It is not easy. But that is no reason for you to give up. Look at the great champions of sport. They have practised hours and hours before becoming world champions and Olympic Gold Medallists. They are world champions for a period of time. You will be a world champion of God for all Eternity. So it is worth the struggle.

Get up early. It is easier in the wee hours of the morning to have an Empty Mind. There are fewer cars, less noise and less people. Switch off all sounds like radio, TV or anything which could disturb your concentration. Just like you swat away flies, swat away all thoughts which may try to crowd your mind. When you buy a cooking pot, you buy it empty so that you can cook some tasty dish in it. So too, the cooking pot of your mind has to be empty so that the delicious dish of Divine Wisdom can fill it. Another good time is late at night when the world sleeps. If you are totally silent, you can hear the Sounds of Silence at night, the Sounds of that Eternal Energy gently humming in your ears and mind. It is a healing and powerful sound.

Have you heard about a Buddhist Zen story regarding A Cup of Tea?

Nan-in, a Japanese Zen master during the Meiji era (1868-1912), received a university professor who came to inquire about Zen. Nan-in served tea. He poured his visitor's cup full, and then kept on pouring. The professor watched the overflow until he no longer could restrain himself. "It is overfull. No more will go in!" "Like this cup," Nan-in said, "you are full of your own opinions and speculations. How can I show and teach you Zen unless you first empty your cup?"

The Zen story about Being Positive.

Moving to a new City or state or country:

There was a person coming to a new village, relocating, and he was wondering if he would like it there, so he went to the Zen master and asked: do you think I will like it in this village? Are the people nice?

The master asked back: How were the people on the town where you come from? "They were nasty and greedy, they were angry and lived for cheating and stealing," said the newcomer. Those are exactly the type of people we have in this village, said the Zen master.

Another newcomer to the village visited the Zen master and asked the same question, to which the master asked: How were the people in the town where you come from? "They were sweet and lived in harmony, they cared for one another and for the land, they respected each other and they were seekers of spirit," he replied.

Those are exactly the type of people we have in this village, said the Zen master.

"Look within. Be still.

Free from fear and attachment,

Know the sweet joy of living in the way." Words of the Buddha – Dhammapada, 300 BC

Fyodor Dostoevsky (1821–1881) was a Russian novelist and philosopher

'And let not men's sin dishearten thee: love a man even in his sin, for that love is a likeness of the divine love, and is the summit of love on earth.' From The Brothers Karamazov

'Love all God's creation, both the whole and every grain of sand. Love every leaf, every ray of light. Love the animals, love the plants, and love each separate thing. If thou love each thing thou wilt perceive the mystery of God in all; and when once thou perceive this, thou wilt thenceforward grow every day to a fuller understanding of it: until thou come at last to love the whole world with a love that will then be all-embracing and universal.'

- Fyodor Dostoevsky (1821–1881)

Prayers for Change and Transformation:

Eternal One, teach me to be silent and still and empty. It is not easy for me. But I will never give up because I know that this is the Greatest Fortune. I will not give up because this is the Secret of the Highest Happiness. I am willing to keep trying until it becomes second nature to me. Help me to advance towards you by leaps and bounds. I believe that if I take a few steps towards you, You will take many more steps towards me. Help me to be one with you.

Eternal One, one with me as I am one with you, grant me the gift of self-realization and Nirvana. May I be totally free. May I uncover eternal freedom or Moksha. Let me find the Kingdom of God within me. I know that it is the greatest gift that you can give to anyone. I know that it is the gift of Eternal Life. I am not worthy. I do not deserve it. But out of your great love for me, I humbly ask you that I discover my Inner Self – my Real Self. I ask for Eternal Happiness which comes from oneness with you.

Eternal One, my father, my friend, my boss and Lord, my Creator and Maker, I come before you with folded hands.

I am sad and depressed today. Yet I know that being one with You, I am the Source of all Joy. I am the Source of all Happiness. Help me understand who I really am. I am true Joy. This depression is not me. It is unreal and fake. It will pass away.

God, O Great Spirit, who has been here from all time, Take away these fears and anxieties from me.

I know that you have taken care of me since I was born. I know that you will take care of me now and always. I was with you even before I was born. I was with you before I was with my mother. Thank you for life and for always being there.

Great Spirit, increase my faith in you. Help me at this moment. I am the Source of all power. These fears are not true. But You and your blessings are real and true.

Great One, Source of All Things, You created everything – the galaxies, the stars and the planets. Nothing is impossible for you. I am now financially in need. What I need is nothing for You. Please help me urgently. May I not be attached to material things but only come to you when I really need assistance. Thank you for all the help in the past. I am very grateful. May I also be compassionate to others in need.

Merciful One, Compassionate One, God who created us, I am deep in sin. Please help me. I cannot give up my addictions. I have tried many times but have failed. I keep sinning again and again. You can do all things, who created me out of nothing, please take over. You cure me of my addictions. I am willing to focus on being silent and still while you clean me up and rid me of my addictions. I wish to be free of sin and all bad habits. That is your wish for me and that is my deepest wish for myself. Forgive me and have mercy on me O God.

Great One, you created all that we see around us. Everything is possible for you. Lord and Master, I wish to be faithful and loyal to you. You are my boss. Right now, I have no job. Kindly help me to find a job in keeping with your wishes. I rely on you. Please assist me. Let me get a job as soon as possible. Thank you.

6 How can I really be Happy? Where can I find Happiness? How do I achieve Happiness?

Qs. How can I be happy? Can I be happy here on earth?

Ans: Repeat these words often to yourself "I am the highest Joy, the Highest Pleasure. I am the Source of Everything. All happiness is in me." Reading about these great Religions, wonderful Teachers, Masters and Prophets has given me great inspiration; their teachings have taught me the correct path to supreme bliss and happiness. Now I realize that the words Self-Realization from Hindu texts, Nirvana from the Buddhist religion, and the Kingdom of God within as propounded by Lord Jesus are one and the same - part of the same vast ocean. Reading and learning from these different teachings has been for me like eating many fruits instead of tasting just one. It has been like being nourished by many plants and vegetables instead of just one plant. This book is my humble attempt to share this great joy and happiness with you and the whole world. May you be blessed with great inner spiritual healing as I have been by these great teachers and masters who have walked this beautiful earth of ours. May this book enable you to discover and live out HEAVEN and PARADISE here on earth itself. All of my dreams in life are being fulfilled one by one. I wish the same for each one of you who read and practice what is taught in this book. My life now is a continuous journey of sweetness and happiness. I no longer feel any sorrow or depressions. It is one unending adventure of joy and blessings from above. I deeply wish the same life for you who read this book. May Heaven for you begin here and now.

A Blessing for Happiness

Metta Sutta (Sutta Nipata) about 400 B.C
'May everyone be happy and safe,
and may their hearts be filled with joy.
May all living beings live in Security and in Peace–
Beings who are frail or strong,
Tall or short, big or small,
Visible or not visible, near or far away,
Already born or yet to be born.
May all of them dwell in perfect tranquility.
Let no one do harm to anyone.
Let no one put the life of anyone in danger.
Let no one, out of anger or ill will,
wish anyone any harm.' Metta Sutta (Sutta Nipata) about 400 BC

Let these thoughts always be in your life - Cheerfulness, Gratitude, Thankfulness, Joyfulness, Appreciation. Any thought which does not have positive feelings just get rid of, the way you would do to a fly or a mosquito. Everything passes. So the negative or sad thoughts will pass and leave you. Life is short so why should one waste time wallowing in sorrow.

You are the Source of Joy. You are the Source of all Happiness. Remind yourself of that. Say it aloud if necessary. Keep repeating to yourself the following: "I am joy. I am happiness. I am not this sadness. I am not this sorrow. I am the source of all joy. I am not this depression. This unease will pass but the joy within me is forever. I am the sky and not the dark clouds. I am the ocean and not a passing storm. I am the majestic snowy mountain and not an avalanche."

"I've learned the great value of the three F's: forgive, forget and forge ahead."

- Author Unknown

"Life is huge! Rejoice about the sun, moon, flowers, and sky. Rejoice about the food you have to eat. Rejoice about the body that houses your spirit. Rejoice about the fact that you can be a positive force in the world around you. Rejoice about the love that is around you. If you want to be happy, commit to making your life one of rejoicing."

- Author Unknown

"Lord, Make me an instrument of Your peace;
Where there is hatred, let me sow love;
Where there is injury, pardon;
Where there is doubt, faith:
Where there is despair, hope;
Where there is darkness, light;
Where there is sadness, joy."

- St. Francis of Assisi

"The best way to cheer yourself up is to cheer someone else up."

- Mark Twain

"One kind word can warm three winter months."

- Japanese proverb

"An Irish Blessing"
I wish you health,
I wish you well and happiness galore.
I wish you luck for you and friends;
What could I wish you more?
May your joys be as deep as the oceans,
Your troubles as light as its foam.
And May you find, sweet peace of mind,
Wherever you may roam.

- Author: Unknown

A Happiness poem by Ella Wheeler Wilcox (November 5, 1850 – October 30, 1919). She was an American author and poet.

Seeking For Happiness

'Seeking for happiness we must go slowly;
The road leads not down avenues of haste;
But often gently winds through by ways lowly,

Whose hidden pleasures are serene and chaste.'
Seeking for happiness we must take heed
of simple joys that are not found in speed.
Eager for noon-time's large effulgent splendour,
Too oft we miss the beauty of the dawn,
Which tiptoes by us, evanescent, tender,
Its pure delights unrecognised till gone.
Seeking for happiness we needs must care
For all the little things that make life fair.
Dreaming of future pleasures and achievements
We must not let to-day starve at our door;
Nor wait till after losses and bereavements
Before we count the riches in our store.
Seeking for happiness we must prize this-
Not what will be, or was, but that which is.
In simple pathways hand in hand with duty
(With faith and love, too, ever at her side),
May happiness be met in all her beauty
The while we search for her both far and wide.
Seeking for happiness we find the way
Doing the things we ought to do each day.' Ella Wheeler Wilcox (1850 – 1919)

There Is Pleasure In The Pathless Woods - Lord George Gordon Byron (22 January 1788 – 19 April 1824)

'There is a pleasure in the pathless woods,
There is a rapture on the lonely shore,
There is society, where none intrudes,
By the deep sea, and music in its roar:
I love not man the less, but Nature more,
From these our interviews, in which I steal
From all I may be, or have been before,

To mingle with the Universe, and feel
What I can ne'er express, yet cannot all conceal.

- George Gordon Byron (1788 – 1824)

Why Tie Things To My Happiness? - Poem by Mr. Nobody

'Tying things to my happiness
is attaching a thick law book
to it, full of rules and
regulations to manage my
happiness
decreasing it, adding a few drops,
regulating and timing it
there is another way
Attach nothing to your happiness
let it abide and reign
and rain on no parade
let it be untouchable
unassailable, undiminishing
forever happiness and suffering
are not bedfellows'

- Why Tie Things To My Happiness? By Mr. Nobody

"O happiness! Our being's end and aim!
Good, pleasure, ease, content! whate'er thy name:
That something still which prompts the eternal sigh,
For which we bear to live, or dare to die."

- Alexander Pope (1688-1744)

"Cheerfulness removes the rust from the mind, lubricates our inward machinery, and enables us to do our work with fewer creaks and groans. If people were universally cheerful, there wouldn't be half the quarreling or a tenth part of the wickedness there is. Cheerfulness, too, promotes health and morality. Cheerful people live longest here on earth, afterward in our hearts."

- Author Unknown

Healing Prayers 7

Healing: God created us out of nothing so healing is not a problem for him provided we have the faith. Everybody can heal; the power of healing is within each one of us. God has given this unique gift to humans, a few develop it. Jesus healed everyone who came to him of all diseases.

Buddhist Prayer for Healing and Peace

"May all beings everywhere plagued with sufferings of body and mind quickly be freed from their illnesses.

May those frightened cease to be afraid, and may those bound be free.

May the powerless find power and may people think of befriending one another.

May those who find themselves in trackless, fearful wildernesses - the children, the aged, the unprotected - be guarded by beneficent celestials, and may they swiftly attain Buddhahood."

May Peace Harmonious

"May peace harmonious bless this land;
May it be ever free from maladies and war;
May there be harvest rich, and increased yield of grain;
May everyone delight in righteousness;
May no perverted thought find entry to your minds;
May all your thoughts e'er pious be and lead
to your success religiously."

- Tibetan Great Yogi, Milarepa (1040-1123)

Tibetan Wind Horse Prayer

"As Wind carries our prayers for Earth and All Life, may respect and love light our way.

May our hearts be filled with compassion for others and for ourselves.

May peace increase on Earth. May it begin with me.

- Tibetan prayer flag is 'Lung ta', meaning 'Wind Horse'

Remember, Jesus healed everybody in the Gospels, so, too, did St. John Bosco and many teachers and masters of other faiths.

In Luke 4:40, "Now when the sun was setting, all they that had any sick with divers diseases brought them unto him; and he laid his hands on every one of them, and healed them." King James Version

In Matthew 15:30, "And great multitudes came unto him, having with them those that were lame, blind, dumb, maimed, and many others, and cast them down at Jesus' feet; and he healed them:" King James Version

Everyone gets sick at some time or the other. In today's world of modern cities there are very few trees which can help absorb the pollution in the air and give out oxygen. As a result viruses are on the rise even in the advanced countries. If you, God forbid, get sick, immediately open this book at this chapter and find any of the prayers which appeal to you.

Place the palm of your right hand on the area of the body where there is pain and discomfort, close your eyes, focus all your mind and soul and pray thus

"Eternal One, One with me, as I am with thee, Creator of all life. You are able to do all things. Nothing is impossible for you. I have some pain/ sickness/ache/wound in the.... (Mention the exact specific place in the body). Please heal this part of my body on which I place the palm of my hands. Eternal One, kindly heal me right now and keep me free from all diseases. Thank You."

Another Healing Prayer:

Eternal One, one with me as I am one with Thee, please heal the part of the body where I have placed my hands. Let every sickness, every disease, every virus, every ailment, every kind of illness or bacteria leave me/my friend/my family now at this moment. Let me/us be completely healed by you, the Creator of All Life. You created me out of nothing. You have the power to cure me totally right now. Forgive me for my sins. Increase my faith in you so that I deserve to receive your healing.

Be as precise as possible in mentioning where your ailment is in the body. When you cancel a confirmed flight on any airline in the world, you do not send an email for a refund merely saying "please send me a refund for my air travel." No airline would refund you on such a request. You need to send the specific details of your cancelled flight. It's the same with prayer. Be as specific as possible. God must be receiving billions of prayers each day. Watch the movie Bruce Almighty. It'll give you an idea. What happens if nothing results? Well, pray again later during the day. Another powerful way is to ask a relation from the family or friend to pray with you together. Believe me. Your prayers will be answered. It may take one day, two days, one week or more, but they will be answered if you have prayed with all your heart, if you have been very specific and if you persist. This does not mean that you should not take the medications prescribed by the doctor. You must continue with your medications until you are completely cured. However, I have found that this simple spiritual exercise heals most common ailments.

Powerful Prayer of Healing for yourself– A beautiful Navajo Indian Prayer

"O you who dwell In the house made of the dawn,

In the house made of the evening twilight...

Where the dark mist curtains the doorway,

The path to which is on the rainbow...

I have made your sacrifice.

I have prepared a smoke for you.

My feet restore for me.

My limbs restore for me.

My body restore for me.

My mind restore for me.

My voice restore for me.

Today, take away your spell from me.

Away from me you have taken it.
Far Off from me you have taken it.
Happily I recover.
Happily my interior becomes cool.
Happily my eyes regain their power.
Happily my head becomes cool.
Happily my limbs regain their power.
Happily I hear again.
Happily for me the spell is taken Off.
Happily I walk.
Impervious to pain, I walk.
Feeling light within, I walk ...
In beauty I walk.
With beauty before me, I walk.
With beauty behind me, I walk.
With beauty below me, I walk.
With beauty all around me, I walk.
It is finished in beauty.
It is finished in beauty.
It is finished in beauty"

- Navajo Healing Prayer

Native American Prayer of Healing for a loved one - Navajo

"In the house made of dawn.
In the story made of dawn.
On the trail of dawn.
O, Talking God.
His feet, my feet, restore.
His limbs, my limbs, restore.
His body, my body, restore.
His mind, my mind, restore.
His voice, my voice, restore.

His plumes, my plumes, restore.
With beauty before him, with beauty before me.
With beauty behind him, with beauty behind me.
With beauty above him, with beauty above me.
With beauty below him, with beauty below me.
With beauty around him, with beauty around me.
With pollen beautiful in his voice, with pollen beautiful in my voice.
It is finished in beauty. It is finished in beauty.
In the house of evening light.
From the story made of evening light.
On the trail of evening light."

Healing Prayer

"Grandfather,
Sacred one,
Teach us love, compassion,
and honor.
That we may heal the earth
And heal each other." - ***Ojibway Native American Prayer***

Healing Prayer - May I Be At Peace

"May I be at peace.
May my heart remain open.
May I be aware of my true nature.
May I be healed.
May I be a source of healing to others.
May I dwell in the Breath of God." - Saint Teresa of Avila, Spanish Carmelite nun and mystic (28 March, 1515 - 4 Oct., 1582)

And don't forget to **thank God** after your prayers are answered. Remember He always answers our prayers in ways we do not expect. Then we think that we did it by ourselves without any help from above. God loves a grateful person. Do you recall the story of the ten lepers whom Jesus healed of leprosy? Only one of them came back to thank him. The others were healed but forgot to thank God.

Luke 17:11-19 "And it happened that, while he was traveling to Jerusalem, he passed through the midst of Samaria and Galilee.

And as he was entering a certain town, ten leprous men met him, and they stood at a distance.

And they lifted up their voice, saying, "Jesus, Teacher, take pity on us."

And when he saw them, he said, "Go, show yourselves to the priests." And it happened that, as they were going, they were cleansed.

And one of them, when he saw that he was cleansed, returned, magnifying God with a loud voice.

And he fell face down before his feet, giving thanks. And this one was a Samaritan.

And in response, Jesus said: "Were not ten made clean? And so where are the nine?

Was no one found who would return and give glory to God, except this foreigner?"

And he said to him: "Rise up, go forth. For your faith has saved you." - Sacred Bible Catholic Public Domain

He even raised people from the dead. Listen to the story of Lazarus being raised from the dead. In John Chapter 11:1-44, 'Now a certain man was sick, named Lazarus, of Bethany, the town of Mary and her sister Martha.'

(It was that Mary which anointed the Lord with ointment, and wiped his feet with her hair, whose brother Lazarus was sick.)

Therefore his sisters sent unto him, saying, Lord, behold, he whom thou lovest is sick.

When Jesus heard that, he said, This sickness is not unto death, but for the glory of God, that the Son of God might be glorified thereby.

Now Jesus loved Martha, and her sister, and Lazarus.

When he had heard therefore that he was sick, he abode two days still in the same place where he was.

Then after that saith he to his disciples, Let us go into Judaea again.

His disciples say unto him, Master, the Jews of late sought to stone thee; and goest thou thither again?

Jesus answered, Are there not twelve hours in the day? If any man walk in the day, he stumbleth not, because he seeth the light of this world.

But if a man walk in the night, he stumbleth, because there is no light in him.

These things said he: and after that he saith unto them, Our friend Lazarus sleepeth; but I go, that I may awake him out of sleep.

Then said his disciples, Lord, if he sleep, he shall do well.

How be it Jesus spake of his death: but they thought that he had spoken of taking of rest in sleep.

Then said Jesus unto them plainly, Lazarus is dead.

And I am glad for your sakes that I was not there, to the intent ye may believe; nevertheless let us go unto him.

Then said Thomas, which is called Didymus, unto his fellowdisciples, Let us also go, that we may die with him.

Then when Jesus came, he found that he had lain in the grave four days already.

Now Bethany was nigh unto Jerusalem, about fifteen furlongs off:

And many of the Jews came to Martha and Mary, to comfort them concerning their brother.

Then Martha, as soon as she heard that Jesus was coming, went and met him: but Mary sat still in the house.

Then said Martha unto Jesus, Lord, if thou hadst been here, my brother had not died.

But I know, that even now, whatsoever thou wilt ask of God, God will give it thee.

Jesus saith unto her, Thy brother shall rise again.

Martha saith unto him, I know that he shall rise again in the resurrection at the last day.

Jesus said unto her, I am the resurrection, and the life: he that believeth in me, though he were dead, yet shall he live:

And whosoever liveth and believeth in me shall never die. Believest thou this?

She saith unto him, Yea, Lord: I believe that thou art the Christ, the Son of God, which should come into the world.

And when she had so said, she went her way, and called Mary her sister secretly, saying, The Master is come, and calleth for thee.

As soon as she heard that, she arose quickly, and came unto him.

Now Jesus was not yet come into the town, but was in that place where Martha met him.

The Jews then which were with her in the house, and comforted her, when they saw Mary, that she rose up hastily and went out, followed her, saying, She goeth unto the grave to weep there.

Then when Mary was come where Jesus was, and saw him, she fell down at his feet, saying unto him, Lord, if thou hadst been here, my brother had not died.

When Jesus therefore saw her weeping, and the Jews also weeping which came with her, he groaned in the spirit, and was troubled.

And said, Where have ye laid him? They said unto him, Lord, come and see.

Jesus wept.

Then said the Jews, Behold how he loved him!

And some of them said, Could not this man, which opened the eyes of the blind, have caused that even this man should not have died?

Jesus therefore again groaning in himself cometh to the grave. It was a cave, and a stone lay upon it.

Jesus said, Take ye away the stone. Martha, the sister of him that was dead, saith unto him, Lord, by this time he stinketh: for he hath been dead four days.

Jesus saith unto her, Said I not unto thee, that, if thou wouldest believe, thou shouldest see the glory of God?

Then they took away the stone from the place where the dead was laid. And Jesus lifted up his eyes, and said, Father, I thank thee that thou hast heard me.

And I knew that thou hearest me always: but because of the people which stand by I said it, that they may believe that thou hast sent me.

And when he thus had spoken, he cried with a loud voice, Lazarus, come forth.

And he that was dead came forth, bound hand and foot with graveclothes: and his face was bound about with a napkin. Jesus saith unto them, Loose him, and let him go.' - King James Version

St. John Bosco, who took care of youth in Turin, Italy, was also a famous miraculous healer. Don Bosco (1815-1888), the patron saint of young people was a brilliant educator. God gave him the Divine gift of Healing. He cured all who came to him. He healed the deaf, the blind and all sorts of diseases.

The Power of Faith:

In Luke 17:5-6, "And the apostles said unto the Lord, Increase our faith. And the Lord said, If ye had faith as a grain of mustard seed, ye might say unto this mulberry tree, Be thou plucked up by the root, and be thou planted in the sea; and it should obey you."

And in Matthew 17:20, "And Jesus said unto them, Because of your unbelief: for verily I say unto you, If ye have faith as a grain of mustard seed, ye shall say unto this mountain, Remove hence to yonder place; and it shall remove; and nothing shall be impossible unto you."

Prayer of Thanks:

Eternal One, one with me as I am one with Thee, thank you so much for life, Mother Earth, the sun, water, air, the healing, the miracle, the guidance, the financial help and for loved ones around me. May I always remember to thank you for so many unexpected gifts big and small. Forgive me for the times when I have forgotten to thank Thee.

"Gratitude is not only the greatest of virtues, but the parent of all the others."

- Cicero, Roman philosopher, politician and orator (January 3, 106 B.C.E. - December 7, 43 B.C.E)

She Who Heals – An American Indian Healing Prayer

"Mother, sing me a song
That will ease my pain,
Mend broken bones,
Bring wholeness again.

Catch my babies
When they are born,
Sing my death song,
Teach me how to mourn.
Show me the Medicine
Of the healing herbs,
The value of spirit,
The way I can serve.
Mother, heal my heart
So that I can see
The gifts of yours
That can live through me."

Prayer for a safe journey and special protection from all harm.

'Great Creator, thank you for the beautiful and fascinating planet that you have made for us to live in. As I/we travel now, we ask for your protection during this journey. Keep us safe on the plane, in the car, on the train, on the bus, on the auto-rickshaw, on the tuk tuk, on the motor bike, on the cycle, on the ship, on the cycle-rickshaw and while we walk. Keep us safe from all harm and accidents. Protect the drivers, the conductors, the pilots and the crew. Protect, too, those who travel with us- our loved ones, our friends and others, who are travelling in the same conveyance. Protect this plane, this bus, this train, this car, this cycle, this motor bike, this ship, this tuk tuk, this auto-rickshaw and this cycle rickshaw. Thank You, Great Maker. May thousands of angels protect us while we are on this journey.'

This is just a simple prayer that I have written. You are most welcome to use your own prayer. You should pray before you start the trip or while just on your way, at the beginning.

To be absolutely safe, do not forget seven intentions while praying before travelling.

1. The pilot or the driver
2. The crew or the conductor

3. The plane, the ship, the car, the bus, the auto-rickshaw, the cycle, the motorbike, the train, the tuk tuk and the cycle rickshaw
4. Your loved ones and friends who are travelling with you
5. Others passengers who are in the same vehicle
6. Pray for your own protection
7. Finally, never fail to thank God at the end, for the safe journey

Sioux Prayer: On a Voyage and while Travelling

"You, O God, are the Lord of the mountains and the valleys. As I travel over mountains and through valleys, I am beneath your feet. You surround me with every kind of creature. Peacocks, pheasants, and wild boars cross my path. Open my eyes to see their beauty, that I may perceive them as the work of your hands.

In your power, in your thought, all things are abundant. Tonight I will sleep beneath your feet, O Lord of the mountains and valleys, ruler of the trees and vines. I will rest in your love, with you protecting me as a father protects his children, with you watching over me as a mother watches over her children. Then tomorrow the sun will rise and I will not know where I am; but I know that you will guide my footsteps."

Ancient Buddhist Healing and Blessing Chant:

"Just as the soft rains fill the streams,
Pour into the rivers and join together in the oceans,
So may the power of every moment of your goodness
Flow forth to awaken and heal all beings,
Those here now, those gone before, those yet to come.
By the power of every moment of your goodness...
May your heart's wishes be soon fulfilled,
As completely shining as the bright full moon,
As magically as by a wish-fulfilling gem.
May all dangers be averted and all disease be gone.
May no obstacle come across your way.
May you enjoy fulfillment and long life.
For all in whose heart dwells respect,

Who follow the wisdom and compassion of the Way,

May your life prosper in the Four Blessings,

Of Old age, Beauty, Happiness and Strength."

Find out, listen to and utilize the powerful healing prayers of Native American Indians from the US and Canada, Aboriginal healing prayer from Australia, Maori healing prayer from New Zealand, ancient Kenyan healing prayer, African healing prayer as well as Buddhist, Hindu, Christian and Islamic healing prayers.

Find the prayer which appeals most to you and pray aloud the Healing Prayers of different faiths so that the One God who allowed many diverse ways of reaching Him, worshipping Him and praising Him will hear you and cure you completely. Unless you have the power of a miraculous saint, in which case on your own you can cure, healing prayers are more efficacious and successful if said with others. You can invite your loved ones like your wife, husband, mother, father, children, grandfather or grandmother. You could also invite your friends for one hour healing sessions, where you all together pray for each others' health problems.

8 How do I find God? How do I find the Kingdom of God? How do I attain the Kingdom of God, Self Realization or Nirvana? How long will it take?

There are many ways to find the Kingdom of God or Self Realization or Nirvana. If you wish to find God, 'Be The Void', 'Be Formless', 'Be Empty', 'Be Blank'.

The Bible, Genesis 1 speaks about the Void before Light and Creation.

'In the beginning God created the heaven and the earth.

And the earth was ***Without Form*, and *Void***; and darkness was upon the face of the deep. And the Spirit of God moved upon the face of the waters.

And God said, Let there be light: and there was light.'

Look at what the Rig Veda says: '**Darkness there was** at first concealed in darkness, this all was indiscriminated chaos.

All that existed then was void and formless:' - Rig-Veda 10.129.7

Ancient Hindu scriptures, teach that there are still four principle orthodox ways of achieving union (Yoga) of the soul (Atman) which is the body's immortal nectar (Amrit) with God (Brahman) and therefore liberation (Moksha /Nirvana for Buddhists) from the cycle of death and rebirth (Samsara). Achieving union or oneness with God frees us from the illusion (Maya) of our perceived reality as opposed to our supreme cosmic reality.

These four paths are:-

- Bhakti Yoga (the path of love and devotion)
- Karma Yoga (the path of right action)

- Raja Yoga (the path of meditation)
- Jnana Yoga (the path of knowledge and wisdom).

According to Hindu scriptures, the various stages of human life are: Brahmacharya (Student Life) where one acquires knowledge, self discipline at the feet of a Guru (Spiritual Teacher) and learns to live a life of Dharma (Righteousness), Grihastha(Household Life) where one fulfils ones duty to family and society, Vanaprastha (Retired Life) where one gradually withdraws from the world and freely shares wisdom with others and finally Sannyasa(Renounced Life) where one completely renounces the world and dedicates themselves to spiritual pursuits.

One is free to follow any path they choose. Sri Ramakrishna Paramahamsa, a Hindu mystic (1836 – 1886), taught 'God can be realized through all paths. All religions are true. The important thing is to reach the roof. You can reach it by stone stairs or by wooden stairs or by bamboo steps or by a rope. You can also climb up by a bamboo pole.'

'With sincerity and earnestness one can realize God through all religions. The Vaishnavas will realize God, and so will the Saktas, the Vedantists and the Brahmos. The Mussalmans and the Christians will realize him too. All will certainly realize God if they are earnest and sincere.'

'Meditate upon the Knowledge and Bliss Eternal, and you will also have bliss. The Bliss indeed is eternal, only it is covered and obscured by ignorance.'

- Sri Ramakrishna, a Hindu saint and reformer (1836–1886)

The Bhagavad Gita (Song of the Lord) better known as the Gita is an epic Hindu scripture probably at some point between 400 BCE and 200 CE.

Various excerpts from Lord Krishna in the Bhagavad Gita speaking to Arjuna:

"All paths, Arjuna, lead to me.

I am the beginning, middle, and end of creation.

Among animals I am the lion; ... and of all that measures, I am time.

I am death, which overcomes all, and the source of all beings still to be born.

Just remember that I am, and that I support the entire cosmos with only a fragment of my being.

Behold, Arjuna, a million divine forms, with an infinite variety of color and shape. Behold the gods of the natural world, and many more wonders never revealed before. Behold the entire cosmos turning within my body, and the other things you desire to see.

I am time, the destroyer of all; I have come to consume the world.

That one is dear to me who runs not after the pleasant or away from the painful, grieves not, lusts not, but let's things come and go as they happen.

Just as a reservoir is of little use when the whole countryside is flooded, scriptures are of little use to the illumined man or woman, who sees the Lord everywhere.

They alone see truly who see the Lord the same in every creature, who see the deathless in the hearts of all that die. Seeing the same Lord everywhere, they do not harm themselves or others. Thus they attain the supreme goal.

With a drop of my energy I enter the earth and support all creatures. Through the moon, the vessel of life-giving fluid, I nourish all plants. I enter breathing creatures and dwell within as the life-giving breath. I am the fire in the stomach which digests all food.

There are three gates to this self-destructive hell: lust, anger, and greed. Renounce these three.

Pleasure from the senses seems like nectar at first, but it is bitter as poison in the end.

That which seems like poison at first, but tastes like nectar in the end – this is the joy of sattva, born of a mind at peace with itself.

The Lord dwells in the hearts of all creatures and whirls them round upon the wheel of maya. Run to him for refuge with all your strength, and peace profound will be yours through his grace.

Whatever you do, make it an offering to me – the food you eat, the sacrifices you make, the help you give, even your suffering.

I am heat; I give and withhold the rain. I am immortality and I am death; I am what is and what is not.

Those who worship other gods with faith and devotion also worship me, Arjuna, even if they do not observe the usual forms. I am the object of all worship, its enjoyer and Lord.

Those who remember me at the time of death will come to me. Do not doubt this. Whatever occupies the mind at the time of death determines the destination of the dying; always they will tend toward that state of being.

When meditation is mastered, the mind is unwavering like the flame of a lamp in a windless place.

They are forever free who renounce all selfish desires and break away from the ego cage of "I," "me," and "mine" to be united with the Lord. This is the supreme state. Attain to this, and pass from death to immortality.

They live in wisdom who see themselves in all and all in them, who have renounced every selfish desire and sense-craving tormenting the heart.

The meaning of Karma (action) is in the intention. The intention behind action is what matters. Those who are motivated only by desire for the fruits of action are miserable, for they are constantly anxious about the results of what they do.

You have the right to work, but never to the fruit of work. You should never engage in action for the sake of reward, nor should you long for inaction.

Perform work in this world, Arjuna, as a man established within himself – without selfish attachments, and alike in success and defeat. For yoga is perfect evenness of mind.

At the beginning of time I declared two paths for the pure heart: jnana yoga, the contemplative path of spiritual wisdom, and karma yoga, the active path of selfless service. There are the fundamental different types of yoga.

Do your work with the welfare of others always in mind. It was by such work that Janaka attained perfection; others too have followed this path.

There is nothing in the three worlds for me to gain, Arjuna, nor is there anything I do not have; I continue to act, but I am not driven by any need of my own.

The ignorant work for their own profit, Arjuna; the wise work for the welfare of the world, without thought for themselves.

It is better to strive in one's own dharma than to succeed in the dharma of another. Nothing is ever lost in following one's own dharma, but competition in another's dharma breeds fear and insecurity.

The senses are higher than the body, the mind higher than the senses; above the mind is the intellect, and above the intellect is the Atman. Thus, knowing that which is supreme, let the Atman rule the ego. Use your mighty arms to slay the fierce enemy that is selfish desire.

You and I have passed through many births, Arjuna. You have forgotten, but I remember them all.

My true being is unborn and changeless. I am the Lord who dwells in every creature. Through the power of my own maya, I manifest myself in a finite form."

"Those who know me as their own divine Self break through the belief that they are the body and are not reborn as separate creatures. Such a one, Arjuna, is united with me." - Bhagavad Gita

Bhagavad Gita (Song of the Lord) on Freedom from the Senses

"Delivered from selfish attachment, fear, and anger, filled with me, surrendering themselves to me, purified in the fire of my being, many have reached the state of unity in me.

Actions do not cling to me because I am not attached to their results. Those who understand this and practice it live in freedom.

The wise see that there is action in the midst of inaction and inaction in the midst of action. Their consciousness is unified, and every act is done with complete awareness.....

The offering of wisdom is better than any material offering, Arjuna; for the goal of all work is spiritual wisdom.

Approach those who have realized the purpose of life and question them with reverence and devotion; they will instruct you in this wisdom.

Even if you were the most sinful of sinners, Arjuna, you could cross beyond all sin by the raft of spiritual wisdom.

As the heat of a fire reduces wood to ashes, the fire of knowledge burns to ashes all karma.

Those who surrender to Brahman (Supreme God, Ultimate Reality) all selfish attachments are like the leaf of a lotus floating clean and dry in water. Sin cannot touch them.

Those who renounce attachment in all their deeds live content in the "city of nine gates," the body, as its master. They are not driven to act, nor do they involve others in action.

Those who possess this wisdom have equal regard for all. They see the same Self in a spiritual aspirant and an outcaste, in an elephant, a cow, and a dog.

Pleasures conceived in the world of the senses have a beginning and an end and give birth to misery, Arjuna. The wise do not look for happiness in them. But those who overcome the impulses of lust and anger which arise in the body are made whole and live in joy. They find their joy, their rest, and their light completely within themselves. United with the Lord, they attain nirvana in Brahman.

Free from anger and selfish desire, unified in mind, those who follow the path of yoga and realize the Self are established forever in that supreme state.

Knowing me as the friend of all creatures, the Lord of the universe, the end of all offerings and all spiritual disciplines, they attain eternal peace.

It is not those who lack energy or refrain from action, but those who work without expectation of reward who attain the goal of meditation.

Those who cannot renounce attachment to the results of their work are far from the path.

Reshape yourself through the power of your will; never let yourself be degraded by self-will. The will is the only friend of the Self, and the will is the only enemy of the Self.

To those who have conquered themselves, the will is a friend. But it is the enemy of those who have not found the Self within them.

The supreme Reality stands revealed in the consciousness of those who have conquered themselves. They live in peace, alike in cold and heat, pleasure and pain, praise and blame.

With all fears dissolved in the peace of the Self and all actions dedicated to Brahman (Supreme God), controlling the mind and fixing it on me, sit in meditation with me as your only goal.

Arjuna, those who eat too much or eat too little, who sleep too much or sleep too little, will not succeed in meditation. But those who are temperate in eating and sleeping, work and recreation, will come to the end of sorrow through meditation.

In the still mind, in the depths of meditation, the Self reveals itself. Beholding the Self by means of the Self, an aspirant knows the joy and peace of complete fulfillment.

Wherever the mind wanders, restless and diffuse in its search for satisfaction without, lead it within; train it to rest in the Self.

I am ever present to those who have realized me in every creature. Seeing all life as my manifestation, they are never separated from me.

When a person responds to the joys and sorrows of others as if they were his

own, he has attained the highest state of spiritual union.

No one who does good work will ever come to a bad end, either here or in the world to come.

Through constant effort over many lifetimes, a person becomes purified of all selfish desires and attains the supreme goal of life.

Meditation is superior to severe asceticism and the path of knowledge. It is also superior to selfless service. May you attain the goal of meditation, Arjuna!

Even among those who meditate, that man or woman who worships me with perfect faith, completely absorbed in me, is the most firmly established in yoga.

With your mind intent on me, Arjuna, discipline yourself with the practice of yoga. Depend on me completely. Listen, and I will dispel all your doubts; you will come to know me fully and be united with me.

The birth and dissolution of the cosmos itself take place in me. There is nothing that exists separate from me, Arjuna. The entire universe is suspended from me as my necklace of jewels.

Arjuna, I am the taste of pure water and the radiance of the sun and moon. I am the sacred word and the sound heard in air, and the courage of human beings. I am the sweet fragrance in the earth and the radiance of fire; I am the life in every creature and the striving of the spiritual aspirant.

My eternal seed, Arjuna, is to be found in every creature. I am the power of discrimination in those who are intelligent, and the glory of the noble. In those who are strong, I am strength, free from passion and selfish attachment. I am desire itself, if that desire is in harmony with the purpose of life.

The Bhagavad Gita on Life and Death

.....Some come to the spiritual life because of suffering, some in order to understand life; some come through a desire to achieve life's purpose, and some come who are men and women of wisdom. Unwavering in devotion, always united with me, the man or woman of wisdom surpasses all the others.

After many births the wise seek refuge in me, seeing me everywhere and in everything. Such great souls are very rare.

The world, deluded, does not know that I am without birth and changeless. I know everything about the past, the present, and the future, Arjuna; but there is no one who knows me completely.

Delusion arises from the duality of attraction and aversion, Arjuna; every creature is deluded by these from birth.....

The Lord is the supreme poet, the first cause, the sovereign ruler, subtler than the tiniest particle, the support of all, inconceivable, bright as the sun, beyond darkness.

Remembering me at the time of death, close down the doors of the senses and place the mind in the heart. Then, while absorbed in meditation, focus all energy upwards to the head. Repeating in this state the divine name, the syllable Om that represents the changeless Brahman (Supreme God, Ultimate Reality), you will go forth from the body and attain the supreme goal.

I am easily attained by the person who always remembers me and is attached to nothing else. Such a person is a true yogi, Arjuna.

Every creature in the universe is subject to rebirth, Arjuna, except the one who is united with me.

The six months of the northern path of the sun, the path of light, of fire, of day, of the bright fortnight, leads knowers of Brahman (Supreme God) to the supreme goal. The six months of the southern path of the sun, the path of smoke, of night, of the dark fortnight, leads other souls to the light of the moon and to rebirth.

Under my watchful eye the laws of nature take their course. Thus is the world set in motion; thus the animate and the inanimate are created.

I am the ritual and the sacrifice; I am true medicine and the mantram. I am the offering and the fire which consumes it, and the one to whom it is offered.

I am the father and mother of this universe, and its grandfather too; I am its entire support. I am the sum of all knowledge, the purifier, the syllable Om; I am the sacred scriptures....

I am the goal of life, the Lord and support of all, the inner witness, the abode of all. I am the only refuge, the one true friend; I am the beginning, the staying, and the end of creation; I am the womb and the eternal seed.

Those who follow the rituals given in the Vedas, who offer sacrifices and take soma, free themselves from evil and attain the vast heaven of the gods, where they enjoy celestial pleasures. When they have enjoyed these fully, their merit is exhausted and they return to this land of death. Thus observing Vedic rituals but caught in an endless chain of desires, they come and go.

Those who worship me and meditate on me constantly, without any other thought – I will provide for all their needs...

Fill your mind with me; love me; serve me; worship me always. Seeking me in your heart, you will at last be united with me.

All the scriptures lead to me; I am their author and their wisdom.

Not by knowledge of the Vedas (sacred texts), nor sacrifice, nor charity, nor rituals, nor even by severe asceticism has any other mortal seen what you have seen, O heroic Arjuna.

Better indeed is knowledge than mechanical practice. Better than knowledge is meditation. But better still is surrender of attachment to results, because there follows immediate peace.

Some realize the Self within them through the practice of meditation, some by the path of wisdom, and others by selfless service. Others may not know these paths; but hearing and following the instructions of an illumined teacher, they too go beyond death.

The brightness of the sun, which lights up the world, the brightness of the moon and of fire – these are my glory.

Calmness, gentleness, silence, self-restraint, and purity: these are the disciplines of the mind.

To refrain from selfish acts is one kind of renunciation, called sannyasa; to renounce the fruit of action is another, called tyaga.

By serving me with steadfast love, a man or woman goes beyond the gunas. Such a one is fit for union with Brahman (Supreme God).

When they see the variety of creation rooted in that unity and growing out of it, they attain fulfillment in Brahman.

I have shared this profound truth with you, Arjuna. Those who understand it will attain wisdom; they will have done that which has to be done.

I give you these precious words of wisdom; reflect on them and then do as you choose." – Bhagavad Gita (Song of the Lord), ancient Hindu texts

Sri Ramakrishna Paramahamsa, a Hindu mystic (1836 – 1886), taught thus: 'So long as God seems to be outside and far away, there is ignorance. But when God is realised within, that is true knowledge.'

'Many are the names of God, and infinite the forms that lead us to know Him. In whatsoever name or form you desire to call Him, in that very form and name you will see Him.'

'I had to practise each religion for a time — Hinduism, Islām, Christianity. Furthermore, I followed the paths of the Śāktas, Vaishnavas, and Vedāntists. I realized that there is only one God toward whom all are travelling; but the paths are different.'

'They say that the universe is a manifestation of the God's power and glory. God has created all these — sky, stars, moon, sun, mountains, ocean, men, animals. They constitute His glory. He is within us, in our hearts. Again, He is outside. The most advanced devotees say that He

Himself has become all this — the 24 cosmic principles, the universe, and all living beings. The devotee of God wants to eat sugar, and not become sugar. Do you know how a lover of God feels? His attitude is: "O God, Thou art the Master, and I am Thy servant. Thou art the Mother, and I Thy child." Or again: "Thou art my Father and Mother. Thou art the Whole, and I am a part." He does not like to say, "I am Brahman." They yogi seeks to realize the Paramatman, the Supreme Soul. His ideal is the union of the embodied soul and the Supreme Soul. He withdraws his mind from sense objects and tries to concentrate on the Paramatman, the Supreme Soul. Therefore, during the first stage of his spiritual discipline, he retires into solitude and with undivided attention practices meditation in a fixed posture.

But the reality is one and the same; the difference is only in name. He who is Brahman (God of Creation) is verily Atman (Inner Soul), and again, He is the Bhagavan, God. He is Brahman, (God of Creation) to the followers of the path of knowledge, Paramatman, the Supreme Soul to the yogis (hermit), and Bhagavan (God) to the lovers of God.'

'One should not think, "My religion alone is the right path and other religions are false." God can be realized by means of all paths. It is enough to have sincere yearning for God. Infinite are the paths and infinite the opinions.' - Sri Ramakrishna, a Hindu saint and reformer (1836 – 1886)

Swami Vivekananda: (1863 – 1902) He was a Hindu monk who was born to an affluent family of Kolkata, West Bengal but left everything to follow in the footsteps of Sri Ramakrishna and taught in India and the US.

These are the immortal words of Vivekananda:

'An aimless life is a miserable life and on the quality of your aim depends on the quality of your life.

Go forward, March forward, Look forward; do not look back.

Look at the ocean and not at the wave.

Live for the sake of the Ideal...Don't live looking at yourselves from the eyes of others.

Do not have friends who are petty minded as they crave for name and fame. If you serve the society selflessly, the liberation will adorn you automatically.

My religion is not Hinduism. The essence of my religion is Strength. If you are not physically and mentally strong, how can you experience the Truth?

You will always have someone to criticize you in this world, however good your work may be. This world resembles the tail of a dog and can never be reformed.

You are not a sinner. He is a sinner who calls you a sinner. You are all the sons of Immortality. There are no such words called sin and fear in my dictionary.

Arise, Awake and stop not till the goal is reached. For how many births do you want to remain in this sleep of ignorance? After you started your journey towards God, how much ever nearest or dearest tendencies may call you back, do not look behind but March forward. Oh! My Mind get back to your source.' - Swami Vivekananda (1863 – 1902)

Who Am I? 9

I am joy. I am happiness. I am the source of all things. I am peace and calm. I am bliss. I am love and kindness. I am the riches of the Universe. I am life and healing. I am gentleness and compassion towards others. I am forgiveness. I am a life full of miracles. I am the unexpected. I am strength and courage. I am light and darkness. I have all things.

I am one with the Eternal God as the Eternal is one with me. I am power. I was never born. I will never die.

You are one with The Eternal as the Eternal is one with you. Jesus said "I am the vine; you are the branches. Whoever abides in me, and I in him, bears much fruit." John 15:5. Keep repeating again and again often during the day "**I am one with the Eternal as the Eternal is one with me.**" To discover who you really are, obedience is the key. Just as you obeyed your nursery school teacher when she taught you to repeat the alphabets 'a b c d', so too, I humbly request you to obey me and repeat this line "**I am one with the Eternal as the Eternal is one with me**" thousands of times till their meaning sinks into you. Slowly you will then go beyond these words into Emptiness and attain your Highest Self. Gradually you will realize who you are. You will understand that you are the Source of all Joy and Happiness, you are Bliss, you are love and kindness, you are peace and calm, you were never born and will never die, you were there before your body came into being and you will be there after your body goes, you are the source of all the galaxies and stars. Before your parents gave you a name, you already existed. After your body dies and is buried or cremated, you will still exist.

Walk as the Eternal here on Earth. Our purpose in life is to be happy with God here and in Heaven.

I am just the signpost guiding you. Go beyond me, beyond words and beyond books. Go beyond religion till you reach the Source, the Heart of God. Just like the river goes to the ocean and then loses itself in the mighty ocean, so too should you keep practicing Silence and Stillness till you reach the Eternal Presence of the Almighty. What I am teaching you is way beyond words. So don't get stuck on my words. Go much further. What I am teaching is indescribable!! Words cannot even attempt to explain the majesty of the Eternal. You can only fully comprehend its true meaning in Silence and Stillness. When your mind is totally blank, Divine Glory, Knowledge and Wisdom will flood in. You don't even have to do anything. Just be blank and God will do the rest.

You are not this body because the body was born when your parents gave birth to you and will return to earth when you die. You existed much before your present body was born. That is why there is the universal teaching "your soul that is within you is immortal"

Constant Awareness of who you are:

When you are Silent, when you are Still, when you are Empty but Conscious of your Oneness with the Eternal, the downloading of God's Wisdom, God's Nature, God's Goodness, God's Powers, God's transformation takes place into you. The longer you stay Silent, Still and Empty in that Presence, the better the downloading of Divinity into you that takes place. The beauty about connection with that Eternal Self is that it never gets disconnected, NEVER. You can always get online to that Source. It's free, it's available anywhere, it's always there. It never goes off. That Void is like bright light and dark matter put together. It exists both in bright light and in darkness. **Immortality** means eternal life with the ability to live forever. What is Immortal cannot die. That is why I say to you that you were never born and will never die. So your name which you have at present is not your real name. You got that name recently when your parents gave birth to you and gave you that name. Your present name will be over when you die. Anything in your life which has a beginning and has an end is not Real but temporary.

Look at the Great Teachers, Masters, Prophets and Leaders whose names live on forever in Eternity and countless others whose lives and example shine as brightly as the stars in the sky. They stored their riches in heaven which is why their names live on forever. But can you name any of those who had stored their riches here on earth? No. They are all dead and forgotten. No one even remembers their name. They lived for 60 or 70 or 80 years and that's it. They carry nothing to their graves or funeral pyres. They are now just dust. However, those who stored up riches in heaven, live on for all Eternity.

The Amritabindu Upanishad (sacred Hindu texts)

The Hidden Self

The mind may be said to be of two kinds,
Pure and impure. Driven by the senses
It becomes impure; but with the senses
Under control, the mind becomes pure.
It is the mind that frees us or enslaves.
Driven by the senses we become bound;
Master of the senses we become free.
Those who seek freedom must master their senses.
When the mind is detached from the senses
One reaches the summit of consciousness.
Mastery of the mind leads to wisdom.
Practice meditation. Stop all vain talk.
The highest state is beyond reach of thought,
For it lies beyond all duality.
Keep repeating the ancient mantram (holy name) 'Om'
Until it reverberates in your heart.
Brahman (Highest Being) is indivisible and pure;
Realize Brahman and go beyond all change.
He is unchangeable and transcendent.
Realizing him, sages attain freedom
And declare that there are no separate minds.
They have but realized what they always are.
Waking, sleeping, dreaming, the Self is one.
Transcend these three and go beyond rebirth.

There is only one Self in all creatures.
The One appears many, just as the moon
Appears many, reflected in water.
The Self appears to change its location
But does not, just as air in a jar
Changes not when the jar is moved about.
When the jar is broken, the air knows not;
But the Self knows well when the body is shed.
We see not the Self, concealed by maya;
When the veil falls, we see we are the Self.
The mantram (holy name) is the symbol of Brahman (Highest Being));
Repeating it can bring peace to the mind.
Knowledge is twofold, lower and higher.
Realize the Self; for all else is lower.
Realization is rice; all else is chaff.
The milk of cows of any hue is white.
The sages say that wisdom is the milk
And the sacred scriptures are the cows.
As butter lies hidden within milk,
The Self is hidden in the hearts of all.
Churn the mind through meditation on it;
Light your fire through meditation on it:
The Self, all whole, all peace, all certitude.
"I have realized the Self," declares the sage,
"Who is present in all beings.
I am united with the Lord of Love;
I am united with the Lord of Love."
"That in whom reside all beings and who
resides in al beings, who is the giver of
grace to all, the Supreme Soul of the
universe, the limitless being-I am that"

- Amritabindu Upanishad, (sacred Hindu text meaning "drop of the nectar of immortality"). Brahman refers to the ultimate reality, the supreme God, beyond all distinctions or forms.

"The world is the wheel of God, turning round
And round with all living creatures upon its rim
The world is the river of God,
Flowing from him and flowing back to him.
On this ever-revolving wheel of being
The individual self goes round and round
Through life after life, believing itself
To be a separate creature, until
It sees its identity with the Lord of Love
And attains immortality in the indivisible whole."

- Shvetashvatara Upanishad 1.4-6. Hindu Sacred Texts

"Ye are all the leaves of one tree and the drops of one ocean."

- Baha'u'llah, founder of the Bahá'***í Faith (12 November 1817 – 29 May 1892)***

"Make your heart like a lake with a calm still surface and great depths of kindness." ***- Lao Tzu***

Adi Shankaracharya (788-820) perhaps the greatest of Indian saints & reformers -

"That which permeates all, which
nothing transcends and which like the
universal space around us, fills
everything completely from within and
without, that Supreme non-dual Brahman-that thou art." - Shri Adi Shankaracharya

The Way Ahead: Walk & Live as the Eternal, spend more & more time just being Empty, totally Aware, Living Consciousness. Into self awareness all blessings flow, Seek first the Kingdom of Heaven & All the rest will fall in line. Nothing else matters, just this-the greatest treasure. Let the vastness of the Universe fill you. Be the Eternal.

The Empty Mind 10

Keep the mind empty and practise thinking of nothing. Focus on being empty of mind. Think about and consider Being Empty of thoughts, anger, worry, fears, lust, desire, of just being Nothing.

So practise Emptying your Mind. Nothing comes to us without constant practice. Keep trying. Never give up. Did a child give up trying to stand and walk because it fell many times? No! Does a child stop smiling, laughing and playing just because it was scolded sometimes? No! So never stop until you reach the Goal of Emptiness of the Mind, utter peace and inner stillness, immeasurable joy and Happiness which only constant Awareness of your Being and Divinity can give.

Besides practicing the exercise of the Empty Mind, you can also begin the exercise of the Positive Mind. Think and consider about the vastness of the void, about how silence is God's language, about how beautiful is being silent, about being eternal & timeless, about being utterly still, about God the Unknown and how little we know of God, about God the Unseen and how no one has seen Him, about God the Unheard, about God's joy & untold bliss. Do you realize that from silence stems all the best music & sounds & words of the world? Think about the God who is beyond space, who is peace & calm, pure energy/deepest breathing, unerring wisdom, sheer goodness & purity, Source of power & strength, Source of Life & healing, Creator of the galaxies/the stars and the universes.

Watch your eyes. Jesus says in Matthew 6:22: 'The light of the body is the eye: if therefore thine eye be single (in good shape), thy whole body shall be full of light'.

Be careful about your thoughts. Guard them well. Remove all negative and bad thoughts. Do not allow suspicious and evil thoughts about others to enter your mind.

Buddha on the Mind:

"All wrong-doing arises because of the mind. If the mind is transformed can wrong-doing remain?"

"The mind is everything. What you think you become."

"It is a man's own mind, not his enemy or foe, that lures him to evil ways."

"There is nothing so disobedient as an undisciplined mind, and there is nothing so obedient as a disciplined mind."

"Nothing can harm you as much as your own thoughts unguarded." – Buddha

The Buddha said: "We are what we think.

All that we are, arises with our thoughts.

With our thoughts, we make our world." - Lord Buddha

Look at what the Bible says about **Meditation**:

Joshua 1:8: 'This book of the law shall not depart out of thy mouth; but thou shalt meditate therein day and night, that thou mayest observe to do according to all that is written therein: for then thou shalt make thy way prosperous, and then thou shalt have good success.'

Psalm 1:2 'But his delight is in the law of the Lord; and in his law doth he meditate day and night.'

Psalm 19:14 'Let the words of my mouth, and the meditation of my heart, be acceptable in thy sight, O Lord, my strength, and my redeemer.'

Psalm 63:6 'When I remember thee upon my bed, and meditate on thee in the night watches.'

Psalm 104:34 'My meditation of him shall be sweet: I will be glad in the Lord.'

Philippians 4:8 'Concerning the rest, brothers, whatever is true, whatever is chaste, whatever is just, whatever is holy, whatever is worthy to be loved, whatever is of good repute, if there is any virtue, if there is any praiseworthy discipline: meditate on these.' Sacred Bible Catholic Public Domain

Psalm 143:5 'I remember the days of old; I meditate on all thy works; I muse on the work of thy hands.'

Psalm 49:3 'My mouth shall speak of wisdom; and the meditation of my heart shall be of understanding.'

Psalm 1:1-6 'Blessed is the man that walketh not in the counsel of the ungodly, nor standeth in the way of sinners, nor sitteth in the seat of the scornful. But his delight is in the law of the Lord; and in his law doth he meditate day and night.

And he shall be like a tree planted by the rivers of water, that bringeth forth his fruit in his season; his leaf also shall not wither; and whatsoever he doeth shall prosper.'

Psalm 119:97-99 'O how I love thy law! It is my meditation all the day. Thou through thy commandments hast made me wiser than mine enemies: for they are ever with me. I have more understanding than all my teachers: for thy testimonies are my meditation.'

Psalm 118:1-50 'Blessed are the immaculate in the way, who walk in the law of the Lord.

Blessed are those who examine his testimonies. They seek him with their whole heart.

For those who work iniquity have not walked in his ways.

You have ordered your commandments to be kept most diligently.

I wish that my ways may be directed so as to keep your justifications.

Then I will not be confounded, when I will look into all your commandments.

I will confess to you with honesty of heart. In this way, I have learned the judgments of your justice.

I will keep your justifications. Do not utterly abandon me.

By what does an adolescent correct his way? By keeping to your words.

With my whole heart, I have sought you. Do not let me be driven away from your commandments.

I have hidden your eloquence in my heart, so that I may not sin against you.

Blessed are you, O Lord. Teach me your justifications.

With my lips, I have pronounced all the judgments of your mouth.

I have been delighted in the way of your testimonies, as if in all riches.

I will be trained in your commandments, and I will consider your ways.

I will meditate on your justifications. I will not forget your words.

Repay your servant, revive me; and I will keep your words.

Reveal to my eyes, and I will consider the wonders of your law.

I am a sojourner on the earth. Do not hide your commandments from me.

My soul has longed to desire your justifications at all times.

You have rebuked the arrogant. Those who decline from your commandments are accursed.

Take me away from disgrace and contempt, for I have sought your testimonies.

For even the leaders sat and spoke against me. But your servant has been trained in your justifications.

For your testimonies are also my meditation, and your justifications are my counsel.

My soul has adhered to the pavement. Revive me according to your word.

I have declared my ways, and you have heeded me. Teach me your justifications.

Instruct me in the way of your justifications, and I will be trained in your wonders.

My soul has slumbered because of weariness. Confirm me in your words.

Remove the way of iniquity from me, and have mercy on me by your law.

I have chosen the way of truth. I have not forgotten your judgments.

I have adhered to your testimonies, O Lord. Do not be willing to confound me.

I have run by way of your commandments, when you enlarged my heart.

O Lord, place the law before me, the way of your justifications, and I will always inquire into it.

Give me understanding, and I will examine your law. And I will keep it with my whole heart.

Lead me according to the path of your commandments, for I have desired this.

Bend my heart with your testimonies, and not with avarice.

Turn my eyes away, lest they see what is vain. Revive me in your way.

Station your eloquence with your servant, along with your fear.

Cut off my disgrace, which I have taken up, for your judgments are delightful.

Behold, I have longed for your commandments. Revive me in your fairness.

And let your mercy overwhelm me, O Lord: your salvation according to your eloquence.

And I will respond to those who reproach me by word, for I have hoped in your words.

And do not utterly take away the word of truth from my mouth. For in your judgments, I have hoped beyond hope.

And I will always keep your law, in this age and forever and ever.

And I have wandered far and wide, because I was seeking your commandments.

And I spoke of your testimonies in the sight of kings, and I was not confounded.

And I meditated on your commandments, which I loved.

And I lifted up my hands to your commandments, which I loved. And I was trained in your justifications.

Be mindful of your word to your servant, by which you have given me hope.

This has consoled me in my humiliation, for your word has revived me." – Sacred Bible Catholic Public Domain

Psalm 46:10 'Be still, and know that I am God: I will be exalted among the heathen, I will be exalted in the earth.'

Genesis 24:63 'And Isaac went out to meditate in the field at the eventide: and he lifted up his eyes, and saw, and, behold, the camels were coming.'

2 Timothy 3:16-17 'All scripture is given by inspiration of God, and is profitable for doctrine, for reproof, for correction, for instruction in

righteousness: That the man of God may be perfect, thoroughly furnished unto all good works.'

1 Timothy 4:13-15 'Till I come, give attendance to reading, to exhortation, to doctrine. Neglect not the gift that is in thee, which was given thee by prophecy, with the laying on of the hands of the presbytery.

Meditate upon these things; give thyself wholly to them; that thy profiting may appear to all.'

Psalm 23:1-6 'The Lord is my shepherd; I shall not want.

He maketh me to lie down in green pastures: he leadeth me beside the still waters.

He restoreth my soul: he leadeth me in the paths of righteousness for his name's sake.

Yea, though I walk through the valley of the shadow of death, I will fear no evil: for thou art with me; thy rod and thy staff they comfort me.

Thou preparest a table before me in the presence of mine enemies: thou anointest my head with oil; my cup runneth over.

Surely goodness and mercy shall follow me all the days of my life: and I will dwell in the house of the Lord for ever.'

Lord Buddha said "The secret of happiness lies in the mind's release from worldly ties."

'Health is the greatest of gifts, contentedness the best riches; trust is the best of relationships, Nirvâna the highest happiness.

He who has tasted the sweetness of solitude and tranquillity, is free from fear and free from sin, while he tastes the sweetness of drinking in the law.'

- Sacred Books of the East: The Dhammapada and Sutta Nipata, Translated from the Pali language by Max Müller and Max Fausböll, [1881]

Meditation:

Qs. How do I meditate?

Ans: This is a very important habit which you must practise if you wish to live always happily here on earth.

Psalm 4:4, Bible 'Stand in awe, and sin not: commune (meditate) with your own heart upon your bed, and be still.'

Meditation

First focus your mind. Focus on how you need to do meditation and stop doing anything else. If possible, be alone in your own room or stand outside early morning. Then try and be comfortable. You can sit down on a chair or sit on a stool or sit cross-legged. The posture does not matter as long as you are comfortable with it. You can even stand. I often am in a standing position while deep in a trance. The next step is to Be silent. It is not enough to be silent from the mouth but you need to be silent in your thoughts too by not thinking of anything. Off course it is not easy. But just as you went to nursery or kindergarten school and then spent years passing Class 1, Class 2, Class 3 and so on, so you must persevere in this most important of Schools & Universities. Think of thoughts that disturb your mind as flies that you must swat and chase away from your body. Do the same with such thoughts. Dismiss them from your mind.

Next you must be Still. Try not moving at all. Why? Because in absolute stillness you move the fastest at lightning speed and in that moment you reach the presence of God. The moment you are totally still with your mind empty, you reach the presence of God. Avoid moving your legs, your hands or any part of your body. Avoid scratching too.

With constant and daily practice, you will become better. Your mind will be silent, your body will be still and you will stand in the august presence of God, the greatest of all Presidents and Prime Ministers, the Emperor of the Universes and all dimensions, the Creator of all the stars. All the great sportsmen in the world became world champions because they practised and practised for hours on end. So practice makes perfection.

Laugh a lot: By the way, God is not a serious person. He loves a good joke. Don't forget he put comedy into man. So laugh and smile. And learn to laugh about yourself. When you can accept a joke on you and not get offended, that shows humility and greatness. When a nation or people learn to laugh about themselves and not get offended by jokes on them, that too shows humility and the greatness of that nation. It does not cost anything to laugh at yourself, to smile and be happy. On the contrary, it has a wonderful effect on you and those around, making life so much more cheerful and easy. Those who find their Kingdom of Heaven or Nirvana, have a natural constant smile on their face. That is why Buddha was known as the Smiling Buddha after he attained Enlightenment. Have you ever driven in India?

Driving in India "A senior monk was driving in India when suddenly a dog crosses the road. The car hit and killed the dog. The monk looked around and seeing a temple went to knock on the door. A young monk opened the door. The senior monk said: "I'm terribly sorry, but my karma ran over your dogma."

"The flapping Flag"

Four monks were meditating in a monastery. All of a sudden, the prayer flag on the roof started flapping.

The youngest monk came out of his meditation and said: "The flag is flapping"

A more experienced monk said: "No, the Wind is flapping"

A third monk who had been there in the monastery for more than 20 years said: "Your Minds are flapping."

Then the fourth monk who was the eldest and senior most among them all said, visibly annoyed: "Your Mouths are flapping!"

Daily Schedule 11

An Ideal day to have peace, calm and joy in your life:

Get up early. The earlier, the better. Nature shows us when to get up. Get up with the sunrise. Say "Hello", "Good Morning" and "Thank you" to the Creator who made us. Thank God for the air, plants, trees, flowers, insects, vegetables, fruits, sky and all of Mother Earth. After you freshen up, focus your mind; become silent and still. Kick out any thoughts of worry, fear and destructions which may enter your mind. It does not matter if you are not too successful. Keep trying. It is the effort and your persistence which are most important in front of God. Gradually over time, keeping your mind Empty will become easier. Remember, into an Empty Mind flows all the Wisdom, the Power, the Joy, the Goodness, the Wealth and the Happiness of the Eternal. This daily practice of an early start will make a perfect beginning for your day. Throughout the day practise the exercise of emptying the mind. This will reduce stress and depression in many lives. This will reduce the clutter in your mind and help you remain fresh throughout the day.

Avoid getting angry with anyone. It is natural to feel anger when you think that you have been wronged. However, a person who is striving to become better should control his anger. At such moments it is better to keep silent. Silence is golden. As I keep repeating, Silence is the language of God. I may not understand your language but everyone in this world knows silence. It is the universal language. Do you recall how many times you have been angry in the past? What was the use of it? All things shall pass. Your anger will pass. Look at a little child. You may scold and get angry with the child. The child may cry. But have you observed that a child forgets what happened in a short time and starts playing again. We, however, carry our anger for a long time. In short, you be the ruler of your anger. Don't let anger rule you.

In the evenings, eat early. Just as you need sleep at night, your stomach too, needs rest. So try not to eat after 5pm as far as possible. This will allow your stomach time to digest the food and by the time you sleep, your stomach and digestive system will sleep with you. If you eat late, your stomach will have to work throughout the night in order to digest the food. And as a result, it will have no rest. This may lead to obesity and other ailments. Do not sleep too late.

Just before sleeping, either stand or sit down or kneel on your bed. Still your mind, thank God for the day and then be empty. Think of nothing. If you are alone, put off all lights. God is both in darkness and light. In fact, darkness existed before light.

The following practice is just a suggestion. It is up to you. Feel free to make your own schedule. Remember, the busier you are, the more time you need to spend in silence and meditation. You are like a torch. The more the torch is used, the more it needs to be charged. Otherwise it will go dead. So it is with you.

1. Oneness - Just Being. Try to spend 1 hr in the morning, 1 hr in the afternoon and 1 hr in the evening just Being Aware in silence and stillness. During these periods of Silence, just Be Empty, yet all powerful, in bliss and calm.
2. Live life 100% as the Eternal. Be the Eternal. Watch always your eyes, thoughts & actions.
3. Being Healed: Strict Diet. Control your eating to control your health. Chew well. Exercise every day.
4. Review the state of your soul 2 hrs at the end of every month. Listen for Guidance on anything that you need to do.

Try the next 30 days living life 100% as the Eternal. Just Be Aware. You need not look outside or elsewhere. When you do wrong or slip below 100%, quickly be aware and get back to 100%. God calls you to the highest, to Total Oneness forever. Pray for healing for yourself, your family and friends.

Reverend John Wesley on Prayer:

'God's command to "pray without ceasing" is founded on the necessity we have of his grace to preserve the life of God in the soul, which can no more subsist one moment without it, than the body can without air.

Whether we think of; or speak to, God, whether we act or suffer for him, all is prayer, when we have no other object than his love, and the desire of pleasing him.

All that a Christian does, even in eating and sleeping, is prayer, when it is done in simplicity, according to the order of God, without either adding to or diminishing from it by his own choice.

Prayer continues in the desire of the heart, though the understanding be employed on outward things.

In souls filled with love, the desire to please God is a continual prayer.

As the furious hate which the devil bears us is termed the roaring of a lion, so our vehement love may be termed crying after God.

God only requires of his adult children, that their hearts be truly purified, and that they offer him continually the wishes and vows that naturally spring from perfect love. For these desires, being the genuine fruits of love, are the most perfect prayers that can spring from it.'

- 'A Plain Account of Christian Perfection' – Rev. John Wesley, (1703-1791)

EUPOLIS' Hymn to the Creator - John Wesley, (1703-1791) and Charles Wesley, (1707-1788)

'AUTHOR of Being, Source of Light,
With unfading Beauties bright,
Fulness, Goodness, rolling round
Thy own fair Orb without a Bound:
Whether Thee thy Supplicants call
Truth, or Good, or One, or All,
Ei or Iao; Thee we hail
Essence that can never fail,
Grecian or Barbaric Name,
Thy stedfast Being still the same.

Thee, when Morning greets the Skies
With rosy Cheeks and humid Eyes;
Thee, when sweet-declining Day
Sinks in purple Waves away;
Thee will I sing, O Parent Jove
And teach the World to praise and love.
Yonder azure Vault on high,
Yonder blue, low, liquid Sky,
Earth on its firm Basis plac'd,
And with circling Waves embrac'd,
All, Creating Pow'r confess,
All their mighty Maker bless.
Thou shak'st all Nature with thy Nod,
Sea, Earth and Air confess the God:
Yet does thy pow'rful Hand sustain
Both Earth and Heaven, both Firm and Main.
Scarce can our daring Thought arise
To thy Pavilion in the Skies;
Nor can Plato's self declare
The Bliss, the Joy, the Rapture there.
Barren above Thou dost not reign,
But circled with a glorious Train,
The Sons of God, the Sons of Light,
Ever joying in thy Sight:
(For Thee their silver Harps are strung,)
Ever beauteous, ever young,
Angelic Forms their Voices raise,
And thro' Heav'n's Arch resound thy Praise.
The Feather'd Souls that swim the Air,
And bathe in liquid Ether there,
The Lark, Precentor of their Choir
Leading them higher still and higher,

Listen and learn; th' angelic Notes
Repeating in their warbling Throats:
And ere to soft Repose they go,
Teach them to their Lords below:
On the green Turf, their mossy Nest,
The Ev'ning Anthem swells their Breast.
Thus like thy Golden Chain from high,
Thy Praise unites the Earth and Sky.
Source of Light, Thou bidst the Sun
On his burning Axles run;
The Stars like Dust around him fly,
And shew the Area of the Sky.
He drives so swift his Race above,
Mortals can't perceive him move:
So smooth his Course, oblique or strait,
Olympus shakes not with his Weight.
As the Queen of solemn Night
Fills at his Vase her Orb of Light,
Imparted Lustre; Thus we see,
The solar Virtue shines by Thee.
Eiresione we'll no more,
Imaginary Pow'r, adore;
Since Oil, and Wool, and chearing Wine,
And Life-sustaining Bread is thine.
Thy Herbage, O Great Pan, sustains
The Flocks that graze our Attic Plains;
The Olive, with fresh Verdure crown'd,
Rises pregnant from the Ground;
At thy Command it shoots and springs,
And a thousand Blessings brings.
Minerva, only is thy Mind,
Wisdom, and Bounty to Mankind.

The fragrant Thyme, the bloomy Rose,
Herb and Flow'r and Shrub that grows
On Thessalian Tempe's Plain,
Or where the rich Sabeans reign,
That treat the Taste or Smell or Sight,
For Food, for Med'cine or Delight;
Planted by thy Parent Care,
Spring and smile and flourish there.
O ye Nurses of soft Dreams,
Reedy Brooks and winding Streams,
Or murm'ring o'er the Pebbles sheen,
Or sliding thro' the Meadows green,
Or where thro' matted Sedge you creep,
Travelling to your Parent Deep:
Sound his Praise, by whom you rose,
That Sea, which neither ebbs nor flows.
O ye immortal Woods and Groves,
Which the enamour'd Student loves;
Beneath whose venerable shade,
For Thought and friendly Converse made,
Fam'd Hecadem, old Hero, lies,
Whose Shrine is shaded from the Skies,
And thro' the Gloom of silent Night
Projects from far its trembling Light;
You, whose Roots descend as low,
As high in Air your Branches grow;
Your leafy Arms to Heav'n extend,
Bend your Heads, in Homage bend:
Cedars and Pines that wave above,
And the Oak belov'd of Jove.
Omen, Monster, Prodigy,
Or nothing are, or Jove from Thee!

Whether various Nature play,
Or re-invers'd thy Will obey,
And to Rebel Man declare
Famine, Plague or Wasteful War.
Laugh, ye Profane, who dare despise
The threatning Vengeance of the Skies,
Whilst the Pious, on his Guard,
Undismay'd is still prepar'd:
Life or Death, his Mind's at rest,
Since what Thou send'st must needs be best.
No Evil can from Thee proceed:
'Tis only Suffer'd, not Decreed.
Darkness is not from the Sun,
Nor mount the Shades till he is gone:
Then does Night obscene arise
From Erebus, and fill the Skies,
Fantastic Forms the Air invade,
Daughters of Nothing and of Shade.
Can we forget thy Guardian Care,
Slow to punish, prone to spare!
Thou brak'st the haughty Persian's Pride,
That dar'd old Ocean's Pow'r deride;
Their Shipwrecks strew'd th' Eubean Wave,
At Marathon they found a Grave.
O ye blest Greeks who there expir'd,
For Greece with pious Ardor fir'd,
What Shrines or Altars shall we raise
To secure your Endless Praise?
Or need we Monuments supply,
To rescue what can never die!
And yet a Greater Hero far
(Unless Great Socrates could err)

Shall rise to bless some future Day,
And teach to live, and teach to pray.
Come, Unknown Instructor, come!
Our leaping Hearts shall make Thee room;
Thou with Jove our Vows shalt share,
Of Jove and Thee We are the Care.
O Father King, whose heav'nly Face
Shines serene on All thy Race,
We thy Magnificence adore,
And thy well-known Aid implore:
Nor vainly for thy Help we call;
Nor can we want: For thou art All!'

- Reverend John Wesley, (1703-1791) and Charles Wesley, (1707-1788)

Special Blessings on You

May you be deeply blessed
May you find Great Joy and Happiness
May you be Highly Favoured
May you be healed and ever rejuvenated
May you be achieve success and reward in all that you do
May you find the Buddha within you
May you find the Kingdom of God inside you
May you live long and well blessed, by God and man.

"To be able to practice five things everywhere under heaven constitutes perfect virtue: gravity, generosity of soul, sincerity, earnestness, and kindness." - **Confucius**, 500 BCE

12 Religions: Why are there so many religions? Which is the best path to God?

Religions are like many rivers leading to the ocean. For example, take the River Thames in England. While it is still a river, it has a name and form and shape. But when it reaches the North Sea, it loses its particular identity and merges with the larger body of water. So it is with all other rivers across the world. God loves diversity. He created many fruits, not just one. He created many types of trees, not just one type. He created countless rivers, streams, nations, peoples, animals, insects, plants, vegetables and so on. In all his creation, you see diversity of an immense nature. God allowed the establishment of so many religions so that there would be **many ways of praising and worshipping Him**. So the Russians praise and worship God through the Russian Orthodox way, the Greeks through the Greek Orthodox way, the Buddhists through the Buddhist beliefs, the Protestants through Christianity, the Hindus through the Hindu way, the Muslims through the teachings of Islam, the Parsis through the Zoroastrian faith, and so it is with every other religion, big or small. But I say to you, if you are a Catholic, be a good Catholic, if you are an Anglican, be the best Anglican, if you are a Presbyterian, be a good Presbyterian and if you are a Baptist, be a great Baptist. These are different ways to reach God. We should not read excerpts from great Religious leaders out of context. When Lord Jesus said, No one can come to the Father, but by me, he meant by His Way, His Life, His Virtues, His Values, His Teaching.

Qs. How do we know that?

Ans: Well, look at whom he praised. To teach the virtue of Love, Charity and Compassion, he told the story of the Good Samaritan. Samaritans were not Jews, The Jews disliked them and yet, Jesus praised the very people who were not of his religion. When Jesus wanted to teach about Faith, he praised a Roman Officer who definitely did not belong to his religion.

It is worth retelling the whole story here.

The Great Faith of the Roman Centurion: Matthew 8:5-13 'And when Jesus was entered into Capernaum, there came unto him a centurion, beseeching him,

And saying, Lord, my servant lieth at home sick of the palsy, grievously tormented.

And Jesus saith unto him, I will come and heal him.

The centurion answered and said, Lord, I am not worthy that thou shouldest come under my roof: but speak the word only, and my servant shall be healed.

For I am a man under authority, having soldiers under me: and I say to this man, Go, and he goeth; and to another, Come, and he cometh; and to my servant, Do this, and he doeth it.

When Jesus heard it, he marvelled, and said to them that followed, Verily I say unto you, I have not found so great faith, no, not in Israel.

And I say unto you, That many shall come from the east and west, and shall sit down with Abraham, and Isaac, and Jacob, in the kingdom of heaven.

But the children of the kingdom shall be cast out into outer darkness: there shall be weeping and gnashing of teeth.

And Jesus said unto the centurion, Go thy way; and as thou hast believed, so be it done unto thee. And his servant was healed in the selfsame hour.'

Jesus taught that Love is the greatest virtue.

In Matthew 22:36-40, when he was asked 'Master, which is the great commandment in the law?

Jesus said unto him, Thou shalt love the Lord thy God with all thy heart, and with all thy soul, and with all thy mind.

This is the first and great commandment.

And the second is like unto it, Thou shalt love thy neighbour as thyself.

On these two commandments hang all the law and the prophets.'

Where is the **Love** in me, if I despise another faith, another people, another religion, just because they praise and worship God in a way which I do not understand and which is different from me? It is like a banana saying that it is the best fruit and that the apple or the orange is false and wrong. No. Each fruit has its own taste and beauty. Or like the oak tree saying that it is the best and that the teak tree is inferior and should be cut down. No. So it is with religions. There are different ways of reaching, praising and worshipping God. Each path has its own beauty and taste. Have you ever travelled to another country and been offered a fruit or dish which you have never tried before? You are reluctant at first but after you taste the strange looking fruit or dish, you say "My God, this is so good!!" God loves diversity. Who are we to preach otherwise? Look at the stars in the Universe. So many. We don't even know how many billions are out there. Our Sun, which is a star, is only one of about 100 billion stars in our galaxy. Look at the Galaxies. Earlier we were told that there were 2 billion galaxies. The latest estimates of astronomers inform us that there are at least 100 to 170 billion galaxies in the visible universe. What they have done is to count the galaxies in a particular region. Then they multiplied this up to estimate the number for the whole universe. So many!! Do we know how many planets, comets, asteroids, moons are out there? No. They are too many. According to some, there could be 200 billion Earth-like worlds in the Milky Way. The more, the merrier. God loves it that way. The best way of living for you is to read about the lives and teachings of great religious leaders with an open mind and take the best out of them. But do not read books written on other faiths by a person of your own faith because unless he has discovered the "Kingdom of God" within him, he will naturally be biased. But read about other faiths from their own Masters and teachers. Just as it is best to eat a basket of different fruits and not just one fruit, just as it is best to eat various vegetables and not just one type, so you will grow faster inwardly in Oneness with God, if you taste and read about his truths from different religions not just one.

A father may be a painter. If he has 5 sons and 3 daughters, just one of whom is a painter; will he love only the one child who is a painter and condemn all the rest? No. A parent cannot but love all his kids equally. One child may be a banker, another may be a farmer, one may be rich and the other may be poor. It does not matter to a father or mother. They would love and cherish all their children because they feel that they are born from them. It is the same with God. He loves all of his creation. We all came from him. How can He not love all of us? Would the God of love condemn 535 million Buddhists followers just because we say so? It would be like the apple telling the jackfruit that you are not God's creation because I say so. Would the God of love and compassion condemn 1 billion Hindus just because a few of us say so? No, he is not intolerant. He embraces all. Teaching that speaks of intolerance of other faiths is not born from the God of Love. Would God reject 2.3 billion Christians just because some say so? No. Neither does He reject more than 2.08 billion Muslims. Whether you are Buddhist, Orthodox, Protestant, Anglican, Lutheran, Methodist, Hindu, Greek, Muslim, Sikh, Jain, Parsi, Mormon, Jewish, Evangelical, Baha'i or atheist, God loves us all. He has allowed many ways of worshipping and praising him just as he has created many stars, planets, asteroids and types of people. He is a God of diversity. All faiths teach that Love is the greatest of virtues.

Lao Tzu (601 BC-531 BC), the great Chinese Teacher and Philosopher said 'Without opening your door, you can open your heart to the world.' - Tao Te Ching, his book.

"Like the bee gathering honey from the different flowers, the wise person accepts the essence of the different scriptures and sees only the good in all religions. - **Mahatma Gandhi** (1869-1948)

"God has made different religions to suit different aspirants, times, and countries. All doctrines are only so many paths; but a path is by no means God himself. Indeed, one can reach God if one follows any of the paths with whole-hearted devotion...One may eat a cake with icing either straight or sidewise. It will taste sweet either way."- Sri Ramakrishna, (1836 – 1886), an Indian mystic and Master

"It is easy to hate and it is difficult to love. This is how the whole scheme of things works. All good things are difficult to achieve; and bad things are very easy to get." **Confucius, a great Chinese philosopher** - (551 BC - 479 BC)

The Blind Men and the Elephant

A number of disciples went to the Buddha and said, "Sir, there are living here in Savatthi many wandering hermits and scholars who indulge in constant dispute, some saying that the world is infinite and eternal and others that it is finite and not eternal, some saying that the soul dies with the body and others that it lives on forever, and so forth. What, Sir, would you say concerning them?"

The Buddha answered, "Once upon a time there was a certain raja who called to his servant and said, 'Come, good fellow, go and gather together in one place all the men of Savatthi who were born blind... and show them an elephant.' 'Very good, sire,' replied the servant, and he did as he was told. He said to the blind men assembled there, 'Here is an elephant,' and to one man he presented the head of the elephant, to another its ears, to another a tusk, to another the trunk, the foot, back, tail, and tuft of the tail, saying to each one that that was the elephant.

"When the blind men had felt the elephant, the raja went to each of them and said to each, 'Well, blind man, have you seen the elephant? Tell me, what sort of thing is an elephant?'

"Thereupon the men who were presented with the head answered, 'Sire, an elephant is like a pot.' And the men who had observed the ear replied, 'An elephant is like a winnowing basket.' Those who had been presented with a tusk said it was a ploughshare. Those who knew only the trunk said it was a plough; others said the body was a grainery; the foot, a pillar; the back, a mortar; the tail, a pestle, the tuft of the tail, a brush.

"Then they began to quarrel, shouting, 'Yes it is!' 'No, it is not!' 'An elephant is not that!' 'Yes, it's like that!' and so on, till they came to blows over the matter.

"Brethren, the raja was delighted with the scene.

"Just so are these preachers and scholars holding various views blind and unseeing... In their ignorance they are by nature quarrelsome, wrangling, and disputatious, each maintaining reality is thus and thus."

Then the Exalted One rendered this meaning by uttering this verse of uplift,

O how they cling and wrangle, some who claim

For preacher and monk the honored name!

For, quarreling, each to his view they cling.

Such folk see only one side of a thing.' – Old Buddhist story used for teaching

John Godfrey Saxe (1816 – 1887) The Blind Men and the Elephant – A Poem

"It was six men of Indostan
To learning much inclined,
Who went to see the Elephant
(Though all of them were blind),
That each by observation
Might satisfy his mind.
The First approached the Elephant,
And happening to fall
Against his broad and sturdy side,
At once began to bawl:
"God bless me! but the Elephant
Is very like a WALL!"
The Second, feeling of the tusk,
Cried, "Ho, what have we here,
So very round and smooth and sharp?
To me 'tis mighty clear
This wonder of an Elephant
Is very like a SPEAR!"
The Third approached the animal,
And happening to take
The squirming trunk within his hands,
Thus boldly up and spake:
"I see," quoth he, "the Elephant
Is very like a SNAKE!"
The Fourth reached out an eager hand,
And felt about the knee
"What most this wondrous beast is like
Is mighty plain," quoth he:
"'Tis clear enough the Elephant
Is very like a TREE!"

The Fifth, who chanced to touch the ear,
Said: "E'en the blindest man
Can tell what this resembles most;
Deny the fact who can,
This marvel of an Elephant
Is very like a FAN!"
The Sixth no sooner had begun
About the beast to grope,
Than seizing on the swinging tail
That fell within his scope,
"I see," quoth he, "the Elephant
Is very like a ROPE!"
And so these men of Indostan
Disputed loud and long,
Each in his own opinion
Exceeding stiff and strong,
Though each was partly in the right,
And all were in the wrong!"

- John Godfrey Saxe, an American poet, known for his re-telling of the Indian parable "The Blind Men and the Elephant", which introduced the story to a Western audience. He wrote the poem "The Blind Man and the Elephant in the 1800's and made it famous. It is based on Indian and Chinese folktales. The poem is in the public domain and able to be used freely. Some variations of the story date back to the Han Dynasty in China from 202 BC - 220 AD.

"Keeping aloof from the community of nations is the only cause for the downfall of India... Everyone that comes out of the country confers a benefit on the whole nation; for it is by doing that alone that your horizon will expand."

- Swami Vivekananda wrote to Manmatha Nath Bhattacharya on Sept 5, 1894.

In 1892 he had written, "So you see, we must travel; we must go to foreign parts. We must see how the engine of society works in other countries, and keep free and open communication with what is going on in the minds of other nations, if we really want to be a nation again".

"Woe unto the world when everyone is of the same religious opinion and takes to the same path. Then all religions and all thought will be destroyed. Variety is the very soul of life. When it dies out entirely, creation will die" - Swami Vivekananda

The Great Poet Saints of Tamil Nadu

Tamil Nadu, a state of South India has many poet-saints. Some of them were known as the Alvars or Alwars, meaning 'those who were one or imbued with God'. Out of the twelve Alvar saints, one of them was as female poet-saint named Andal. They taught devotion to the Hindu gods Vishnu and Krishna. Their songs were full of divine longing, bliss and service.

Besides the Alvars, there were sixty three Shaiva Nayanars. The Nayanars were famous as 'the hounds of Lord Shiva'. They were also known as 'the teachers of Lord Shiva'.

The Alvars and the Nayanars are perhaps the most significant saints of Tamil Nadu. They were said to have lived between the 6th and 8th century. However there is another school of thought who say they actually sang, taught and lived at least 3000-3500 years ago.

The four great Masters of the movement called Saivism were Manikka Vachaka, Appar, Jnanasam Bhanda and Sundar Murthy. Foremost among these Masters, was Manikka Vasahar or Manikya Vachaka (in Sanskrit form). He was a kind of a Chief Minister in the Royal Court of one of the Pandya Kings. After meeting a Brahman religious teacher, he suddenly understood the shortness of this worldly life and the vainness of earthly riches and abruptly left his high office with all its perks. He became a wandering poet saint. He renounced all earthly possessions to go around travelling from one shrine to the next.

These four Masters founded the four main paths of Saivism. They established the four main paths of Saivism, namely the sat marga or the path of truth, dasa marga or the path of the servant, the satputra marga or path of the son and the saha marga or path of a friend.

Among these great saints there was also Auvai, a famous woman saint from Tamil Nadu. She composed many fervent devotional poems. Ammaiyar from Karikkal and Auvai were two great women saints of Saivism. Nandanar was an untouchable of Saivism who reached great heights in sanctity. There were also five renowned Lingayat saints.

In ancient India, particularly in the south, there were many saints who advanced the rapid spread of Saivism through their sanctity and selfless acts of service to the people especially the poorest. Below are brief excerpts from the Tamil Poet Saint Manikka Vachaka and his Songs as translated in the 'Hymns of the Tamil Saivite Saints', by F. Kingsbury and G.P. Phillips, (1921)

"Though like Thy saints I seem, 'tis but the acting of a part.
Yet wondrous swift I run to reach the heaven where Thou art.
O hill of gold and precious gems, grant in Thy grace to me
A heart to melt, lord of my life, in ceaseless love to Thee
I have no fear of births, but quake at thought that I must die.
E'en heav'n to me were naught; for earth's whole empire what care I?
O Śiva wreathed with honeyed blossoms, "When shall come the morn
When Thou wilt grant Thy grace to me?" I cry with anguish torn.
The sky, earth, wind, the light, our very flesh and life art Thou,
Being art Thou, non-being too, Thou king, who see'st how
Men dance like puppets with their foolish thoughts of 'I' and 'Mine,'
While Thou the cords dost pull. What words can tell Thy praise divine?...
Hail to Thee, treasure rare,
Source of all prosperity,
Dawn has come, at Thy feet,
Flowers themselves, fair flowers lay we.
Praising Thee, we await
Smiles that blossom fair and sweet
In Thy face, as we fall
Prone adoring at Thy feet.
Śiva, Lord, dweller in

Perunduṛai, where expand
Lotus flowers, petalled white,
In the cool moist pasture land,
Thou whose flag is the bull,
Thou the Lord of all my ways,
Now O Lord of us all,
From Thy couch rise in Thy grace."

- Hymns of the Tamil Saivite Saints, by F. Kingsbury and G.P. Phillips, (1921)

Respectfully, I am telling you that you don't learn about the taste of a banana by eating an apple. You learn to saviour the taste of the banana by eating the banana. In the same way, you will never learn about the sweetness of another religious Master's teachings just by reading those of your own faith. You savour the taste of another God inspired faith by reading their sacred texts.

How do I pray? 13

Prayer: To GOD – THE ETERNAL

Lord Jesus in Mathew 6:6 "But you, when you pray, enter into your room, and having shut the door, pray to your Father in secret, and your Father, who sees in secret, will repay you."

1. When praying, try different types of prayer. One is praying aloud. The Word said out loud is very powerful so use it when praying for healing, for others, for self and for any problem faced. The other way is silent prayer. When one is not alone, praying silently is the best way. God hears you in the silence of your heart. Another method besides praying TO God, is to COMMAND the way Jesus did. Go to the source of all things within you, to the Source of Creation, then command or order for what you need. Off course, needless to say, you must have the faith and purity. But practise this method. Nothing in life comes without practice. You may have the gift of healing. But unless you try and keep trying, how will you ever come to know that you have this gift. Your prayers will be much more powerful and effective, if you pray with others than all by yourself. Invite your wife, husband, children, father, mother, grandfather and grandmother. You can also invite your friends and jointly pray for each other's needs. Pray for everything even the most mundane and little things. You can pray for healing, for a job, for change in your character, for self realization, for more and more Oneness with God, for financial stability, for others, for peace, for a difficult situation, for solving a problem and so on. Remember, God listens and answers every prayer. It may take time because we are not as powerful as saints, but believe me; ALL prayers are answered in some form or the other. Off course, if you are

asking for something wicked or evil, then no, your prayer will not be answered. Otherwise, the Kind One answers all our prayers.

2. **Being Grateful**. Saying Thank You to God from one's heart is very important when the prayer has been answered. God loves a grateful person.
3. **Meditation** is very important in life. The best form of meditation is Just Being. Empty your mind totally of all fears, thoughts, worries, distractions. God comes in with all his graces only when your mind is completely empty. He can only fill you with his beauty, his happiness, his wisdom, and his blessings if the mind is free and uncluttered. This is perhaps the greatest secret of all – the Secret of the Empty Mind. This is the Kingdom of God which Jesus spoke about, this is Nirvana which Buddha preached, this is Paradise, and this is Ram Rajya as mentioned by great Hindu Saints.
4. **Listening for Guidance:** This is extremely useful when seeking directions for anything. Suppose you are seeking guidance on a particular subject. Write down on a piece of paper or diary, the exact and precise subject that you want guidance about. Be very specific. Then close your eyes and ask God for direction & wisdom. After the prayer, be silent for a few moments, and then begin writing down whatever thoughts come to your mind. If all the thoughts are 'Yes' about the subject that you are asking about, then go ahead and do it. If all the thoughts are 'No' about the topic that you are seeking direction for, then do not do it. If the thoughts are mixed, neither all 'yes' nor all 'no', then don't do anything. Wait, be patient, God will send you signs. Maintain status quo. Normally, allow for between 30 to 50 'Yes' thoughts or 30 to 50 'No' thoughts before making a decision. This method is 100% accurate. It is more accurate than Google. It is tapping into Eternal wisdom, a wisdom that never fails. Psalm 139:17 'How precious also are thy thoughts unto me, O God! How great is the sum of them!'
5. **GOD:** The best life, the best career in life is to discover 'Who is God?' Who is this Intelligence that has created us? God is Eternal. His language is Silence. Just like people have German, English, French, Mandarin, Japanese, Russian or Hindi as their language,

God's language is Silence. Practise his language, practice silence. God is Still. It is amazing that the fastest speed in the Universe is Stillness. In that moment of stillness, we can reach anywhere in this Universe or beyond. This is the Secret of Not Doing and Just Being. The trees are still unlike us who think we need to work, to struggle, to strive and to move. Yet, we live only 70 to 90 years whereas the trees live much longer than us without moving at all. It is the same with the mountains. The Himalayas do not move as much as we do, but will exist and live for much longer than we will. God is formless and invisible. God is Bliss, so be happy. Our earthly life is short so we need to be happy. Finding happiness is very important. The greatest happiness comes when we practise the Art of the Empty Mind. Seek first the Kingdom of God and all the rest will come to you. The Empty Mind is the Kingdom of God. We can have Heaven here on earth when we are empty of ourselves and full of God.

Eternal Divine Prayers:

Dear God, what a beautiful language you have – the language of SILENCE. Before any wonderful word spoken, there has to be silence. Your language comes first. Before any award-winning music is played, there is silence. Your sound comes first. After every word is spoken, after every music is played, again there is silence. Your sound, your language prevails. Silence is the beginning, the middle and the end of everything. Between every word, between every note of music, there is silence.

You are ETERNAL. You have no beginning and no end. You are the Alpha and the Omega.

You are absolute STILLNESS. That is the fastest speed ever known. You are everywhere; you are in all things, just by being still. Nothing moves faster than the speed of stillness. Nothing lives longer than stillness. The tree in our garden remains absolutely still. It has never worked, nor has gone anywhere. Yet, it will live longer than all of us. It has seen my grandmother, my parents and us. Just by being still, it has all the food it needs.

You are BEAUTIFUL. You are the source of all beauty. The snow-clad mountains, the lovely flowers, the green meadows, the gushing waterfalls, the mighty rivers, the vast oceans, the clear blue sky, the green-green trees, the amazing wildlife and all the species speak of your beauty. Outside this planet, the billions of stars and galaxies showcase your wondrous beauty. You are beautiful. Your beauty is beyond all words.

You are the God of LOVE. In spite of all our sins and wrongdoings, you never criticize or scold us directly. You are full of love, you are mercy and compassion. You give rain, sunshine, air to breathe to everyone, to the Saint and the sinner. No one, no matter how sinful, is rejected by you. Rain falls on everyone. We love you though not as much as you love us. Thank you for your great love. You are mercy, tenderness and compassion.

You are ONENESS. You are One with everybody as everything is One with you. We wish to be more and more One with you. The more we look at this planet and the Universe, the more we realize how interconnected we are. We are all linked to you. Make us One with you as you are One with us.

You are the CREATOR of everything, seen and unseen around us. From a tiny seed you create a mighty tree. From a tree with green leaves, you produce tasty fruits. Almost out of nothing, a child is born and becomes a man or a woman. You create the billions of stars, galaxies, comets, asteroids, black holes, planets that we know very little about. We have not even been or travelled to any planet or star, such is vastness of your creation. You created millions of trees, flowers, fruits, vegetables, animal species and all that exists on this earth. We stand in awe at your creation and praise and worship you.

You are the ultimate PERFECTION. Everything you created is so perfect and marvelous. From the little ant, insect, the snail to the mighty lion, the giraffe, the tiger, elephant, crocodile, hippopotamus, rhinoceros, everything is sheer perfection. We marvel at the perfection of the rose, the lily, the daffodil, the orchids and the sweetness of the banana, the apple, the orange, the mango, the pomegranate and so on. We thank you for the wonder and the perfection of every tree, every blade of grass, every fruit, every flower and every animal. When we empty our minds, we are immediately connected with you. The connection is so good. It is free. We do not have to pay anything, neither a registration fee nor a monthly fee to be connected with you. The connection never goes off as long as our minds are empty. There is no power failure. No one cuts us off. The connection with you is 24 hours, 365 days.

You are BEYOND SPACE & TIME. You have always been there. You were never born, you will never die. You are here and everywhere. You are on this planet earth and you are present in a galaxy billions of light years away.

You are UNSEEN. No one alive has ever seen you. You are formless, yet exist in every form. You are unseen but you are seen in everything around us. We see you in the sparkling stream, the snowy mountains, the lush green forests, the dazzling stars and in all of nature.

You are UNKNOWN. No one knows you fully. Our knowledge of you is but a tiny speck of sand on the seashore. You are mysterious, worthy of study and meditation. There is no more important knowledge than the knowledge of you. You are the most important subject of education. Knowledge of you gives us knowledge of everything. No other knowledge is as important as knowledge and understanding of you. Yet, you are largely unknown.

You are UNHEARD. No one has heard your voice. Your language is silence. So perhaps one can only listen to your silent whisper in the stillness of one's heart. There is no recording of your words or voice. Yet, we hear you in thunder and lightning, in the blowing of the wind, in the pitter patter of rain, in the roar of mighty waterfalls and in the sound of music.

You are the Source of ALL WISDOM. You are the Source of ALL WISDOM. Thank you that for 29 years, since 1986, you have given precise and accurate guidance on every issue for which I have sought direction. You have never failed me. Your wisdom has always been available. Whenever I listened to my Inner Voice, you have spoken and shown me the way. All wisdom flows from you. Your wisdom is the best University, the highest PhD and the Source of all knowledge.

You are EMPTINESS. When we empty our minds of this world, you come and fill it. You are emptiness and yet you are fullness. The moment we are empty of worries, thoughts, fears, anxieties, anger and impurity, in that instant we are filled with your calm, your peace, your silence, your joy, your purity and your love.

You are ALL THINGS & EVERYTHING. You are Source of all Wealth. You created the billions of stars, gold, silver, diamonds and all precious things found on this planet. All life and good health come from you. Just as you are the biggest banker in the Universe, you are also the best Doctor and Healer ever known. You are the best father, mother, husband, wife, friend, teacher, healer, banker to us.

You are Supreme JOY & HAPPINESS. There is only one word that describes being with you – Bliss. When the birds chirp merrily, they sing out with joy to you. Life with you is full of joy. Being with you evokes a constant smile on one's face. You are the Source of all pleasure. All other pleasures are short-lived, temporary, full of regret and pain and a mere imitation of the ultimate pleasure which is Oneness with you.

You are ETERNAL. You live forever. You are unimaginable. You are beyond comprehension and understanding. You are all wisdom, all knowledge, all goodness, all kindness and compassion. I bow before you with folded hands. I come in front of you with all humility. I am not worthy of your great love. I seek to know you ever more. I seek to be one with you all the more. I seek to love you with all my heart and mind.

Dear God, help me to know that I do not know. Help me to realise that I am nothing. Help me to learn to stop speaking and be silent. Teach me to be absolutely still not only in my body but also in my mind. May I consider you as my best friend, the friend who will never betray me, the friend who will never condemn me, the friend who always loves me, the friend who truly takes care of me and the friend who is constantly there when I am in need. Thank you for everything that you have done for me.

Eternal God, One with me as I am One with Thee, kindly grant me to gift of uncovering my Inner Divine Self. Help me discover my Real Self. Help me realise the Divinity within me. I wish to walk and live as the Eternal here on earth.

Prayers from many Faiths 14

Buddhist Prayer

"We reverently pray for
eternal harmony in the universe.
May the weather be seasonable,
may the harvest be fruitful,
may countries exist in harmony,
and may all people enjoy happiness. "- ***Buddhist Prayer***

"Love the saints of every faith:
Put away thy pride.
Remember the essence of religion
Is meekness and sympathy,
Not fine clothes,
Not the Yogi's garb and ashes,
Not the blowing of the horns,
Not the shaven head,
Not long prayers,
Not recitations and torturings,
Not the ascetic way,
But a life of goodness and purity,
Amid the world's temptations." – Guru Nanak (1469 - 1539), the founder of Sikhism and the first of the ten Gurus of the Sikhs.

Sikh Prayers:

"True Bliss is experienced when ego is non-existent. True Bliss fills the void created by the exit of ego, of total surrender of ego at the lotus feet of the Lord. With ego surrendered, there is no more seeking, all desires disappear, the Sweet Will and Bliss of the Lord takes over."

"Save us, O Father, from lust, wrath greed, undue attachment and pride: and keeping us always attached to Thy feet...

Give us light, give us understanding, so that we may know what pleaseth Thee... Forgive up our sins. Help us keeping ourselves pure...

And may all men prosper by the grace." – Sikh prayers

Parsi prayers: Parsis belong to the Zoroastrian religion which arrived in India from Persia following persecution in the 7th century AD. This religion was started by Zarathustra also known as Zoroaster in the 6th or 7th century BC.

"O Ohrmazd, Lord! I am contrite for all sins and I desist from them, from all bad thoughts, bad words and bad acts which I have thought, spoken or done in the world, or which have happened through me, or have originated with me. For those sins of thinking, speaking and acting, of body and soul, worldly or spiritual, O Ohrmazd! I am contrite, I renounce them. With three words I distance myself (from them).

- excerpt from AVESTA: KHORDA AVESTA (Book of Common Prayers of Zoroastrians)

"Bestow on him riches and good things; bestow health of body, toughness of body, and resistance of body; bestow on him possessions giving abundant ease, future noble offspring, and a lengthy long life; ... Thus may it come as I wish."

- Excerpt of a prayer from Avesta: Khorda Avesta (Book of Common Prayers of Zoroastrians)

'In the name of God, the bestower, the giver, the benevolent! May there be health and long life, complete Glory giving righteousness! ...May this household be happy, may there be blessing! May there be happiness among the people of the religion of Zartosht! We beseech you, Lord, to grant to the present ruler, to all the community, and to all those of the Good Religion, health and fair repute. May so-and-so (**Here name the person or persons to be blessed**), [and his wife (or, her husband), and children], live for a thousand years! Keep them long happy, long healthy, long just! Keep them thus, keep them caring for the deserving! Keep them living and abiding for many years and countless hours! A hundred thousand thousand blessings upon them!'

– Prayer from AVESTA: KHORDA AVESTA (Book of Common Prayers of Zoroastrians)

"May the year be auspicious, the day fortunate, the month propitious in all these years and days and months! For many years keep them worthy to perform worship and utter prayers, to give charity and offerings, being just. May they have health to fulfil all their duties! May they be liberal, kind and good! May it be so, may it be more so," – powerful Parsi prayer from AVESTA: KHORDA AVESTA (Book of Common Prayers of Zoroastrians)

Bodhisattva Prayer for Humanity

"May I be a guard for those who need protection

A guide for those on the path

A boat, a raft, a bridge for those who wish to cross the flood

May I be a lamp in the darkness

A resting place for the weary

A healing medicine for all who are sick

A vase of plenty, a tree of miracles

And for the boundless multitudes of living beings

May I bring sustenance and awakening

Enduring like the earth and sky

Until all beings are freed from sorrow

And all are awakened." - Shantideva, Indian Buddhist sage 700 A.D. This is one of the prayers recited each morning by His Holiness the Dalai Lama

Well, Happy, and Peaceful

"May I be well, happy, and peaceful.

May my teachers be well, happy, and peaceful.

May my parents be well, happy, and peaceful.

May my relatives be well, happy, and peaceful.

May my friends be well, happy, and peaceful.

May the indifferent persons be well, happy, and peaceful.

May the unfriendly persons be well, happy, and peaceful.

May all meditators be well, happy, and peaceful.

May all beings be well, happy, and peaceful." - Buddhist Prayer

Offering the Mandala

"Here is the great Earth,

filled with the smell of incense,

covered with a blanket of flowers,

the Great Mountain, the Four Continents,

wearing a jewel of the Sun and Moon.

In my mind I make them the Paradise of a Buddha,

and offer it all to You.

By this deed, May every living being

Experience the Pure World." - ***Tibetan Prayer***

"Words have the power to both destroy and heal. When words are both true and kind, they can change our world." - ***The Buddha***

Blessings by The Buddha

"May every creature abound in well-being and peace.

May every living being, weak or strong, the long and the small

The short and the medium-sized, the mean and the great.

May every living being, seen or unseen, those dwelling far off,

Those nearby, those already born, those waiting to be born,

May all attain inward peace.

Let no one deceive another, Let no one despise another in any situation,

Let no one, from antipathy or hatred, wish evil to anyone at all.

Just as a mother, with her own life, protects her only son from hurt,

So within yourself foster a limitless concern for every living creature.

Display a heart of boundless love for all the world,

In all its height and depth and broad extent,

Love unrestrained, without hate or enmity.

Then as you stand or walk, sit or lie, until overcome by drowsiness,

Devote your mind entirely to this, it is known as living here life divine." - Lord Buddha

Golden Chain

"I am a link in Lord Buddha's golden chain of love that stretches around the world.

I must keep my link bright and strong.

I will try to be kind and gentle to every living thing, and protect all who are weaker than myself.

I will try to think pure and beautiful thoughts, to say pure and beautiful words, and to do pure and beautiful deeds, knowing that on what I do now depends my happiness and misery.

May every link in Lord Buddha's golden chain of love become bright and strong and may we all attain perfect peace." **- *Buddhist Prayer***

"O Lord, please forgive three sins that are due to my human limitations:

Thou art everywhere, but I worship you here;

Thou art without form, but I worship you in these forms;

Thou needest no praise, yet I offer you these prayers and salutations.

Lord, please forgive three sins that are due to my human limitations".

- A mystical and powerful Hindu prayer

Prayer for Peace

"Almighty God,
from whom all thoughts of truth and peace proceed,
kindle in the hearts of all men the true love of peace,
and guide with Your pure and peaceable wisdom
those who make decisions for the nations of the earth;
that in tranquility Your kingdom may go forward,
till the earth be filled with the knowledge of Your love;
through Jesus Christ our Lord. Amen" - Christian Prayer

"Cardinal Newman: *Shine Through Me* John Henry Newman (1801 – 1890), was an English prelate who is also referred to as Blessed John Henry Newman,

'Dear Jesus, help me to spread Your fragrance everywhere I go.

Flood my soul with Your spirit and life.

Penetrate and possess my whole being so utterly,

That my life may only be a radiance of Yours.

Shine through me, and be so in me

That every soul I come in contact with

May feel Your presence in my soul.

Let them look up and see no longer me, but only Jesus!

Stay with me and then I shall begin to shine as You shine,

So to shine as to be a light to others;

The light, O Jesus will be all from You; none of it will be mine;

It will be you, shining on others through me.

Let me thus praise You the way You love best, by shining on those around me.

Let me preach You without preaching, not by words but by my example,

By the catching force of the sympathetic influence of what I do,

The evident fullness of the love my heart bears to You. Amen.' - Newman (1801 – 1890)

"Truth alone triumphs, not untruth.

Lead me from the unreal to the Real.

Lead me from darkness to Light.

Lead me from death to Immortality". - A prayer from the Upanishads, ancient Hindu texts. The Upanishads comprise of religious, spiritual and philosophical scripture, written in India probably between (800 BCE-500 BCE)

Our Lord's Prayer in Matthew 6:9-15,

'Our Father which art in heaven, Hallowed be thy name.

Thy kingdom come, Thy will be done in earth, as it is in heaven.

Give us this day our daily bread.

And forgive us our debts, as we forgive our debtors.

And lead us not into temptation, but deliver us from evil: For thine is the kingdom, and the power, and the glory, forever. Amen.

For if ye forgive men their trespasses, your heavenly Father will also forgive you:

But if ye forgive not men their trespasses, neither will your Father forgive your trespasses.'

Prophet Muhammad (570 – 632) was the founder of Islam. When he began to spend time in solitude and reflection, he started receiving messages. During a period of solitary contemplation around the year 610, Muhammad heard a voice as he meditated. The voice said, "You are the Messenger of God". Muhammad later concluded that he had heard the archangel Gabriel. He continued to receive such messages from time to time until his death. They were collected into chapters and make up the Koran (Qur'an). The Five Pillars of Islam define Islamic practices - faith, prayer, fasting, pilgrimage and alms. Muslims believe that the Koran, the sacred religious book of Islam came from God.

The opening words of the Qur'an, also known as the Koran (609 – 632).

This is "In the name of Allah, Most gracious, Most merciful

Praise be to Allah, the Cherisher and Sustainer of the Worlds

Most Gracious, Most Merciful.

Master of the Day of Judgement

Thee do we worship, and Thine aide we seek

Show us the straight way

The way of those on whom Thou has bestowed thy Grace, those whose portion

Is not wrath, and who do not go astray."

"In the Name of Allah, the beneficent, the merciful: Praise be to the Lord of the Universe

who has created us and made us into tribes and nations that we may know each other,

not that we may despise each other.

If the enemy incline towards peace, do thou also incline towards peace, and trust in God,

for the Lord is one that hears and knows all things.

And the servants of God Most Gracious are those who walk on the Earth in humility,

and when we address them, we say, 'Peace.'"

Muslim Prayer **for Peace**

"O God, O our Master!

You Have eternal life and Everlasting peace by your essence and attributes.

The everlasting peace is from you And it returns to you, O our Sustainer!

Grant us the life of True peace and usher us into The abode of peace.

O Glorious and Bounteous One!

You are blessed and sublime." - ***Muslim Prayer***

Oh God, You Are Peace

"Oh God,

You are peace.

From you comes peace,

To you returns peace.

Revive us with a salutation of peace,

And lead us to your abode of peace." - Prophet Muhammad

A Shinto (Japan) Prayer for Peace

"Although the people living across the ocean surrounding us,

I believe, are all our brothers and sisters,

why are there constant troubles in this world?

Why do winds and waves rise in the ocean surrounding us?

I only earnestly wish that the wind will soon puff away all the clouds

which are hanging over the tops of the mountains." – A Shinto prayer

Prayer for Peace – Taoist

"If there is to be peace in the world, there must be peace in the nations.

If there is to be peace in the nations, there must be peace in the cities.

If there is to be peace in the cities, there must be peace between neighbors.

If there is to be peace between neighbors, there must be peace in the home.

If there is to be peace in the home, there must be peace in the heart."

- Lao-Tzu, revered Chinese Master

The Blessing of Light, Rain and Earth – Ancient Celtic Prayer

"May the blessing of Light be on you
light without and light within.
May the blessed sunlight shine on you
And warm your heart till it glows
Like a great peat fire, so that the stranger
may come and warm himself at it
and also a friend
And may the light shine out of the two eyes of you
Like a candle set in the windows of a house
Bidding the wanderer to come in out of the storm.
And may the blessing of the Rain be upon you, the soft sweet rain.
May it fall upon your spirit so that all the little flowers may spring up
And shed their sweetness on the air
And may the blessing of the Great Rains be on you
May they beat upon your spirit and wash it fair and clean
And leave there many a shining pool where the blue of heaven shines
And sometimes a star.
And may the blessing of the Earth be upon you, the great round earth
May you ever have a kindly greeting for them you pass
As you're going along the roads
May the earth be soft under you when you rest upon it
Tire at the end of the day
And may it rest easy over you
When at the last you lay out under it
May it rest so lightly over you
That your soul may be out from under it quickly
And up, and off, and on its way to God." - Traditional Irish and Scottish Blessing

Celtic Peace Prayer from Antiquity

"Deep Peace of the running wave to you
Deep Peace of the flowing air to you
Deep Peace of the quiet earth to you
Deep Peace of the shining stars to you
Deep peace of the shades of night to you
Moon and stars always giving Light to you." - ***Celtic Peace Prayer***

The Vedas are a set of four Hindu holy texts including ancient chants, written between about 1500 and 1000 BCE.

"Oh Creator of the Universe, may we receive thy supreme sin-destroying light, May Thou guide our intellect in the right direction." **The Vedas**

Jewish Prayer

"God, hear my prayer,
And let my cry come to You.
Do not hide from me in the day of my distress
Turn to me and speedily answer my prayer.
Eternal God, Source of healing,
Out of my distress I call upon You.
Help me sense Your presence
At this difficult time.
Grant me patience when the hours are heavy;
In hurt or disappointment give me courage.
Keep me trustful in Your love.
Give me strength for today, and hope for tomorrow.
To your loving hands I commit my spirit
When asleep and when awake. You are with me; I shall not fear." Jewish prayer

Mother Earth

"Dear mother earth, who day by day
Unfolds rich blessing on our way,

O praise God! Alleluia!

The fruits and flowers that verdant grow,

Let them his praise abundant show.

O praise God, O praise God,

Alleluia, Alleluia, Alleluia."

- St. Francis of Assisi (born at Assisi, Italy in 1181 or 1182 and died on 3 October, 1226)

Beautiful Protestant Prayer

"O God,

We thank you for this earth, our home; for the wide sky and the blessed sun, for the ocean and streams, for the towering hills and the whispering wind, for the trees and green grass.

We thank you for our senses by which we hear the songs of birds, and see the splendor of fields of golden wheat, and taste autumn's fruit, rejoice in the feel of snow, and smell the breath of spring flowers.

Grant us a heart opened wide to all this beauty; and save us from being so blind that we pass unseeing when even the common thornbush is aflame with your glory.

For each new dawn is filled with infinite possibilities for new beginnings and new discoveries. Life is constantly changing and renewing itself. In this new day of new beginnings with God, all things are possible. We are restored and renewed in a joyous awakening to the wonder that our lives are and, yet, can be." - Protestant Prayer

A **Hindu Prayer** for Peace

"Oh God, lead us from the unreal to the Real.

Oh God, lead us from darkness to light.

Oh God, lead us from death to immortality.

Shanti, Shanti, Shanti unto all.

Oh Lord God almighty, May there be peace in celestial regions.

May there be peace on earth.

May the waters be appeasing.

May herbs be wholesome, and may trees and plants bring peace to all.

May all beneficent beings bring peace to us.

May the Vedic Law propagate peace all through the world.

May all things be a source of peace to us.

And may thy peace itself bestow peace on all and may that peace come to me also."

"O! Mother Earth

O! Mother Earth,

who has the ocean as clothes and mountains and forests on her body,

who is the wife of Lord Vishnu, I bow to you.

Please forgive me for touching you with my feet." - Hindu Prayer

Bhagavad-Gita (Song of the Lord)

"The brightness of the sun, which lights up the world, the brightness of the moon and of fire

- these are my glory. With a drop of my energy, I enter the earth and support all creatures.

Through the moon, the vessel of life-giving fluid, I nourish all plants." - Lord Krishna sings

"O Lord, you love justice and you establish peace on earth.

We bring before you the disunity of today's world;

the absurd violence, and the many wars,

which are breaking the courage of the peoples of the world;

human greed and injustice,

which breed hatred and strife.

Send your spirit and renew the face of the earth;

teach us to be compassionate towards the whole human family;

strengthen the will of all those

who fight for justice and for peace,

and give us that peace which the world cannot give." - Ecumenical Centre Prayer

A Prayer about Nature and God's Creation

"Loving Father and Creator of all we come to you today deeply grateful for your creation.

As we look around us we are amazed at the greatness and majesty of all that you have made.

Nature around us speaks of your greatness - the vast expanse of the sky, the mountains, trees, lakes and streams speak of your great design.

You have given us such beauty in the colors of the rainbow, the beauty of flowers and fields.

Words cannot adequately express the magnificence of all you have created.

We join in praise with the writer of the psalms when he says, 'O Lord, our Lord, how majestic is your name in all the earth.' - A Catholic prayer

Ashanti Prayer from Africa

"O God, creator of our land,

our earth, the trees, the animals and humans, all is for your honour.

The drums beat it out, and people sing about it,

and they dance with noisy joy that you are the Lord.

You also have pulled the other continents out of the sea.

What a wonderful world you have made out of wet mud,

and what beautiful men and women!

We thank you for all the beauty of this earth.

The grace of your creation is like a cool day between rainy seasons.

We drink in your creation with our eyes.

We listen to the bird's jubilee with our ears.

How strong and good and sure your earth smells,

and everything that grows there.

Be with us in our countries and in all Africa, and in the whole world

Prepare us for the service that we should render." - ***Ashanti Prayer, Africa***

Dadirri arising from the **Aboriginal people** of Australia teaches us deep listening and quiet. It means being still and aware. It is a 'tuning in' to the inner depths within and leads to a deeper understanding of the beauty of nature. It calls us to reflect and contemplate on the amazing wonders of all God's creation.

"Dadirri is deep listening.

Listening to the land.

Listening to the spirit speaking through the land.

Listening to the stillness.

Dadirri is awareness of the land as sacred Silent awareness of deep springs within me. I am the story of the land. I feel the harmony that is in the land.

My life is sacred.

A deep theme unfolding.

Dadirri makes me feel whole. Renews me and brings peace. My life is new."

- Aboriginal Prayer from Australia

Peace

"Looking behind, I am filled with gratitude.

Looking forward, I am filled with vision.

Looking upwards, I am filled with strength.

Looking within, I discover peace." - **Queio Apache Prayer**

Druid Prayer for Peace

"Deep within the still center of my being,

may I find peace.

Silently within the quiet of the Grove,

may I share peace.

Gently and powerfully,

within the greater circle of humankind,

may I radiate peace." - Druid Prayer

May we show our love and reverence to you, our Lord, by caring for all that you have created. We humbly give you praise and thanks." - **Catholic Prayer**

Let Us Together Praise the Lord

"Let us together praise the Lord,

from whom we have rain from the heavens

and abundance from the earth.

Blessed be God now and forever." - Christian Prayer

Prayers for Peace

"Supreme Lord, let there be peace in the sky and in the atmosphere. Let there be peace in the plant world and in the forests. Let the cosmic powers be peaceful. Let the Brahman, the true essence and source of life, be peaceful. Let there be undiluted and fulfilling peace everywhere."

- The Atharva Veda

Hindu Morning Prayer

"May all in this world be happy,
may they be healthy,
may they be comfortable
and never miserable.
May the rain come down in the proper time,
may the earth yield plenty of corn,
may the country be free from war,
may the Brahmans be secure." - Hindu Morning Prayer

Pure and Strong

"Lord, make me so pure and strong
That all creatures may look upon me with friendship.
And may I also look upon all creatures with friendship." - Yajur Ved

There is a Light

"There is a light that shines beyond all things on earth,
beyond all of us, beyond the heavens,
beyond the highest, the very highest heavens.
This is the light that shines in our hearts." - Chandogya Upanishad

Nature's Beauty

"Nature's beauty is an art of God. Let us feel the touch of God's invisible hands in everything beautiful.

By the first touch of His hand rivers throb and ripple. When He smiles the sun shines, the moon glimmers, the stars twinkle, the flowers bloom. By the first rays of the rising sun, the universe is stirred; the shining gold is sprinkled on the smiling buds of rose; the fragrant air is filled with sweet melodies of singing birds, the dawn is the dream of God's creative fancy." - **Rig Veda** 1.6.3

Hindu Prayer for the Unity of All Life

'May the winds, the oceans, the herbs, and night and days, the mother earth, the father heaven, all vegetation, the sun, be all sweet to us.

Let us follow the path of goodness for all times, like the sun and the moon moving eternally in the sky.

Let us be charitable to one another. Let us not kill or be violent with one another.

Let us know and appreciate the points of view of others. And let us unite.

May the God who is friendly, benevolent, all-encompassing, measurer of everything, the sovereign, the lord of speech, may He shower His blessings on us...

Oh Lord, remove my indiscretion and arrogance, control my mind. Put an end to the snare of endless desires. Broaden the sphere of compassion and help me to cross the ocean of existence." – Such a beautiful ancient Hindu prayer

Prayer For Peace

"I offer you peace. I offer you love. I offer you friendship.

I see your beauty. I hear your need. I feel your feelings.

My wisdom flows from the Highest Source. I salute that Source in you.

Let us work together for unity and love." - **Mahatma Gandhi**

A Prayer for Peace in Our World

"Make your ways known upon earth, Lord God,

Your saving power among all peoples.

Renew your Church in holiness

And help us to serve you with joy.

Guide the leaders of all nations,

That justice may prevail throughout the world.

Let not the needy be forgotten,

Nor the hope of the poor be taken away.

Make us instruments of your peace

And let your glory be over all the earth." - **Church of England Prayer**

Do All the Good You Can

"Do all the good you can. By all the means you can.

In all the ways you can. In all the places you can.

At all the times you can. To all the people you can.

As long as ever you can." - **John Wesley**, 18th-century founder of the Methodist movement

O God Eternal

"O God eternal, good beyond all that is good;

fair beyond all that is fair,

in whom is calmness and peace:

reconcile the differences which divide us from one another

and bring us back into the unity of love

which may bear some likeness to your divine nature.

Grant that we may be spiritually one,

both within ourselves and with one another,

through the grace, mercy and tenderness

of your Son, Jesus Christ." - **Christian Orthodox Tradition**

Native American/First People Prayers: During Native American tribal gatherings traditional worship practices form part of their dance, rhythm, songs and trance. Deeply rooted in Nature, their ancient sacred legends and beliefs are full of imagery of earth, plants, seasons, weather, fire, animals, sky and water. Native Americans believe in the principle of an all embracing and universal Great Spirit and in their abiding connection to the Earth. Common among the tribes are creation stories and revered memories of ancient ancestors.

A Native American/First People Prayer for Peace

"O Great Spirit of our Ancestors, I raise my pipe to you.

To your messengers the four winds,

and to Mother Earth who provides for your children.

Give us the wisdom to teach our children to love, to respect, and to be kind to each other so that they may grow with peace in mind.

Let us learn to share all the good things you provide for us on this Earth."

Cheyenne Prayer for Peace

"Let us know peace.

For as long as the moon shall rise,

For as long as the rivers shall flow,

For as long as the sun shall shine,

For as long as the grass shall grow,

Let us know peace." - Cheyenne Prayer

The Great Spirit and Mother Earth

"The Great Spirit is in all things, He is in the air we breathe.

The Great Spirit is our Father, but the Earth is our Mother.

She nourishes us, that which we put into the ground, She returns to us..."

- Big Thunder (Bedagi) - Wabanaki Algonquin

Prayer to the Great Spirit

"O Great Spirit, help me always to speak the truth quietly, to listen with an open mind when others speak and to remember the peace that may be found in silence." - Cherokee Prayer

What is Life

"What is life?

It is the flash of a firefly in the night.

It is the breath of a buffalo in the wintertime.

It is the little shadow which runs across the grass

and loses itself in the sunset." - ***Crowfoot, Blackfoot warrior and orator*** (1821 – 1890)

Eagle Prayer

"Oh Eagle, come with wings outspread in sunny skies.
Oh Eagle, come and bring us peace, thy gentle peace.
Oh Eagle, come and give new life to us who pray.
Remember the circle of the sky, the stars, and the brown eagle,
the great life of the Sun, the young within the nest.
Remember the sacredness of things." - Pawnee Prayer

Prayer For Peace

"Oh Great Spirit who dwells in the sky,
lead us to the path of peace and understanding,
let all of us live together as brothers and sisters.
Our lives are so short here, walking upon Mother Earth's surface,
let our eyes be opened to all the blessings you have given us.
Please hear our prayers, Oh Great Spirit." - Native American Prayer

The Journey

"When the earth is sick and dying,
There will come a tribe of people
From all races...
Who will put their faith in deeds,
Not words, and make the planet
Green again..." - Cree Prophecy

Navajo Chant

"The mountains, I become a part of it...
The herbs, the fir tree, I become a part of it.
The morning mists, the clouds, the gathering waters,
I become a part of it.
The wilderness, the dew drops, the pollen...
I become a part of it." - ***Navajo Chant***

Sioux Prayer

"Grandfather Great Spirit
All over the world the faces of living ones are alike.
With tenderness they have come up out of the ground
Look upon your children that they may face the winds
And walk the good road to the Day of Quiet.
Grandfather Great Spirit
Fill us with the Light.
Give us the strength to understand, and the eyes to see.
Teach us to walk the soft Earth as relatives to all that live." - Sioux Prayer

Native American Prayer

"Give us the wisdom to teach our children to love, to respect and to be kind to one another that we may grow with peace in mind." - ***Native American Prayer***

Mohawk Prayer

"Oh Great Spirit, Creator of all things;
Human Beings, trees, grass, berries.
Help us, be kind to us.
Let us be happy on earth.
Let us lead our children
To a good life and old age.
These our people; give them good minds
To love one another.
Oh Great Spirit,
Be kind to us
Give these people the favor
To see green trees,
Green grass, flowers, and berries
This next spring;
So we all meet again

Oh Great Spirit,

We ask of you." - ***Mohawk Prayer***

Zuni Prayer

"Cover my earth mother four times with many flowers.

Let the heavens be covered with the banked-up clouds.

Let the earth be covered with fog; cover the earth with rains.

Great waters, rains, cover the earth. Lighting cover the earth.

Let thunder be heard over the earth; let thunder be heard;

Let thunder be heard over the six regions of the earth." - ***Zuni Prayer for Rain***

May All I Say

"May all I say and all I think

be in harmony with thee,

God within me,

God beyond me,

maker of the trees." - ***Chinook prayer, Pacific Northwest Coast, North America***

Apache Blessing

"May the sun bring you new energy by day,

may the moon softly restore you by night,

may the rain wash away your worries,

may the breeze blow new strength into your being,

may you walk gently through the world and

know its beauty all the days of your life." - Apache Blessing

Sioux prayer

"O our Father, the Sky, hear us

and make us strong.

O our Mother the Earth, hear us

and give us support.

O Spirit of the East,

send us your Wisdom.

O Spirit of the South,

may we tread your path of life.

O Spirit of the West,

may we always be ready for the long journey.

O Spirit of the North, purify us

with your cleansing winds." - The Native American Indians are an important part of the culture of the United States. Their people have nursed and lived on the land for thousands of years.

Blessings From Rig Veda

"May your counsel be common,

May you belong to one fraternity,

May your minds move, with one accord.

May your hearts work in harmony for one goal.

May you be inspired, by common ideal.

May you offer worship, with common oblation." - From RIG VEDA. 10 –191– 3

"May you resolve, with one accord.

May your hearts be in unison.

May your thoughts be harmonious,

So that you live together with happiness and hilarity." - From RIG. VEDA. 10 –191 -4

Be pleased to show mercy, O God! – Magnificent Hindu prayer

Thou art the Imperishable, the supreme Object of Knowledge;

Thou art the ultimate resting-place of this universe;

Thou art the immortal guardian of the eternal right,

Thou art the everlasting Spirit, I hold.

Without beginning, middle, or end, of infinite power,

Of infinite arms, whose eyes are the moon and sun,

I see Thee, whose face is flaming fire,

Burning this whole universe with Thy radiance.

For this region between heaven and earth

Is pervaded by Thee alone, and all the directions;
Seeing this Thy wondrous, terrible form,
The triple world trembles, O exalted one!
Homage be to Thee from, in front and from behind,
Homage be to Thee from all sides, Thou All!
O Thou of infinite might, Thy prowess is unmeasured;
Thou attainest all; therefore Thou art All!
Thou art the father of the world of things that move and move not,
And Thou art its revered, most venerable Guru;
There is no other like Thee-how then a greater?
Even, in the three worlds, O Thou of matchless greatness
Therefore, bowing and prostrating my body,
I beg grace of Thee, the Lord to be revered:
As a father to his son, as a friend to his friend,
As a lover to his beloved, be pleased to show mercy, O God!" - From the Bhagavad Gita.

The Bhagavad Gita (Song of the Lord): This is one of the most important and popular of ancient Indian religious texts. From the Bhagavad Gita we learn about the three yogas, Karma yoga (yoga of action), Jnana yoga (yoga of knowledge) and Bhakthi yoga (yoga of devotion). In the passage below, Arjun "sees" God in His full glory, sings praises to God and marvels at how mighty God is!!

The Infinity Of God - The Bhagavad Gita (Song of the Lord)

"I see you in all things, O my God. Infinity itself is your creation. And all around are the signs of your infinity: the bursting life of countless plants; the unending song of innumerable birds; the tireless movement of animals and insects.

Nowhere can I see a beginning or an end of your creation.

I see the infinite beauty which infuses the entire universe. You are the king of the universe, and its beauty is your crown and sceptre. I bow down in homage and adoration.

You are immortal, imperishable, the summit of all knowledge, the power behind all movement. You designed all things, and set them in motion.

The sun is your eye during the day, and the moon your eye at night. The wind is your breath, and the fertile brown earth is your heart.

By your power all things are created, and by your power they are destroyed. Birth and death are in your hands. I tremble with awe and wonder when I contemplate your power.

As the waters of a river flow to the sea, the path determined by the line of the valley, so we pass through life to death, our destiny mapped out by your will.

Lord, reveal yourself to me. Show me that love, not hatred, inspires your creation. Show me that mercy, not anger, guides my life. I do not ask to understand the mystery of your works; I want only to be assured of your goodness."

The Truth Of God – The Bhagavad Gita (Song of the Lord)

"Supreme God, your light is brighter than the sun, your purity whiter than mountain snow, you are present wherever I go.

All people of wisdom praise you. So I too put faith in all your words, knowing that everything you teach is true. Neither the angels in heaven nor the demons in hell can know the perfection of your wisdom, for it is beyond all understanding.

Only your Spirit knows you; only you can know your true self. You are the source of all being, the power of all power, the ruler of all creatures. So you alone understand what you are.

In your mercy reveal to me all that I need to know, in order to find peace and joy. Tell me the truths that are necessary for the world in which I live.

Show me how I can meditate upon you, learning from you the wisdom that I need. I am never tired of hearing you, because your words bring life."

Noble Masters and Teachers - Inspiring Lives

15

Plato, ancient great Greek philosopher. Plato was born about 427 BCE in Athens. He was the teacher of Aristotle and the student of Socrates. He is one of the world's most famous and most widely read philosophers.

'One of the penalties for refusing to participate in politics is that you end up being governed by your inferiors.'

'A hero is born among a hundred, a wise man is found among a thousand, but an accomplished one might not be found even among a hundred thousand men.'

'Good actions give strength to ourselves and inspire good actions in others.'

'All the gold which is under or upon the earth is not enough to give in exchange for virtue.'

'Astronomy compels the soul to look upwards and leads us from this world to another.'

'The greatest wealth is to live content with little.' Plato (427 - 347 B.C.E)

Man is a Civilised Animal: "Man is a tame or civilized animal; nevertheless, he requires proper instructions and a fortunate nature, and then of all animals he becomes the most divine and most civilized; but if he be insufficiently or ill- educated he is the most savage of earthly creatures."

'Wherefore my counsel is that we hold fast ever to the heavenly way and follow after justice and virtue always, considering that the soul is immortal and able to endure every sort of good and every sort of evil. Thus shall we live dear to one another and to the gods, both while remaining here and when, like conquerors in the games who go round to gather gifts, we receive our reward. And it shall be well with us both in this life and in the pilgrimage of a thousand years which we have been describing.' – REPUBLIC by Plato (427—347 B.C.E.) (Public Domain English Translation by Benjamin Jowett)

Count Leo Tolstoy, illustrious Russian novelist must have been a great soul to have had such a deep influence on giants of history among whom are Mahatma Gandhi and Martin Luther King Jr. After 1870, it is said he radically transformed his life to become one of the Greats of all time.

Leo Tolstoy famous Sayings:

"If you want to be happy, be."

"Everyone thinks of changing the world, but no one thinks of changing himself."

"The two most powerful warriors are patience and time."

"There is no greatness where there is no simplicity, goodness and truth."

"Truth, like gold, is to be obtained not by its growth, but by washing away from it all that is not gold."

"Without knowing what I am and why I am here, life is impossible."

- Count Lev Nikolayevich Tolstoy, the greatest Russian philosopher, 1903.

Shri Adi Shankaracharya, perhaps the greatest of Indian saints. He is said to have lived between 788 and 820 though some say that he lived much earlier than this.

Outline of Shankara's teachings: After Shankaracharya decided to enter 'samadhi,' Sudhanva, the main disciple of Shankara, requested that the essentials of his teaching may be summarized and given to them. Shankaracharya then said the Dasa Shlokas, or Ten Verses, which elaborated the omniscience, omnipotence and omnipresence of Brahman – the core concept of Hinduism (Sanatana Dharma).

1. The five elements do not express my real nature; I am changeless and persist forever.
2. I am above castes and creeds. I am seen when 'maya (illusion)' is removed, and do not need concentration or worship....

3. I have no parents; I need no Vedas as proclaimed in the scriptures, no sacrifices, no pilgrimages. I am the eternal witness.
4. All the teachings of various religions and philosophies do not reveal my true nature and are but shallow views of my deep being.
5. I pervade the whole universe and am above, in the middle and below, in all directions.
6. I am colourless, formless, light being my form.
7. I have no teacher, scripture or any disciples, nor do I recognize Thou or I, or even the universe and am changeless and the absolute knowledge.
8. I am neither awake, in deep sleep nor dreaming, but above consciousness with which the three are associated. All these are due to ignorance and I am beyond that.
9. I pervade everything, everywhere and the eternal reality and self-existent. The whole universe depends on me and become nothing without me.
10. I cannot be called one, for that implies two, which is not. I am neither isolated nor non-isolated, neither am I empty or full.'

"Men worship Incarnations such as Christ or Buddha. They are the most perfect manifestations of the eternal Self. They are much higher than all the conceptions of God that you or I can make." - **Swami Vivekananda, a** revered Hindu teacher **(**12 January 1863 – 4 July 1902)

"The greatest men in the world have passed away unknown. Silently they live and silently they pass away; and in time their thoughts find expression in Buddhas or Christs, and it is these latter that become known to us." - Swami Vivekananda **(**1863 – 1902)

Lord Buddha (about 600 BCE – around 300 BCE): What a life he led!! Can you imagine in today's world a Prince giving up everything to search for an end to human suffering? Well that is what Prince Siddhartha did. He left all the glory and throne and wealth of a Kingdom, shaved his head and went in search for Enlightenment. He found it and began teaching a way to reach Nirvana and end suffering. Today people in countries like Japan, Thailand, Vietnam, Singapore, Myanmar, China, South Korea, Cambodia, Laos, Bhutan, Sri Lanka, Taiwan and Mongolia practise Buddhism. Below are excerpts from an excellent and gentle description of the life of Lord Buddha by Colonel Henry S. Olcott presented in the form of Questions and Answers. Colonel Henry Olcott (1832–1907) was perhaps the first Western and first American Buddhist convert. He co-founded the Theosophical Society. Read them again and again. May they kindle in you the eternal spark of wisdom and goodness which lies within you. May many such enlightened souls emerge on earth to bring real joy and happiness into this world.

The Buddhist Catechism, by Henry S. Olcott [1908]

THE LIFE OF THE BUDDHA.

1. Q. Of what religion are you?

A. The Buddhist

2. Q. What is Buddhism?

A. It is a body of teachings given out by the great personage known as the Buddha.

3. Q. Is 'Buddhism' the best name for this teaching?

A. No; that is only a western term: the best name for it is Bauddha Dharma.

4. Q Would you call a person a Buddhist who had merely been born of Buddhist parents?

A. Certainly not. A Buddhist is one who not only professes belief in the Buddha as the noblest of Teachers, in the Doctrine preached by Him, and in the Brotherhood of Arahats, but also practises His precepts in daily life

5. Q. What is a male lay Buddhist called?

A. An Upâsaka.

6. Q. What is a female called?

A. An Upâsikâ.

7. Q. Was the Buddha God?

A. No. Buddha Dharma teaches no "divine" incarnation.

8. Q. Was he a man?

A. Yes; but the wisest, noblest and most holy being who had developed himself in the course of countless births far beyond all other beings, the previous Buddhas alone excepted.

9. Q. Were there other Buddhas before him?

A. Yes; as will be explained later on.

10. Q. Was Buddha his name?

A. No. It is the name of a condition or state of mind, of the mind after it has reached the culmination of development.

11. Q. What is its meaning?

A. Enlightened; or, he who has the all-perfect wisdom. The Pâlî phrase is Sabbannu, the One of Boundless Knowledge. In Sanskrit it is Sarvajña.

12. Q. What was the Buddha's real name, then?

A. Siddhartha was his royal name, and Gautama, or Gotama, his family name. He was Prince of Kapilavastu and belonged to the illustrious family of the Okkâka, of the Solar race.

13. Q. Who were his father and mother?

A. King Suddhodana and Queen Mâyâ, called Mahâ Mâyâ.

14. Q. What people did this King reign over?

A. The Sâkyas; an Aryan tribe of Kshattriyas.

15. Q. Tell me again when Prince Siddhârtha was born.

A. Six hundred and twenty-three years before the Christian era.

16. Q. Had the Prince luxuries and splendors like other Princes?

A. He had; his father, the King, built him three magnificent palaces—for the three Indian seasons—the cold, the hot, and the rainy—of nine, five, and three stories respectively, and handsomely decorated,

17. Q. How were they situated?

A. Around each palace were gardens of the most beautiful and fragrant flowers, with fountains of spouting water, the trees full of singing birds, and peacocks strutting over the ground.

18. Q. Was he living alone?

A. No; in his sixteenth year he was married to the Princess Yasodharâ, daughter of the King Suprabuddha. Many beautiful maidens, skilled in dancing and music, were also in continual attendance to amuse him.

19. Q. How did he get his wife?

A. In the ancient Kshattriya or warrior fashion, by overcoming all competitors in games and exercises of skill and prowess, and then selecting Yasodharâ out of all the young princesses, whose fathers had brought them to the tournament or mela.

20. Q. How, amid all this luxury, could a Prince become all-wise?

A. He had such natural wisdom that when but a child he seemed to understand all arts and sciences almost without study. He had the best teachers, but they could teach him nothing that he did not seem to comprehend immediately.

21. Q. Did he become Buddha in his splendid palaces?

A. No. He left all and went alone into the jungle.

22. Q. Why did he do this?

A. To discover the cause of our sufferings and the way to escape from them.

23. Q. Was it not selfishness that made him do this?

A. No; it was boundless love for all beings that made him devote himself to their good.

24. Q. But how did he acquire this boundless love?

A. Throughout numberless births and æons of years he had been cultivating this love, with the unfaltering determination to become a Buddha.

25. Q. What did he this time relinquish?

A. His beautiful palaces, his riches, luxuries, and pleasures, his soft beds, fine dresses, his rich food, and his kingdom; he even left his beloved wife and only son, Râhula

26. Q. Did any other man ever sacrifice so much for our sake?

A. Not one in this present world-period: this is why Buddhists so love him and why good Buddhists try to be like him.

27. Q. How old was he when he went to the jungle?

A. He was in his twenty-ninth year.

28. Q. What finally determined him to leave all that men usually love so much and go to the jungle?

A. A deva (a deity) appeared to him when driving out in his chariot, under four impressive forms, on four different occasions.

29. Q. What were these different forms?

A. Those of a very old man broken down by age, of a sick man, of a decaying corpse, and of a dignified hermit.

30. Q. Did he alone see these?

A. No, his attendant, Channa, also saw them.

31. Q. Why should these sights, so familiar to everybody, have caused him to go to the jungle?

A. We often see such sights: he had not seen them, so they made a deep impression on his mind.

32. Q. Why had he not also seen them?

A. The Brâhmana astrologers had foretold at his birth that he would one day resign his kingdom and become a Buddha, The King, his father, not wishing to lose an heir to his kingdom, had carefully prevented his seeing any sights that might suggest to him human misery and death. No one was allowed even to speak of such things to the Prince. He was almost like a prisoner in his lovely palaces and flower gardens. They were surrounded by high walls, and inside, everything was made as beautiful as possible, so that he might not wish to go and see the sorrow and distress that are in the world.

33. Q. Was he so kind-hearted that the King feared he might really wish to leave everything for the world's sake?

A. Yes; he seems to have felt for all beings so strong a pity and love as that.

34. Q. And how did he expect to learn the cause of sorrow in the jungle?

A. By removing far away from all that could prevent his thinking deeply of the causes of sorrow and the nature of man.

35. Q. How did he escape from the palace?

A. One night, when all were asleep, he arose, took a last look at his sleeping wife and infant son; called Channa, mounted his favourite white horse, Kanthaka, and rode to the palace gate. The devas had thrown a deep sleep upon the King's guard who watched the gate, so that they could not hear the noise of the horse's hoofs.

36. Q. But the gate was locked, was it not?

A. Yes; but the devas caused it to open without the slightest noise, and he rode away into the darkness.

37. Q. Whither did he go?

A. To the river Anomâ, a long way from Kapilavastu.

38. Q. What did he then do?

A. He sprang from his horse, cut off his beautiful hair with his sword, put on the yellow dress of an ascetic, and giving his ornaments and horse to Channa, ordered him to take them back to his father, the King.

39. Q. What then?

A. He went afoot towards Râjagriha, the capital city of King Bimbisâra, of Magadha.

40. Q. Who visited him there?

A. The King with his whole Court.

41. Q. Thence whither did he go?

A. To Uruvela, near the present Mahâbôdhi Temple at Buddha Gayâ.

42. Q. Why did he go there?

A. In the forests were hermits—very wise men, whose pupil he afterwards became, in the hope of finding the knowledge of which he was in search.

43. Q. Of what religion were they?

A. The Hindu religion: they were Brâhmanas.

44. Q. What did they teach?

A. That by severe penances and torture of the body a man may acquire perfect wisdom.

45. Q. Did the Prince find this to be so?

A. No; he learned their systems and practised all their penances, but he could not thus discover the cause of human sorrow and the way to absolute emancipation.

46. Q. What did he then do?

A. He went away into the forest near Uruvela, and spent six years in deep meditation and undergoing the severest discipline in mortifying his body.

47. Q. Was he alone?

A. No; five Brahman (priests or monks) companions attended him.

48. Q. What were their names?

A. Kondañña, Bhaddiya, Vappa, Mahânâma, and Assaji.

49. Q. What plan of discipline did he adopt to open his mind to know the whole truth?

A. He sat and meditated, concentrating his mind upon the higher problems of life, and shutting out from his sight and hearing all that was likely to interrupt his inward reflections.

50. Q. Did he fast?

A. Yes, through the whole period. He took less and less food and water until, it is said, he ate scarcely more than one grain of rice or of sesamum seed each day.

51. Q. Did this give him the wisdom he longed for?

A. No. He grew thinner and thinner in body and fainter in strength until, one day, as he was slowly walking about and meditating, his vital force suddenly left him and he fell to the ground unconscious.

52. Q. What did his companions think of that?

A. They fancied he was dead; but after a time he revived.

53. Q. What then?

A. The thought came to him that knowledge could never be reached by mere fasting or bodily suffering, but must be gained by the opening of the mind. He had just barely escaped death from self-starvation, yet had not obtained the Perfect Wisdom. So he decided to eat, that he might live at least long enough to become wise.

54. Q. Who gave him food?

A. He received food from Sujâtâ, a nobleman's daughter, who saw him sitting at the foot of a nyagrodha (banyan) tree, He arose, took his alms bowl, bathed in the river Nêranjarâ, ate the food, and went into the jungle.

55. Q. What did he do there?

A. Having formed his determination after these reflections, he went at evening to the Bodhi, or Asvattha tree, where the present Mahâbodhi Temple stands.

56. Q. What did he do there?

A. He determined not to leave the spot until he attained perfect wisdom.

57. Q. At which side of the tree did he seat himself?

A. The side facing the east.

58. Q. What did he obtain that night?

A. The knowledge of his previous births, of the causes of re-births, and of the way to extinguish desires. Just before the break of the next day his mind was entirely opened, like the full-blown lotus flower; the light of supreme knowledge, or the Four Truths, poured in upon him. He had become Buddha—the Enlightened, the all-knowing—the Sarvajña.

59. Q. Had he at last discovered the cause of human misery?

A. At last he had. As the light of the morning sun chases away the darkness of night, and reveals to sight the trees, fields, rocks, seas, rivers, animals, men and all things, so the full light of knowledge rose in his mind, and he saw at one glance the causes of human suffering and the way to escape from them.

60. Q. Had he great struggles before gaining this perfect wisdom?

A. Yes, mighty and terrible struggles. He had to conquer in his body all those natural defects and human appetites and desires that prevent our seeing the truth. He had to overcome all the bad influences of the sinful world around him. Like a soldier fighting desperately in battle against many enemies, he struggled: like a hero who conquers, he gained his object, and the secret of human misery was discovered.

61. Q. What use did he make of the knowledge thus gained?

A. At first he was reluctant to teach it to the people at large.

62. Q. Why?

A. Because of its profound importance and sublimity. He feared that but few people would understand it.

63. Q. What made him alter this view?

A. He saw that it was his duty to teach what he had learnt as clearly and simply as possible, and trust to the truth impressing itself upon the popular mind in proportion to each one's individual Karma. It was the only way of salvation, and every being had an equal right to have it pointed out to him. So he determined to begin with his five late companions, who had abandoned him when he broke his fast.

64. Q. Where did he find these?

A. In the deer-park at Isipatana, near Benares.

65. Q. Can the spot be now identified?

A. Yes, a partly ruined stupa, or dagoba, is still standing on that very spot.

66. Q. Did those five companions readily listen to him?

A. At first, no; but so great was the spiritual beauty of his appearance, so sweet and convincing his teaching, that they soon turned and gave him the closest attention.

67. Q. What effect did this discourse have upon them?

A. The aged Kondañña, "one who understood" (Anna), was the first to lose his prejudices, accept the Buddha's teaching, become his disciple, and enter the Path leading to Arahatship. The other four soon followed his example.

68. Q. Who were his next converts?

A. A rich young layman, named Yasa, and his father, a wealthy merchant. By the end of three months the disciples numbered sixty persons.

69. Q. Who were the first women lay disciples?

A. The mother and wife of Yasa.

70. Q. What did the Buddha do at that time?

A. He called the disciples together, gave them full instructions, and sent them out in all directions to preach his doctrine.

71. Q. What was the essence of it?

A. That the way of emancipation lies in leading the holy life and following the rules laid down, which will be explained later on.

72. Q. Tell me what name he gave to this course of life.

A. The Noble Eight-fold Path.

73. Q. Whither did the Buddha then go?

A. To Uruvela.

74. Q. What happened there?

A. He converted a man named Kâshyappa, renowned for his learning, and teacher of the Jatilas, a great sect of fire-worshippers, all of whom became also his followers.

75. Q. Who was his next great convert?

A. King Bimbisâra of Magadha

76. Q. Which two of the Buddha's most learned and beloved disciples were converted at about this time?

A. Sâriputra and Moggallâna, formerly chief disciples of Sanjaya, the ascetic.

77. Q. For what did they become renowned?

A. Sâriputra for his profound learning (Prajña), Moggallâna for his exceptional spiritual powers (Iddhi).

78. Q. Are these wonder-working powers miraculous?

A. No, but natural to all men and capable of being developed by a certain course of training.

79. Q. Did the Buddha hear again from his family after leaving them?

A. Oh yes, seven years later, while he was living at Râjagriha, his father, King Suddhodana, sent a message to request him to come and let him see him again before he died.

80. Q. Did he go?

A. Yes. His father went with all his relatives and ministers to meet him and received him with great joy.

81. Q. Did he consent to resume his old rank?

A. No. In all sweetness he explained to his father that the Prince Siddhârtha had passed out of existence, as such, and was now changed into the condition of a Buddha, to whom all beings were equally akin and equally dear. Instead of ruling over one tribe or nation, like an earthly king, he, through his Dharma, would win the hearts of all men to be his followers.

82. Q. Did he see Yasodharâ and his son Râhula?

A. Yes. His wife, who had mourned for him with deepest love, wept bitterly. She also sent Râhula to ask him to give him his inheritance, as the son of a prince.

83. Q. What happened?

A. To one and all he preached the Dharma as the cure for all sorrows. His father, son, wife, Ânanda (his half-brother), Devadatta (his cousin and brother-in-law), were all converted and became his disciples. Two other famous ones were Anuruddha, afterwards a great metaphysician, and Upâli, a barber, afterwards the greatest authority on Vinaya. Both of these gained great renown.

84. Q. Who was the first Bhikkhuni?

A. Prajâpatî, the aunt and foster-mother of Prince Siddhartha. With her, Yasodharâ and many other ladies were admitted into the order as Bhikkhunis or female devotees.

85. Q. What effect did the taking up of the religious life by his sons Siddhartha and Ânanda, his nephew Devadatta, his son's wife Yasodharâ and his grandson Râhula, have upon the old king Suddhodana?

A. It grieved him much and he complained to the Buddha, who then made it a rule of the order that no person should thenceforth be ordained without the consent of his parents if alive.

86. Q. For how many years was the Buddha engaged in teaching?

A. Forty-five years, during which time he preached a great many discourses. His custom and that of his disciples was to travel and preach during the eight dry months, but during the season of Wâs—the rains—he and they would stop in the pânsulas and vihâras which had been built for them by various kings and other wealthy converts.

87. Q. What kind of people were converted by him and his disciples?

A. People of all ranks, nations and castes; rajas and coolies, rich and poor, mighty and humble, the illiterate and the most learned. His doctrine was suited to all.

88. Q. Give some account of the decease of the Buddha?

A. In the forty-fifth season after his attaining Buddhahood, on the full-moon day of May, knowing that his end was near, he came at evening to Kusinâgâra, a place about one hundred and twenty miles from Benares. In the sâla grove of the Mallas, the Uparvartana of Kusinâgâra, between two sâla trees, he had his bedding spread with the head towards the north according to the ancient custom. He lay upon it, and with his mind perfectly clear, gave his final instructions to his disciples and bade them farewell.

89. Q. Did he also make new converts in those last hours?

A. Yes, a very important one, a great Brâhman pandit named Subhâdra. He had also preached to the Mallya princes and their followers.

90. Q. At daybreak what happened?

A. He passed into the interior condition of Samâdhi and thence into Nirvâna.

91. Q. What were his last words to his disciples?

A. "Bhikkhus," he said, "I now impress it upon you, the parts and powers of man must be dissolved. Work out your salvation with diligence."

92. Q. What convincing proofs have we that the Buddha, formerly Prince Siddhartha, was a historical personage?

A. His existence is apparently as clearly proved as that of any other character of ancient history.

93. Q. Name some of the proofs?

A. (1) The testimony of those who personally knew him.

(2) The discovery of places and the remains of buildings mentioned in the narrative of his time.

(3) The rock-inscriptions, pillars and dagobas made in memory of him by sovereigns who were near enough to his time to be able to verify the story of his life.

(4) The unbroken existence of the Sangha which he founded and their possession of the facts of his life transmitted from generation to generation from the beginning.

(5) The fact that in the very year of his death and at various times subsequently, conventions and councils of the Sangha were held, for the verification of the actual teachings of the Founder, and the handing down of those verified teachings from teacher to pupil, to the present day.

(6) After his cremation his relics were divided among eight kings and a stûpa was erected over each portion. The portion given to King Ajâtasatru, and by him covered with a stûpa at Râjagriha, was taken, less than two centuries later, by the Emperor Asoka and distributed throughout his Empire. He, of course, had ample means of knowing whether the relics were those of the Buddha or not, since they had been in charge of the royal house of Patna from the beginning.

(7) Many of the Buddha's disciples, being Arahats and thus having control over their vital powers, must have lived to great ages, and there was nothing to have prevented two or three of them, in succession to each other, to have covered the whole period between the death of the Buddha and the reign of Asoka, and thus to have enabled the latter to get from his contemporary every desired attestation of the fact of the Buddha's life.

(8) The "Mahâvansa," the best authenticated ancient history known to us, records the events of Sinhalese history to the reign of King Vijaya, 543 B.C.—almost the time of the Buddha—and gives most particulars of his life, as well as those of Emperor Asoka and all other sovereigns related to Buddhistic history.

94. Q. By what names of respect is the Buddha called?

A. Sâkyamuni (the Sâkya sage); Sâkya Simha (the Sâkya Lion); Sugata (the Happy One); Satthta (the Teacher); Jina (the Conqueror); Bhagavat (the Blessed One); Lôka-nâtha (the Lord of the world); Sarvajña (the Omniscient One); Dharmarâja (the King of Truth); Tathâgata (the great Being), etc.

PART II. THE DHARMA OR DOCTRINE.

95. Q. What is the meaning of the word Buddha?

A. The enlightened or he who has the perfect wisdom.

96. Q. You have said that there were other Buddhas: before this one.

A. Yes; our belief is that, under the operation of eternal causation, a Buddha takes birth at intervals, when mankind have become plunged into misery through ignorance and need the wisdom which it is the function of a Buddha to teach (See also Q. 11).

97. Q. How is a Buddha developed?

A. A person, hearing and seeing one of the Buddhas on earth, becomes seized with the determination to so live that at some future time, when he shall become-fitted for it, he also will be a Buddha for the guiding-of mankind out of the cycle of re-birth.

98. Q. How does he proceed?

A. Throughout that birth and every succeeding one, he strives to subdue his passions, to gain wisdom by experience, and to develop his higher faculties. He thus grows by degrees wiser, nobler in character, and stronger in virtue, until, finally, after numberless rebirths he reaches the state when he can become Perfected, Enlightened, All-wise, the ideal Teacher of the human race.

99. Q. While this gradual development is going on throughout all these births, by what name do we call him?

A. Bodhisat, or Bodhisattva, Thus the Prince Siddhârtha Gautama was a Bodhisattva up to the moment when, under the blessed Bodhi tree at Gaya, he became Buddha.

100. Q. Have we any account of his various rebirths as a Bodhisattva?

A. In the Jâtakatthakathâ, a book containing stories of the Bodhisattva's re-incarnations, there are several hundred tales of that kind.

101. Q. What lesson do these stories teach?

A. That a man can carry, throughout a long series of re-incarnations, one great, good purpose which enables him to conquer bad tendencies and develop virtuous ones.

102. Q. Can we fix the number of re-incarnations through which a Bodhisattva must pass before he can become a Buddha?

A. Of course not: that depends upon his natural character, the state of development to which he has arrived when he forms the resolution to become a Buddha, and other things.

103. Q. Have we a way of classifying Bodhisattvas? If so, explain it.

A. Bodhisattvas—the future Buddhas—are divided into three classes.

104. Q. Proceed. How are these three kinds of Bodhisats called?

A. Pannâdhika, or Udghatitagnya—"he who attains least quickly;" Saddhâdhika, or Vipachitagnya—"he who attains less quickly;" and Vîriyâdhika, or Gneyya—"he who attains quickly." The Pannâdhika Bodhisats take the course of Intelligence; the Saddhâdhika take the course of Faith; the Vîryâdhika take the course of energetic action. The first is guided by Intelligence and does not hasten; the second is full of Faith, and does not care to take the guidance of Wisdom; and the third never delays to do what is good. Regardless of the consequences to himself, he does it when he sees that it is best that it should be done.

105. Q. When our Bodhisattva became Buddha, what did he see was the cause of human misery? Tell me in one word.

A. Ignorance (Avidyâ).

106. Q. Can you tell me the remedy?

A. To dispel Ignorance and become wise (Prajña)

107. Q. Why does ignorance cause suffering?

A. Because it makes us prize what is not worth prizing, grieve for what we should not grieve, consider real what is not real but only illusionary, and pass our lives in the pursuit of worthless objects, neglecting what is in reality most valuable.

108. Q. And what is that which is most valuable?

A. To know the whole secret of man's existence and destiny, so that we may estimate at no more than their actual value this life and its relations; and so that we may live in a way to ensure the greatest happiness and the least suffering for our fellowmen and ourselves.

109. Q. What is the light that can dispel this ignorance of ours and remove all sorrows?

A. The knowledge of the "Four Noble Truths," as Buddha called them.

110. Q. Name these Four Noble Truths.

A. 1. The miseries of evolutionary existence resulting in births and deaths, life after life

2. The cause productive of misery, which is the selfish desire, ever renewed, of satisfying one's self, without being able ever to secure that end.

3. The destruction of that desire or the estranging of one's self from it.

4. The means of obtaining this destruction of desire.

111. Q. Tell me some things that cause sorrow.

A. Birth, decay, illness, death, separation from objects we love, association with those who are repugnant, craving for what cannot be obtained.

112. Q. Do these differ with each individual?

A. Yes: but all men suffer from them in degree.

113. Q. How can we escape the sufferings which result from unsatisfied desires and ignorant cravings?

A. By complete conquest over, and destruction of, this eager thirst for life and its pleasures, which causes sorrow.

114. Q. How may we gain such a conquest?

A. By following in the Noble Eight-fold Path which Buddha discovered and pointed out.

115. Q. What do you mean by that word: what is this Noble Eight fold Path?

A. The eight parts of this path are called angas they are: 1. Right Belief (as to the law of Causation, or Karma); 2. Right Thought; 3. Right Speech; 4. Right Action; 5. Right Means of Livelihood; 6. Right Exertion; 7. Right Remembrance and Self-discipline; 8. Right Concentration of Thought. The man who keeps these aligns in mind and follows them will be free from sorrow and ultimately reach salvation.

116. Q. Can you give a better word for salvation?

A. Yes, emancipation (freedom).

117. Q. Emancipation (freedom), then, from what?

A. Emancipation (freedom) from the miseries of earthly existence and of re-births, all of which are due to ignorance and impure lusts and cravings.

118. Q. And when this salvation or emancipation is attained, what do we reach?

A. Nirvâna.

119. Q. What is Nirvâna?

A. A condition of total cessation of changes, of perfect rest; of the absence of desire and illusion and sorrow; of the total obliteration of everything that goes to make up the physical man. Before reaching Nirvâna man is constantly being re-born: when he reaches Nirvâna he is re-born no more.

120. Q. Where can be found a learned discussion of the word Nirvâna, and a list of the other names by which the old Pâlî writers attempted to define it?

A. In the famous Dictionary of the Pâlî Language, by the late Mr. R. C. Childers is a complete list.

121. Q. But some people imagine that Nirvâna is some sort of heavenly place, a Paradise. Does Buddhism teach that?

A. No. When Kûtadanta asked the Buddha "Where is Nirvâna," he replied that it was "Wherever the precepts are obeyed."

122. Q. What causes us to be re-born?

A. The unsatisfied selfish desire (Sk., trishna; Pâlî, tanha) for things that belong to the state of personal existence in the material world. This unquenched thirst for physical existence (bhâva) is a force, and has a creative power in itself so strong that it draws the being back into mundane life.

123. Q. Are our re-births in any way affected by the nature of our unsatisfied desires?

A. Yes; and by our individual merits or demerits.

124. Q. Does our merit or demerit control the state, condition or form in which we shall be re-born?

A. It does. The broad rule is that if we have an excess of merit we shall be well and happily born the next time; if an excess of demerit, our next birth will be wretched and full of suffering.

125. Q. One chief pillar of Buddhistic doctrine is, then, the idea that every effect is the result of an actual cause, is it not?

A. It is; of a cause either immediate or remote.

126. Q. What do we call this causation?

A. Applied to individuals, it is Karma, that is, action. It means that our own actions or deeds bring upon us whatever of joy or misery we experience.

127. Q. Can a bad man escape from the out-workings of his Karma?

A. The Dhammapada says: "There exists no spot on the earth, or in the sky, or in the sea, neither is there any in the mountain-clefts, where an (evil) deed does not bring trouble (to the doer)."

128. Q. Can a good man escape?

A. As the result of deeds of peculiar merit, a man may attain certain advantages of place, body, environment and teaching in his next stage of progress, which ward off the effects of bad Karma and help his higher evolution.

129. Q. What are they called?

A. Gati Sampatti, Upâdhi Sampatti, Kâla Sampatti and Payoga Sampatti.

130. Q. Is that consistent or inconsistent with common sense and the teachings of modern science?

A. Perfectly consistent: there can be no doubt of it.

131. Q. May all men become Buddhas?

A. It is not in the nature of every man to become a Buddha; for a Buddha is developed only at long intervals of time, and seemingly, when the state of humanity absolutely requires such a teacher to show it. The forgotten Path to Nirvâna. But every being may equally reach Nirvâna, by conquering Ignorance and: gaining Wisdom.

132. Q. Does Buddhism teach that man is re-born, only upon our earth?

A. As a general rule that would be the case, until he had evolved beyond its level; but the inhabited worlds are numberless. The world, upon which a person is to have his next birth, as well as the nature of the re-birth itself, is decided by the preponderance- of the individual's merit or demerit. In other words, it will be controlled by his attractions, as science would describe it; or by his Karma, as we, Buddhists, would say.

133. Q. Are there worlds more perfect and developed and others less so than our Earth?

A. Buddhism teaches that there are whole Sakwalas or systems of worlds, of various kinds, higher: and lower and also that the inhabitants of each world correspond in development with itself.

134. Q. Has not the Buddha summed up his whole doctrine in one gâthâ, or verse?

A. Yes.

135. Q. Repeat it.

A. "To cease from all evil actions,
To generate all that is good,

To cleanse one's mind:

This is the constant advice of the Buddhas."

136. Q. Do these precepts show that Buddhism is an active or a passive religion?

A. To 'cease from sin' may be called passive, but to 'get virtue' and to 'cleanse one's own heart,' or mind, are altogether active qualities. Buddha taught that we should not merely not be evil, but that we should be positively good.

137. Q. Who or what are the "Three Guides" that a Buddhist is supposed to follow?

A. They are disclosed in the formula called the Tisarana: "I follow Buddha as my Guide: I follow the Law as my Guide: I follow the order as my Guide." These three are, in fact, the Buddha Dharma.

138. Q. What does he mean when repeating this formula?

A. He means that he regards the Buddha as his all-wise Teacher, Friend and Exemplar; the Law, or Doctrine, as containing the essential and immutable principles of Justice and Truth and the path that leads to the realisation of perfect peace of mind on earth; and the Order as the teachers and exemplars of that excellent Law taught by Buddha.

139. Q. But are not some of the members of this "Order", men intellectually and morally inferior?

A. Yes; but we are taught by the Buddha that only those who diligently attend to the Precepts, discipline their minds, and strive to attain or have attained one of the eight stages of holiness and perfection, constitute his "Order." It is expressly stated that the Order referred to in the "Tisarana" refers to the "Attha Ariya Puggala"—the Noble Ones who have attained one of the eight stages of perfection. The mere wearing of yellow robes, or even ordination, does not of itself make a man pure, wise or entitled to reverence.

140. Q. Then it is not such unworthy bhikkhus as they, whom the true Buddhist would take as his guides?

A. Certainly not.

141. Q. What are the five observances, or universal precepts, called the Pancha Sila, which are imposed on the laity in general?

A. They are included in the following formula, which Buddhists repeat publicly at the vihâras (temples):—

I observe the precept to refrain from destroying the life of beings.

I observe the precept to refrain from stealing.

I observe the precept to abstain from unlawful sexual intercourse.

I observe the precept to refrain from falsehood.

I observe the precept to abstain from using intoxicants.

142. Q. What strikes the intelligent person on reading these Silas?

A. That one who observes them strictly must escape from every cause productive of human misery.

If we study history we shall find that it has all sprung from one or another of these causes.

143. Q. In which Silas is the far-seeing wisdom of the Buddha most plainly shown?

A. In the first, third and fifth: for the taking of life, sensuality, and the use of intoxicants, cause of at least 95 per cent of the suffering among men.

144. Q. What benefits does a man derive from the observance of these Precepts?

A. He is said to acquire more or less merit according to the manner and time of observing the precepts, and the number observed. That is, if he observes only one precept, violating the other four, he acquires the merit of the observance of that precept only; and the longer he keeps that precept the greater will be the merit. He who keeps all the precepts inviolate will cause himself to have a higher and happier existence hereafter.

145. Q. What are the other observances which it is considered meritorious for the laity as such to undertake voluntarily to keep?

A. The Atthanga Silo, or the Eight-fold Precept, which embraces the five above enumerated (omitting the word "unlawful" in the third), with three additional; viz.:— I observe the precept to abstain from eating at an unseasonable time.

I observe the precept to abstain from dancing, singing, music and unbecoming shows, and from the use of garlands, scents, perfumes, cosmetics, ointments, and ornaments.

I observe the precept to abstain from using high and broad beds.

The seats and couches here referred to are those used by the worldly-minded for the sake of pleasure and sensual enjoyment. The celibate should avoid these.

146. Q. How would a Buddhist describe trite merit?

A. There is no great merit in any merely outward act; all depends upon the inward motive that provokes the deed.

147. Q. Give an example.

A. A rich man may expend lakhs (hundred thousands) of rupees in building dâgobas or vihâras, in erecting statues of Buddha, in festivals and processions, in feeding priests, in giving alms to the poor, or in planting trees, digging tanks, or constructing rest-houses by the roadside for travellers, and yet have comparatively little merit if it be done for display, and to make himself praised by men, or for any other selfish motives. But he who does the least of these things with a kind motive, as from love for his fellow-men, gains great merit. A good deed done with a bad motive benefits others, but not the doer. One who approves of a good deed when done by another shares in the merit, if his sympathy is real, not pretended. The same rule as to evil deeds.

148. Q. But which is said to be the greatest of all meritorious actions?

A. The Dhammapada declares that the merit of disseminating the Dharma, the Law of Righteousness, is greater than that of any other good work.

149. Q. What books contain all the most excellent wisdom of Buddha's teachings?

A. The three collections of books called Tripitakas, or "Three Baskets."

150. Q. What are the names of the three Pitakas, or groups of books?

A. The Vinâya Pitaka, the Sutta Pitaka and the Abhidhamma Pitaka.

151. Q. What do they respectively contain?

A. The first contains all that pertains to morality and rules of discipline for the government of the Sangha, or Order; the second contains instructive discourses on ethics applicable to all; the third explains the psychological teachings of the Buddha, including the twenty-four transcendental laws explanatory of the workings of Nature.

152. Q. Do Buddhists believe these books to be inspired, or revealed by a Divine Being?

A. No; but they revere them as containing all the parts of that most Excellent Law, by the knowing of which man may break through the trammels of Samsâra.

153. Q In the whole text of the three Pitakas how many words are there?

A. Dr. Rhys-Davids estimates them at 1,752,800.

154. Q. When were the Pitakas first reduced to writing?

A. In 88–76 B.C., under the Sinhalese King, Wattagamini; or 330 years after the Parinirvâna of the Buddha. (Sinhala are the people who inhabit modern Sri Lanka)

155. Q. Have we reason to believe that all the discourses of the Buddha are known to us?

A. Probably not, and it would be strange if they were. Within the forty-five years of his public life he must have preached many hundreds of discourses. Of these, in times of war and persecution, many must have been lost, many scattered to distant countries, and many mutilated. History says that enemies of the Buddha Dharma burnt piles of our books as high as a cocoanut tree.

156. Q. Do Buddhists consider the Buddha as one who by his own virtue can save us from the consequences of our individual sins?

A. Not at all. Man must emancipate himself. Until he does that he will continue being born over and over and over again—the victim of ignorance, the slave of unquenched passions.

157. Q. What, then, was the Buddha to us, and all other beings?

A. An all-seeing, all-wise Counsellor; one who discovered the safe path and pointed it out; one who showed the cause of, and the only cure for, human suffering. In pointing to the road, in showing us how to escape dangers, he became our Guide. He is to us like one leading a blind man across a narrow bridge over a swift and deep stream and so saving his life.

158. Q. If we were to try to represent the whole spirit of the Buddha's doctrine by one word, which word should we choose?

A. Justice.

159. Q. Why?

A. Because it teaches that every man gets, under the operations of unerring KARMA, exactly that reward or punishment which he has deserved, no more and no less. No good deed or bad deed, however trifling, and however secretly committed, escapes the evenly-balanced scales of Karma.

160. Q. What is Karma?

A. A causation operating on the moral, as well as on the physical and other planes. Buddhists say there is no miracle in human affairs what a man sows that he must and will reap.

161. Q. What other good words have been used to express the essence of Buddhism?

A. Self-culture and universal love.

162. Q. What doctrine ennobles Buddhism, and gives it its exalted place among the world's religions?

A. That of Mitta or Maitreya—compassionate kindness. The importance of this doctrine is moreover emphasised in the giving of the name "Maitri" (the Compassionate One), to the coming Buddha.

163. Q. Were all these points of Doctrine that you have explained meditated upon by the Buddha near the Bo-tree?

A. Yes, these and many more that may be read in the Buddhist Scriptures. The entire system of Buddhism came to his mind during the Great Enlightenment.

164. Q. How long did the Buddha remain near the Bo-tree?

A. Forty-nine days.

165. Q. What do we call the first discourse preached by the Buddha—that which he addressed to his five former companions?

A. The Dhammacakka-ppavattana sutta,—the Sûtra of the Definition of the Rule of Doctrine.

166. Q. What subjects were treated by him in this discourse?

A. The "Four Noble Truths" and the "Noble Eight-fold Path." He condemned the extreme physical mortification of the ascetics, on the one hand, and the enjoyment of sensual pleasures on the other; pointing out and recommending the Noble Eight-fold Path as the Middle Path.

167. Q. Did the Buddha hold to idol worship?

A. He did not; he opposed it. The worship of gods, demons, trees, etc, was condemned by the Buddha. External worship is a fetter that one has to break if he is to advance higher.

168. Q. But do not Buddhists make reverence before the statue to the Buddha, his relics, and the monuments enshrining them?

A. Yes, but not with the sentiment of the idolator.

169. Q. What is the difference?

A. Our Pagan brother not only takes his images as visible representations of his unseen God or gods, but the refined idolater, in worshipping, considers that the idol contains in its substance a portion of the all-pervading divinity.

170. Q. What does the Buddhist think?

A. The Buddhist reverences the Buddha's statue and the other things you have mentioned, only as mementos of the greatest, wisest, most benevolent and compassionate man in this world-period (Kalpa). All races and peoples preserve, treasure up, and value the relics and mementos of men and women who have been considered in any way great. The Buddha, to us, seems more to be revered and beloved than anyone else, by every human being who knows sorrow.

171. Q. Has the Buddha himself given us something definite upon this subject?

A. Certainly. In the Mahâ Pari-Nirvâna Sutta he says that emancipation is attainable only by leading the Holy life, according to the Noble Eight-fold Path, not by external worship (âmisa pûja), nor by adoration of himself, or of another, or of any image.

172. Q. What was the Buddha's estimate of ceremonialism?

A. From the beginning, he condemned the observance of ceremonies and other external practices, which only tend to increase our spiritual blindness and our clinging to mere lifeless forms.

173. Q. What as to controversies?

A. In numerous discourses he denounced this habit as most pernicious. He prescribed penances for Bhikkhus who waste time and weaken their higher intuitions in wrangling over theories and metaphysical subtleties.

174. Q. Are charms, incantations, the observance of lucky hours and devil-dancing a part of Buddhism?

A. They are positively repugnant to its fundamental principles. They are the surviving relics of fetishism and pantheistic and other foreign religions. In the Brâhmajâta Sutta the Buddha has categorically described these and other superstitions as pagan, mean and spurious.

175. Q. What striking contrasts are there between Buddhism and what may be properly called "religions?"

A. Among others, these: It teaches the highest goodness without a creating God; a continuity of life without adhering to the superstitious and selfish doctrine of an eternal, metaphysical soul-substance that goes out of the body; a happiness without an objective heaven; a method of salvation without a vicarious Savior; redemption by oneself as the Redeemer, and without rites, prayers, penances, priests or intercessory saints; and a summun bonum, i.e., Nirvâna, attainable in this life and in this world by leading a pure, unselfish life of wisdom and compassion to all beings.

176. Q. Specify the two main divisions of 'meditation,' i.e., of the process by which one extinguishes passion and attains knowledge.

A. Samatha and Vidarsama: (1) the attenuation of passion by leading the holy life and by continued effort to subdue the senses; (2) the attainment of supernormal wisdom by reflection: each of which embraces twenty aspects, but I need not here specify them.

177. Q. What are the four paths or stages of advancement that one may attain to?

A. (1) Sottâpatti, the beginning or entering into which follows after one's clear perception of the 'Four Noble Truths;'

(2) Sakardâgâmi—the path of one who has so subjugated lust, hatred and delusion that he need only return once to this world;

(3) Anâgami—the path of those who have so far conquered self that they need not return to this world;

(4) Arahat—the path of the holy and worthy Arahat, who is not only free from the necessity of re-incarnation, but has capacitated himself to enjoy perfect wisdom, boundless pity for the ignorant and suffering, and measureless love for all beings.

178. Q. Does popular Buddhism contain nothing but what is true, and in accord with science?

A. Like every other religion that has existed many centuries, it certainly now contains untruth mingled with truth; ever gold is found mixed with dross. The poetical imagination, the zeal, or the lingering superstition of Buddhist devotees have, in various ages, and in various lands, caused the noble principles of the Buddha's moral doctrines to be coupled more or less with what might be removed to advantage.

179. Q. When such perversions are discovered, what should be the tree Buddhist's earnest desire?

A. The true Buddhist should be ever ready and anxious to see the false purged away from the true, and to assist, if he can. Three great Councils of the Sangha were held for the express purpose of purging the body of Teachings from all corrupt interpolations.

180. Q. When?

A. The first, at Sattapanni cave, just after the death of the Buddha; the second at Valukarama, in Vaisali; the third at Asokarama Vihâra, at Pataliputra, 235 years after the Buddha's decease.

181. Q. In what discourse does the Buddha himself warn us to expect this perversion of the true Doctrine?

A. In the Sanyutta Nikâya.

182. Q. Are there any dogmas in Buddhism which we are required to accept on faith?

A. No: we are earnestly enjoined to accept nothing whatever on faith; whether it be written in books, handed down from our ancestors, or taught by the sages.

183. Q. Did he himself really teach that noble rule?

A. Yes. The Buddha has said that we must not believe in a thing said merely because it is said; nor in traditions because they have been handed down from antiquity; nor rumours, as such; nor writings by sages, merely because sages wrote them; nor fancies that we may suspect to have been inspired in us by a deva (that is, in presumed spiritual inspiration); nor from inferences drawn from some haphazard assumption we may have made; nor because of what seems an analogical necessity; nor on the mere authority of our own teachers or masters.

184. Q. When, then, must we believe?

A. We are to believe when the writing, doctrine or saying is corroborated by our own reason and consciousness. "For this," says he in concluding, "I taught you not to believe merely because you have heard, but when you believed of your own consciousness, then to act accordingly and abundantly." (See the Kâlâma Sutta of the Anguttara Nikâya, and the Mahâ Pari Nirvâna Sutta.)

185. Q. What does the Buddha call himself?

A. He says that he and the other Buddhas are only "preachers" of truth who point out the way: we ourselves must make the effort.

186. Q. Where is this said?

A. In chapter XX of the Dhammapada.

187. Q. Does Buddhism countenance hypocrisy?

A. The Dhammapada says: "Like a beautiful flower full of color without scent, the fine words of him who does not act accordingly are fruitless."

188. Q. Does Buddhism teach us to return evil for evil?

A. In the Dhammapada the Buddha said: "If a man foolishly does me wrong, I will return to him the protection of my ungrudging love; the more evil comes from him, the more good shall go from me." This is the path followed by the Arahat. To return evil for evil is positively forbidden in Buddhism.

189. Q. Does it encourage cruelty?

A. No, indeed. In the Five Precepts and in many of his discourses, the Buddha teaches us to be merciful to all beings, to try and make them happy, to love them all, to abstain from taking life, or consenting to it, or encouraging its being done.

190. Q. In which discourse is this stated?

A. The Dhammika Sutta says: "Let him (the householder) not destroy, or cause to be destroyed, any life at all, or sanction the acts of those who do so. Let him refrain from even hurting any creature," etc.

191. Q. Does it approve of drunkenness?

A. In his Dhammika Sutta we are warned against drinking liquors, causing others to drink, or sanctioning the acts of those who drink.

192. Q. To what are we told that drunkenness leads?

A. To demerit, crime, insanity, and ignorance—which is the chief cause of re-birth.

193. Q. What does Buddhism teach about marriage?

A. Absolute chastity being a condition of full spiritual development is most highly commended; but a marriage to one wife and fidelity to her is recognised as a kind of chastity. Polygamy was censured by the Buddha as involving ignorance and promoting lust.

194. Q. In what discourse?

A. The Anguttara Nikâya, chap. IV, 55.

195. Q. What does it teach as to the duty of parents to children?

A. They should restrain them from vice; train them in virtue; have them taught arts and sciences; provide them with suitable wives and husbands, and give them their inheritance.

196. Q. What is the duty of children?

A. To support their parents when old or needy; perform family duties incumbent on them; guard their property; make themselves worthy to be their heirs, and when they are gone, honor their memory.

197. Q. What of pupils to the teacher?

A. To show him respect; minister to him; obey him; supply his wants; attend to his instruction.

198. Q. What of husband to wife?

A. To cherish her; treat her with respect and kindness; be faithful to her; cause her to be honored by others; provide her with suitable ornaments and clothes.

199. Q. What of the wife to her husband?

A. To show affection to him; order her household aright; be hospitable to guests; be chaste; be thrifty; show skill and diligence in all things.

200. Q. Where are these precepts taught?

A. In the Sigâlovâda Sutta.

201. Q. Do riches help a man to future happiness?

A. The Dhammapada says: "One is the road that leads to wealth, another the road that leads to Nirvâna."

202. Q. Does that mean that no rich man can attain Nirvâna?

A. That depends on which he loves most. If he uses his wealth for the benefit of mankind—for the suffering, the oppressed, the ignorant—then his wealth aids him to acquire merit.

203. Q. But if the contrary?

A. But if he loves and greedily hoards money for the sake of its possession, then it weakens his moral sense, prompts him to crime, brings curses upon him in this life, and their effects are felt in the next birth.

204. Q. What says the "Dhammapada" about ignorance?

A. That it is a taint worse than all taints that a man can put upon himself.

205. Q. What does it say about uncharitableness towards others?

A. That the fault of others is easily perceived, but that of oneself difficult to perceive; a man winnows his neighbor's faults like chaff, but his own fault he hides, as a cheat hides the bad die from the gambler.

206. Q. What advice does the Buddha give us as to man's duty to the poor?

A. He says that a man's net income should be divided into four parts, of which one should be devoted to philanthropic objects.

207. Q. What five occupations are said to be low and base?

A. Selling liquor, selling animals for slaughter, selling poison, selling murderous weapons, and dealing in slaves.

208. Q. Who are said to be incapable of progress in spirituality?

A. The killers of father, mother, and holy Arahats; bhikkhus who sow discord in the Sangha; those who attempt to injure the person of a Buddha; those who hold extremely nihilistic views as to the future existence; and those who are extremely sensual.

209. Q. Does Buddhism specify places or conditions of torment into which a bad man's Karma draws him on leaving this life?

A. Yes., They are: Sanjîva; Kâlasûtra; Sanghâta; Raurava; Mahâ-Raurava; Tâpa; Pratâpa; Avîchi.

210. Q. Is the torment eternal?

A. Certainly not. Its duration depends on a man's Karma.

211. Q. Does Buddhism declare that non-believers in Buddha will of necessity be damned for their unbelief?

A. No; by good deeds they may enjoy a limited term of happiness before being drawn into re-birth by their unexhausted tanhâ. To escape re-birth, one must tread the Noble Eight-fold Path.

212. Q. What is the spiritual status of woman among Buddhists?

A. According to our religion they are on a footing of perfect equality with men. "Woman," says the Buddha, in the Chullavêdalla Sutta, "may attain the highest path of holiness "—Arahatship— that is open to man.

213. Q. What does a modern critic say about the effect of Buddhism on woman?

A. That "it has done more for the happiness and enfranchisement of woman than any other creed" (Sir Lepel Griffin).

214. Q. What did the Buddha teach about caste?

A. That one does not become of any caste, whether Pariah, the lowest, or Brâhmana, the highest, by birth, but by deeds. "By deeds, "said He, "one becomes an outcast, by deeds one becomes a Brâhmana" (See Vasala Sutta).

215. Q. Tell me a story to illustrate this.

A. Ânanda, passing by a well, was thirsty and asked Prakriti, a girl of the Mâtanga, or Pariah caste, to give him water. She said she was of such low caste that he would become contaminated by taking water from her hand. But Ânanda replied: "I ask not for caste but for water;" and the Mâtanga girl's heart was glad and she gave him to drink. The Buddha blessed her for it.

216. Q. What did the Buddha say in Vasalasutta about a man of the Pariah Sopâka caste?

A. That by his merits he reached the highest fame; that many Khattiyas (Kshattriyas) and Brahmans went to serve him; and that after death he was born in the Brahma world: while there are many Brâhmanas who for their evil deeds are born in hell.

217. Q. Does Buddhism teach the immortality of the soul?

A. It considers "soul" to be a word used by the ignorant to express a false idea. If everything is subject to change, then man is included, and every material part of him must change. That which is subject to change is not permanent: so there can be no immortal survival of a changeful thing.

218. Q. What is so objectionable in this word 'soul'?

A. The idea associated with it that man can be an entity separated from all other entities, and from the existence of the whole of the Universe. This idea of separateness is unreasonable, not provable by logic, nor supported by science.

219. Q. Then there is no separate "I," nor can we say "my" this or that?

A. Exactly so.

220. Q. If the idea of a separate human soul is to be rejected, what is it in man which gives him the impression of having a permanent personality?

A. Tanhâ or the unsatisfied desire for existence. The being having done that for which he must be rewarded or punished in future, and having Tanhâ, will have a re-birth through the influence of Karma.

221. Q. What is it that is born?

A. A new aggregation of Skandhas, or personality caused by the last generative thought of the dying person.

222. Q. How many Skandhas are there?

A. Five.

223. Q. Name the five Skandhas.

A. Rûpa, Vêdanâ, Saññâ, Samkhârâ, and Viññâna.

224. Q. Briefly explain what they are.

A. Rûpa, material qualities; Vedanâ, sensation; Saññâ, abstract ideas; Samkhârâ, tendencies of mind; Viññâna, mental powers, or consciousness. Of these we are formed; by them we are conscious of existence; and through them communicate with the world about us.

225. Q. To what cause must we attribute the differences in the combination of the five Skandhas which make every individual differ from every other individual?

A. To the ripened Karma of the individual in his preceding births.

226. Q. What is the force or energy that is at work, under the guidance of Karma, to produce the new being?

A. Tanhâ—the will to live.

227. Q. Upon what is the doctrine of re-births founded?

A. Upon the perception that perfect justice, equilibrium and adjustment are inherent in the universal system of Nature. Buddhists do not believe that one life—even though it were extended to one hundred or five hundred years—is long enough for the reward or punishment of a man's deeds. The great circle of re-births will be more or less quickly run through according to the preponderating purity or impurity of the several lives of the individual.

228. Q. Is this new aggregation of Skandhas—this new personality—the same being as that in the previous birth, whose Tanhâ has brought it into existence?

A. In one sense it is a new being; in another it is not. In Pâlî it is—"nacha so nacha añño," which means not the same nor yet another. During this life the Skandhas are constantly changing; and while the man A. B., of forty, is identical, as regards. personality, with the youth A. B., of eighteen, yet, by the continual waste and reparation of his body, and change of mind and character, he is a different being. Nevertheless, the man in his old age justly reaps the reward or suffering consequent upon his thoughts and actions at every previous stage of his life. So the new being of a re-birth, being the same individuality as before, with but a changed form, or new aggregation of Skandhas, justly reaps the consequences of his actions and thoughts in the previous existence.

229. Q. But the aged man remembers the incidents of his youth, despite his being physically and mentally changed. Why, then, is not the recollection of past lives brought over by us from our last birth into the present birth?

A. Because memory is included within the Skandhas; and the Skandhas having changed with the new reincarnation, a new Memory, the record of that particular existence, develops. Yet the record or reflection of all the past earth-lives must survive; for, when Prince Siddhârthâ became Buddha, the full sequence of his previous births was seen by him. If their several incidents had left no trace behind, this could not have been so, as there would have been nothing for him to see. And anyone who attains to the fourth state of Dhyâna (psychical insight) can thus retrospectively trace the line of his lives.

230. Q. What is the ultimate point towards which bend all these series of changes in form?

A. Nirvâna.

231. Q. Does Buddhism teach that we should do good with the view of reaching Nirvâna?

A. No; that would he as absolute selfishness as though the reward hoped for had been money, a throne, or any other sensual enjoyment. Nirvâna cannot be so reached, and the unwise speculator is foredoomed to disappointment.

232. Q. Please make it a little clearer.

A. Nirvâna is the synonym of unselfishness, the entire surrender of selfhood to truth. The ignorant man aspires to nirvânic happiness without the least idea of its nature. Absence of selfishness is

Nirvâna. Doing good with the view to getting results, or leading the holy life with the object of gaining heavenly happiness, is not the Noble Life that the Buddha enjoined. Without hope of reward the Noble Life should be lived, and that is the highest life. The nirvânic state can be attained while one is living on this earth.

233. Q. Name the ten great obstacles to advancement, called Sanyojanas, the Fetters.

A. Delusion of self (Sakkâya-ditthi); Doubt (Vicikicchâ); Dependence on superstitious rites (Sîlabbata-parâmâsa); Sensuality, bodily passions (Kâma); Hatred, ill-feeling (Patigha); Love of life on earth (Rûparâga); Desire for life in a heaven (Arûparâga); Pride (Mâna); Self-righteousness (Uddhacca); Ignorance (Avijjâ).

234. Q. To become an Arahat, how many of these fetters must be broken?

A. All.

235. Q. What are the five Niwarânas or Hindrances?

A. Greed, Malice, Sloth, Pride, and Doubt.

236. Q. Why do we see this minute division of feelings, impulses, workings of the mind, obstacles and aids to advancement so much used in the Buddha's teachings? It is very confusing to a beginner.

A. It is to help us to obtain knowledge of ourselves, by training our minds to think out every subject in detail. By following out this system of self-examination, we come finally to acquire knowledge and see truth as it is. This is the course taken by every wise teacher to help his pupil's mind to develop.

237. Q. How many of the Buddha's disciples were specially renowned for their superior qualities?

A. There are eighty so distinguished. They are called the Asîti Maha Sâvakas.

238. Q. What did the Buddha's wisdom embrace?

A. He knew the nature of the Knowable and the Unknowable, the Possible and the Impossible, the cause of Merit and Demerit; he could read the thoughts of all beings; he knew the laws of Nature, the illusions of the senses and the means to suppress desires; he could distinguish the births and re-births of individuals, and other things.

239. Q. What do we call the basic principle on which the whole of the Buddha's teaching is constructed?

A. It is called Paticca Samuppâdâ.

240. Q. Is it easily grasped?

A. It is most difficult; in fact, the full meaning and extent of it is beyond the capacity of such as are not perfectly developed.

241. Q. What said the great commentator Buddha Ghosha about it?

A. That even he was as helpless in this vast ocean of thought as one who is drifting on the ocean of waters.

242. Q. Then why should the Buddha say, in the Parinibbâna Sutta, that he "has no such thing as the closed fist of a teacher, who keeps something back?" If his whole teaching was open to every one's comprehension, why should so great and learned a man as Buddha Ghosha declare it so hard to understand?

A. The Buddha evidently meant that he taught everything freely; but equally certain is it that the real basis of the Dharma can only be understood by him who has perfected his powers of comprehension. It is, therefore, incomprehensible to common, unenlightened persons.

243. Q. How does the teaching of the Buddha support this view?

A. The Buddha looked into the heart of each person, and preached to suit the individual temperament and spiritual development of the hearer." - Colonel Henry Steel Olcott (1832–1907)

When Lord Buddha had achieved Enlightenment, he then met five disciples of his who had been with him earlier. Here is the story of his encounter with them at Benares or present day Varanasi.

BUDDHA, THE GOSPEL THE SERMON AT BENARES By Paul Carus [1894] 'ON seeing their old teacher approach, the five bhikkus (monks) agreed among themselves not to salute him, nor to address him as a master, but by his name only. "For," so they said, "he has broken his vow and has abandoned holiness. He is no bhikkhu (monk), but Gotama, and Gotama has become a man who lives in abundance and indulges in the pleasures of worldliness." But when the Blessed One approached in a dignified manner, they involuntarily rose from their seats and greeted him in spite of their resolution. Still they called him by his name and addressed him as "friend Gotama."

When they had thus received the Blessed One, he said: "Do not call the Tathagata by his name nor address him as 'friend,' for he is the Buddha, the Holy One. The Buddha looks with a kind heart equally on all living beings, and they therefore call him 'Father.' To disrespect a father is wrong; to despise him, is wicked. The Tathagata, the Buddha continued, does not seek salvation in austerities, but neither does he for that reason indulge in worldly pleasures, nor live in abundance. The Tathagata has found the middle path.

"There are two extremes, O bhikkhus (monks), which the man who has given up the world ought not to follow-the habitual practice, on the one hand, of self-indulgence which is unworthy, vain and fit only for the worldly-minded and the habitual practice, on the other hand, of self-mortification, which is painful, useless and unprofitable.

"Neither abstinence from fish and flesh, nor going naked, nor shaving the head, nor wearing matted hair, nor dressing in a rough garment, nor covering oneself with dirt, nor sacrificing to Agni (Fire), will cleanse a man who is not free from delusions. Reading the Vedas, making offerings to priests, or sacrifices to the gods, self-mortification by heat or cold and many such penances performed for the sake of immortality, these do not cleanse the man who is not free from delusions. Anger, drunkenness, obstinacy, bigotry, deception, envy, self-praise, disparaging others, superciliousness and evil intentions constitute uncleanness; not verily the eating of flesh.

"A middle path, O bhikkhus avoiding the two extremes, has been discovered by the Tathagata-a path which opens the eyes, and bestows understanding, which leads to peace of mind, to the higher wisdom, to full enlightenment, to Nirvana! What is that middle path, O bhikkhus, avoiding these two extremes, discovered by the Tathagata-that path which opens the eyes, and bestows understanding, which leads to peace of mind, to the higher wisdom, to full enlightenment, to Nirvana? Let me teach you, O bhikkhus (monks), the middle path, which keeps aloof from both extremes. By suffering, the emaciated devotee produces confusion and sickly thoughts in his mind. Mortification is not conducive even to worldly knowledge; how much less to a triumph over the senses!

"He who fills his lamp with water will not dispel the darkness, and he who tries to light a fire with rotten wood will fail. And how can anyone be free from self by leading a wretched life, if he does not succeed in quenching the fires of lust, if he still hankers after either worldly or heavenly pleasures? But he in whom self has become extinct is free from lust; he will desire neither worldly nor heavenly pleasures, and the satisfaction of his natural wants will not defile him. However, let him be moderate, let him eat and drink according to the need of the body.

"Sensuality is enervating; the self-indulgent man is a slave to his passions, and pleasure-seeking is degrading and vulgar. But to satisfy the necessities of life is not evil. To keep the body in good health is a duty, for otherwise we shall not be able to trim the lamp of wisdom, and keep our minds strong and clear. Water surrounds the lotus flower, but does not wet its petals. This is the middle path, O bhikkhus, that keeps aloof from both extremes." And the Blessed One spoke kindly to his disciples, pitying them for their errors, and pointing out the uselessness of their endeavors, and the ice of ill-will that chilled their hearts melted away under the gentle warmth of the Master's persuasion.

Now the Blessed One set the wheel of the most excellent law rolling, and he began to preach to the five bhikkhus (monks), opening to them the gate of immortality, and showing them the bliss of Nirvana.

The Buddha said: "The spokes of the wheel are the rules of pure conduct: justice is the uniformity of their length; wisdom is the tire; modesty and thoughtfulness are the hub in which the immovable axle of truth is fixed. He who recognizes the existence of suffering, its cause, its remedy, and its cessation has fathomed the four noble truths. He will walk in the right path.

"Right views will be the torch to light his way. Right aspirations will be his guide. Right speech will be his dwelling-place on the road. His gait will be straight, for it is right behaviour. His refreshments will be the right way of earning his livelihood. Right efforts will be his steps: right thoughts his breath; and right contemplation will give him the peace that follows in his footprints.

"Now, this, O bhikkhus, is the noble truth concerning suffering: Birth is attended with pain, decay is painful, disease is painful, death is painful. Union with the unpleasant is painful, painful is separation from the pleasant; and any craving that is unsatisfied, that too is painful. In brief, bodily conditions which spring from attachment are painful. This, then, O bhikkhus, is the noble truth concerning suffering.

"Now this, O bhikkhus, is the noble truth concerning the origin of suffering: Verily, it is that craving which causes the renewal of existence, accompanied by sensual delight, seeking satisfaction now here, now there, the craving for the gratification of the passions, the craving for a future life, and the craving for happiness in this life. This, then, O bhikkhus, is the noble truth concerning the origin of suffering.

"Now this, O bhikkhus, is the noble truth concerning the destruction of suffering: Verily, it is the destruction, in which no passion remains, of this very thirst; it is the laying aside of, the being free from, the dwelling no longer upon this thirst. This, then, O bhikkhus, is the noble truth concerning the destruction of suffering.

"Now, this, O bhikkhus, is the noble truth concerning the way which leads to the destruction of sorrow. Verily, it is this noble eightfold path; that is to say: Right views; right aspirations; right speech; right behaviour; right livelihood; right effort; right thoughts; and right contemplation. This, then, O bhikkhus, is the noble truth concerning the destruction of sorrow.

"By the practice of loving-kindness I have attained liberation of heart, and thus I am assured that I shall never return in renewed births. I have even now attained Nirvana."

When the Blessed One had thus set the royal chariot wheel of truth rolling onward, a rapture thrilled through all the universes. The devas (divine beings) left their heavenly abodes to listen to the sweetness of the truth; the saints that had parted from life crowded around the great teacher to receive the glad tidings; even the animals of the earth felt the bliss that rested upon the words of the Tathagata: and all the creatures of the host of sentient beings, gods, men, and beasts, hearing the message of deliverance, received and understood it in their own language.

And when the doctrine was propounded, the venerable Kondanna, the oldest one among the five bhikkhus, discerned the truth with his mental eye, and he said: "Truly, O Buddha, our Lord, thou hast found the truth!" Then the other bhikkhus too, joined him and exclaimed: "Truly, thou art the Buddha, thou hast found the truth."

And the devas (divine beings) and saints and all the good spirits of the departed generations that had listened to the sermon of the Tathagata, joyfully received the doctrine and shouted: "Truly, the Blessed One has founded the kingdom of righteousness. The Blessed One has moved the earth; he has set the wheel of Truth rolling, which by no one in the universe, be he god or man, can ever be turned back. The kingdom of Truth will be preached upon earth; it will spread; and righteousness, good-will, and peace will reign among mankind." – Paul Carus (1894)

Teachings of Gautama Buddha (566 BCE - 486 BCE)

"When you go into the space of nothingness, everything becomes known

Holding on to anger is like grasping a hot coal with the intent of throwing it at someone else; you are the one who gets burned

You only lose what you cling to

Buddha was speaking in a village one day, when one of the inhabitants started to abuse him. Buddha paused and said to the man,

"If you offer me a piece of paper and I refuse to accept it, what happens to the paper?"

"Why, it stays with me, of course," the villager replied.

Buddha smiled gently, "And that is exactly what I am doing with your abuse," he said.

"I am not accepting it, therefore it stays with you."

'Even as a solid rock is unshaken by the wind, so are the wise unshaken by praise or blame.

Everything that has a beginning has an end.

Make your peace with that and all will be well

Wear your ego like a loose fitting garment

Three things cannot hide for long: the Moon, the Sun and the Truth

Happiness does not depend on what you have or who you are...

It solely relies on what you think

The trouble is, you think you have time

Do not believe in anything simply because you have heard it. Do not believe in anything simply because it is spoken and rumored by many. Do not believe in anything simply because it is found written in your religious books. Do not believe in anything merely on the authority of your teachers and elders. Do not believe in traditions because they have been handed down for many generations. But after observation and analysis, when you find that anything agrees with reason and is conducive to the good and benefit of one and all, then accept it and live up to it

If we could see the miracle of a single flower clearly,

our whole life would change

No one saves us but ourselves. No one can and no one may. We ourselves must walk the path

If you light a lamp for someone else, it will also brighten your path

People with opinions just go around bothering one another

Let us rise up and be thankful, for if we didn't learn a lot at least we learned a little, and if we didn't learn a little, at least we didn't get sick, and if we got sick, at least we didn't die; so, let us all be thankful

The greatest treasures are those invisible to the eye

and found by the heart.

Remembering a wrong is like carrying a burden on the mind

Doubt everything. Find your own light

The heart of a child is like that of Buddha

One moment can change a day, one day can change a life and one life can change the world

Every morning we are born again. What we do today is what matters most

There is only one time when it is essential to AWAKEN...

that time is... NOW

Imagine that every person in the world is enlightened but you. They are all your teachers, each doing just the right things to help you

There is no path to happiness: happiness is the path

Whatever words we utter should be chosen with care for people will hear them and be influenced by them for good or ill

Your purpose in life is to find your purpose and give your whole heart and soul to it"

Hatred does not cease through hatred at any time. Hatred ceases through love. This is an unalterable law

You cannot travel on the path until you become the path itself.

If you truly loved yourself, you could never hurt another

You, yourself, as much as anybody in the entire universe,

deserve your love and affection

Every human being is the author of his own health or disease

A man is not called wise because he talks and talks again; but if he is peaceful, loving and fearless then he is in truth called wise

If you are facing in the right direction, all you need to do is keep on walking

The secret of health for both mind and body is not to mourn for the past, not to worry about the future, or not to anticipate troubles, but to live in the present moment wisely and earnestly

If your compassion does not include yourself, it is incomplete

He is able... who thinks he is able

The thought manifests as the word. The word manifests as the deed.

The deed develops into habit. And the habit hardens into character.

So watch the thought and its ways with care.

And let it spring from love, born of our concern for all beings

Now, Kalamas, don't go by reports, by legends, by traditions, by scripture, by logical conjecture, by inference, by analogies, by agreement through pondering views, by probability, or by the thought, 'This contemplative is our teacher.' When you know for yourselves that, 'These qualities are skilful; these qualities are blameless; these qualities are praised by the wise; these qualities, when adopted & carried out, lead to welfare & to happiness' — then you should enter & remain in them.

What we are today, comes from our thoughts of yesterday.

And our present thoughts, build our life of tomorrow.

Our life is the creation of our mind

Nothing can harm you as much as your own thoughts unguarded

To conquer oneself is a greater task than conquering others

Greater in battle

than the man who would conquer

a thousand-thousand men,

is he who would conquer

just one —

himself.

Better to conquer yourself

than others.

However many holy words you read, however many you speak, what good will they do you if you do not act on upon them?

Whatever a monk keeps pursuing with his thinking and pondering, that becomes the inclination of his awareness

Peace comes from within. Do not seek it without

"These... things, householder, are welcome, agreeable, pleasant, & hard to obtain in the world:

Long life is welcome, agreeable, pleasant, & hard to obtain in the world.

Beauty is welcome, agreeable, pleasant, & hard to obtain in the world.

Happiness is welcome, agreeable, pleasant, & hard to obtain in the world.

Status is welcome, agreeable, pleasant, & hard to obtain in the world.

...Now, I tell you, these... things are not to be obtained by reason of prayers or wishes. If they were to be obtained by reason of prayers or wishes, who here would lack them? It's not fitting for the disciple of the noble ones who desires long life to pray for it or to delight in doing so. Instead, the disciple of the noble ones who desires long life should follow the path of practice leading to long life. In so doing, he will attain long life..."

Those who have failed to work toward the truth have missed the purpose of living

There are only two mistakes one can make along the road to truth; not going all the way, and not starting

Even death is not to be feared by one who has lived wisely

If the problem can be solved why worry? If the problem cannot be solved worrying will do you no good

The whole secret of existence is to have no fear

Look within, thou art the Buddha

It is better to conquer yourself than to win a thousand battles. Then the victory is yours. It cannot be taken from you

Learn this from water: loud splashes the brook but the oceans depth are calm

If you knew what I know about the power of giving you would not let a single meal pass without sharing it in some way

If you find no one to support you on the spiritual path, walk alone. There is no companionship with the immature

I never see what has been done; I only see what remains to be done

When you realize how perfect everything is you will tilt your head back and laugh at the sky

In separateness lies the world's greatest misery; in compassion lies the world's true strength

What we think, we become.

The only real failure in life is not to be true to the best one knows

An idea that is developed and put into action is more important than an idea that exists only as an idea.

There have been many Buddhas before me and will be many Buddhas in the future.

All living beings have the Buddha nature and can become Buddhas.

We are the same as plants, as trees, as other people, as the rain that falls. We consist of that which is around us; we are the same as everything.

Neither my life of luxury in the palace nor my life as an ascetic in the forest is the way to freedom.

If we destroy something around us, we destroy ourselves. If we cheat another, we cheat ourselves.

As soon as we think we are safe, something unexpected happens.

No one can escape death and unhappiness. If people expect only happiness in life, they will be disappointed.

Life is dear to all beings. They have the right to live the same as we do.

Do not dwell in the past; do not dream of the future, concentrate the mind on the present moment.

In the sky, there is no distinction of east and west; people create distinctions out of their own minds and then believe them to be true.

Hunger (for things) is the supreme disease.

Do not overrate what you have received, nor envy others. He who envies others does not obtain peace of mind.

Work out your own salvation. Do not depend on others.

Awake. Be the witness of your thoughts. You are what observes, not what you observe.

Life can only take place in the present moment. If we lose the present moment, we lose life.

The cause of all pain and suffering is ignorance.

A dog is not considered a good dog because he is a good barker. A man is not considered a good man because he is a good talker.

If a man speaks or acts with an evil thought, pain follows him. If a man speaks or acts with a pure thought, happiness follows him, like a shadow that never leaves him.

The mind is everything. What we think we become.

All things appear and disappear because of the concurrence of causes and conditions. Nothing ever exists entirely alone; everything is in relation to everything else.

An insincere and evil friend is more to be feared than a wild beast; a wild beast may wound your body, but an evil friend will wound your mind.

Every human being is the author of his own health or disease.

Hatred does not cease by hatred, but only by love; this is the eternal rule.

Have compassion for all beings, rich and poor alike; each has their suffering. Some suffer too much, others too little.

He who experiences the unity of life sees his own Self in all beings, and all beings in his own Self, and looks on everything with an impartial eye.

Health is the greatest gift, contentment the greatest wealth, faithfulness the best relationship.

I do not believe in a fate that falls on men however they act; but I do believe in a fate that falls on them unless they act.

In a controversy the instant we feel anger we have already ceased striving for the truth, and have begun striving for ourselves.

It is better to travel well than to arrive.

Just as a candle cannot burn without fire, men cannot live without a spiritual life.

Just as treasures are uncovered from the earth, so virtue appears from good deeds, and wisdom appears from a pure and peaceful mind. To walk safely through the maze of human life, one needs the light of wisdom and the guidance of virtue.

On life's journey faith is nourishment, virtuous deeds are a shelter, wisdom is the light by day and right mindfulness is the protection by night. If a man lives a pure life, nothing can destroy him.

Teach this triple truth to all: A generous heart, kind speech, and a life of service and compassion are the things which renew humanity.

The tongue like a sharp knife... It kills without drawing blood.

The way is not in the sky. The way is in the heart.

The world, indeed, is like a dream and the treasures of the world are an alluring mirage! Like the apparent distances in a picture, things have no reality in themselves, but they are like heat haze.

There has to be evil so that good can prove its purity above it.

There is nothing more dreadful than the habit of doubt. Doubt separates people. It is a poison that disintegrates friendships and breaks up pleasant relations. It is a thorn that irritates and hurts; it is a sword that kills.

Those who are free of resentful thoughts surely find peace.

Thousands of candles can be lighted from a single candle, and the life of the candle will not be shortened. Happiness never decreases by being shared.

To enjoy good health, to bring true happiness to one's family, to bring peace to all, one must first discipline and control one's own mind. If a man can control his mind he can find the way to Enlightenment, and all wisdom and virtue will naturally come to him.

To live a pure unselfish life, one must count nothing as one's own in the midst of abundance.

Unity can only be manifested by the Binary. Unity itself and the idea of Unity are already two.

We are formed and molded by our thoughts. Those whose minds are shaped by selfless thoughts give joy when they speak or act. Joy follows them like a shadow that never leaves them.

You can search throughout the entire universe for someone who is more deserving of your love and affection than you are yourself, and that person is not to be found anywhere. You yourself, as much as anybody in the entire universe deserve your love and affection.

You will not be punished for your anger; you will be punished by your anger.

Your work is to discover your work and then with all your heart to give yourself to it." – Adapted from the Dhammapada (5th century AD,), a Treasury of Truth, a Path of Wisdom, a collection of verses and sayings of the Lord Buddha

ENLIGHTENMENT: 'THE Bodhisattva, having put Mara (demon) to flight, gave himself up to meditation. All the miseries of the world, the evils produced by evil deeds and the sufferings arising therefrom, passed before his mental eye, and he thought:

"Surely if living creatures saw the results of all their evil deeds, they would turn away from them in disgust. But selfhood blinds them, and they cling to their obnoxious desires. They crave pleasure for themselves and they cause pain to others; when death destroys their individuality, they find no peace; their thirst for existence abides and their selfhood reappears in new births. Thus they continue to move in the coil and can find no escape from the hell of their own making. And how empty are their pleasures, how vain are their endeavors! Hollow like the plantain-tree and without contents like the bubble. The world is full of evil and sorrow, because it is full of lust. Men go astray because they think that delusion is better than truth. Rather than truth they follow error, which is pleasant to look at in the beginning but in the end causes anxiety, tribulation, and misery."...

This is the Dharma. This is the truth. This is religion. And the Enlightened One uttered this stanza:

"Through many births I sought in vain
The Builder of this House of Pain.
Now, Builder, You are plain to see,
And from this House at last I'm free;
I burst the rafters, roof and wall,
And dwell in the Peace beyond them all."...

Blessed is he who has understood the Dharma. Blessed is he who does no harm to his fellow-beings. Blessed is he who overcomes wrong and is free from passion. To the highest bliss has he attained who has conquered all selfishness and vanity. He has become the Buddha, the Perfect One.' - Excerpts from BUDDHA, THE GOSPEL by Paul Carus (1894)

Buddha Story: 'One of his students asked Buddha, "Are you the messiah?"

"No", answered Buddha.

"Then are you a healer?"

"No", Buddha replied.

"Then are you a teacher?" the student persisted.

"No, I am not a teacher."

"Then what are you?" asked the student, exasperated.

"I am awake", Buddha replied.'

"Pay no attention to the faults of others,
Things done or left undone by others.

Consider only what by oneself is done or left undone." **Lord Buddha** (lived about 2,500 years ago in India)

"Fools wait for a lucky day
but every day is a lucky day
for an industrious man." - Lord Buddha

As the Buddha was dying,
Ananda asked
who would be their teacher after death.
He replied to his disciple -
"Be lamps unto yourselves.
Be refuges unto yourselves.
Take yourself no external refuge.
Hold fast to the truth as a lamp.
Hold fast to the truth as a refuge.
Look not for a refuge in anyone besides yourselves.
And those, Ananda, who either now or after I am dead,
Shall be a lamp unto themselves,
Shall betake themselves as no external refuge,
But holding fast to the truth as their lamp,
Holding fast to the truth as their refuge,
Shall not look for refuge to anyone else besides themselves,
It is they who shall reach to the very topmost height;
But they must be anxious to learn." – The dying sacred words of the Buddha

For **Thai Buddhists**, the Three Most Significant sacred days of the year all include the word "Bucha", which means to give homage.

Asaraha Bucha celebrates the day Lord Buddha preached his first sermon.

Makha Bucha also called Sangtha Day or the full moon day of Tabodwe in Myanmar, marks both the occasion when 1,250 disciples came to see the Buddha that evening without notice. All of them were Arhantas, Enlightened Ones, and all were ordained by the Buddha himself. They listened to the Buddha elaborate some of his most important teachings in a sermon, as well as foretell the day he foresaw his own death and attainment of Nibbana (Nirvana).

The Buddha gave those Arhantas (Enlightened Ones) the principles of Buddhism. Those principles are: To cease from all evil; To do what is good; To cleanse one's mind. In Thailand, this teaching has been dubbed the "heart of Buddhism".

But the most auspicious day is **Visakha Bucha**, which simultaneously commemorates three important anniversaries in the life of Siddharta Gautama, the Lord Buudha: 1. His birth (80 B.C) 2. His enlightenment (35 BC) and 3. His death (1 BC)

The word Visakabucha stands for Visakapoonnameebucha which implies the worship of the Lord Buddha.

Cambodia

From the 13th century, the Cambodian state religion has been Theravada Buddhism. This has been true throughout this time except during the Khmer Rouge period when the genocidal Khmer Rouge government tried to destroy Buddhism. Today 95 per cent of the Khmer population are believed to be Buddhists. Buddhism has existed in Cambodia from the 5th century.

At the heart of Cambodian Buddhism are the Buddhist Bhikkhus and the Wat. From ancient times, each village has a Wat or a spiritual center where between five to more than eighty bhikkhus live. Bhikkhus are monks. 'A Khmer Wat in rural Cambodia comprises a walled quarter which would have a sacred interior,...'

In the countryside of Cambodia, a Wat would consist of a walled quarter which would have a sacred interior, a number of dwellings for bhikkhus, a hall, a kitchen, quarters for nuns, and a pond. The size of the Wat and the number of monks would depend on the size of the village and the population. The larger the population is, the larger the number of monks in a Wat.

From ancient times, monks join at a very early age. Sometimes you will find novice monks who are as young as seven. Nevertheless, the common practise is to accept novices who are thirteen and above. They need not take perpetual vows to remain Buddhist monks. However, those who agree with the ascetic life opt to become permanent monks.

The Beatitudes of Lord Jesus: Can you even begin to imagine what Jesus did for us? He offered his life to receive pardon for the sins of the whole of mankind. He loved and cared profoundly for every single one of us. He never sinned in his life. He was innocent as a child. He was just 33 years old - at the prime of his life with perhaps the best years ahead of him. Yet, he gave up his life as a sacrifice in such an excruciating and painful way to pay for the sins of each one of us. God honored his suffering. All of us, if we wish to, can freely obtain forgiveness for the grievous wrongs we have committed in our lives. What greater love can anyone have, that he shed his own blood for the misdeeds of humanity?

There was no place for him to be born. His parents, Mary and Joseph had to use a cowshed. He was born in a manger. Jesus never built a building, he did not even own a house and he wandered around teaching people the Way. Often his disciples must have thought when and what they were going to eat. He died penniless. He gave up his life as a sacrifice for our sins even though he himself was innocent. Even in death, there was no place to bury him. Thank God, a rich man gave his burial sepulchre for Jesus to be buried in. He lived one of the most beautiful lives in history. He asked nothing for himself but gave all for humanity. The world is a better place because he lived more than 2000 years ago.

In Matthew 5:1-12 'And seeing the multitudes, he went up into a mountain: and when he was set, his disciples came unto him:

And he opened his mouth, and taught them, saying,

Blessed are the poor in spirit: for theirs is the kingdom of heaven.

Blessed are they that mourn: for they shall be comforted.

Blessed are the meek: for they shall inherit the earth.

Blessed are they which do hunger and thirst after righteousness: for they shall be filled.

Blessed are the merciful: for they shall obtain mercy.

Blessed are the pure in heart: for they shall see God.

Blessed are the peacemakers: for they shall be called the children of God.

Blessed are they which are persecuted for righteousness' sake: for theirs is the kingdom of heaven.

Blessed are ye, when men shall revile you, and persecute you, and shall say all manner of evil against you falsely, for my sake.

Rejoice, and be exceeding glad: for great is your reward in heaven: for so

persecuted they the prophets which were before you.'

Lao Tzu: He was a 6th century Chinese philosopher. Fed up with the politics and corruption of the Imperial Court, he left and on the border at the insistence of a border guard, wrote and composed in 5,000 characters the Tao Te Ching (The Way and Its Power) following which he vanished into history. Founder and guiding light of **Taoism**, he was an older contemporary of Confucius. Some historians say that Confucius was his student. Others say that on leaving China, he disappeared into Nepal and India where he became a wandering monk and teacher. Numbering between at least twenty million Taoists, and perhaps even half a billion, around the world, especially in China and Taiwan, Taoists do go on pilgrimages to five sacred and holy mountains in eastern China in order to pray at the temples and imbibe spiritual energy from these sanctified places, where the immortals are said to reside and dwell.

The following five mountains are highly revered by Taoists from ancient times:

- Tai Shan, Taoist mountain of the east, Shandong province, 1545 meters.
- Heng Shan Bei, Taoist mountain of the north, Shanxi province, 2017 meters.
- Hua Shan, Taoist mountain of the west, Shanxi province, 1997 meters.
- Heng Shan Nan, Taoist mountain of the south, Hunan province, 1290 meters.
- Song Shan, Taoist mountain of the center, Henan province, 1494 meters.

Legends tell of sages and mystics, often called 'immortals', who lived deep in the mountains. They fed on rare herbs and exotic elixirs, and lived to be 400 to 800 years old. (The same stories of longevity of life are told about monks and hermits who resided up in the Himalayas and survived for hundreds of years on pure mountain herbs.)

Lao Tzu teaches:

"The Tao abides in non-action,

Yet nothing is left undone...

If they still desired to act,

They would return to the simplicity of formless substance.

Without form there is no desire.

Without desire there is tranquillity.

In this way all things would be at peace.

Nature does not hurry, yet everything is accomplished."

"The usefulness of a pot comes from its emptiness."

Lao Tzu said. "Empty yourself of everything, let your mind become still."

Lao Tzu wrote the 'Tao Te Ching' or the Book of the Way. It could be translated as The Law of Virtue and its Way.

Written by Lao-Tzu, (580-500 B.C.), Tao Te Ching is simple and yet deep. It is one of the most widely read sacred texts. Its appeal is universal, and has been recently rediscovered and valued not only by Taoists but by Christians, Hindus, Muslims, Buddhists, and followers of other faiths.

"When I let go of what I am," Lao Tzu wrote, "I become what I might be."

"Seek not happiness too greedily, and be not fearful of happiness.

A journey of a thousand miles begins with a single step.

He who knows does not speak.

He who speaks does not know.

He who knows others is wise;

He who knows himself is enlightened.

He who loves the world as his body may be entrusted with the empire.

I have three treasures. Guard and keep them:

The first is deep love,

The second is frugality,

And the third is not to dare to be ahead of the world.

Because of deep love, one is courageous.

Because of frugality, one is generous.

Because of not daring to be ahead of the world, one becomes the leader of the world.

Manifest plainness,

Embrace simplicity,

Reduce selfishness,

Have few desires.

People are difficult to govern because they have too much knowledge.

Before the universe was born

there was something in the chaos of the heavens.

It stands alone and empty,

solitary and unchanging.

It is ever present and secure.

It may be regarded as the Mother of the universe.

Because I do not know its name,

I call it the Tao.

If forced to give it a name,

I would call it 'Great'.

Because it is Great means it is everywhere.

Being everywhere means it is eternal.

Being eternal means everything returns to it.

Tao is great.

Heaven is great.

Earth is great.

Humanity is great.

Within the universe, these are the four great things.

Humanity follows the earth.

Earth follows Heaven.

Heaven follows the Tao.

The Tao follows only itself.
Wise men are not scholars,
and scholars are not wise.
The Master desires no possessions. .
Who is able to give to the needy from their excess?
Only someone who is following the way of the Tao.
The Tao of the universe
does not compete, yet wins;
does not speak, yet responds;
does not command, yet is obeyed;
and does act, but is good at directing.
Knowing you don't know is wholeness.
Thinking you know is a disease.
Only by recognizing that you have an illness
can you move to seek a cure.
Because you do not know me,
you are not able to understand my teachings.
Because those who know me are few,
my teachings become even more precious.
My teachings come from the ancients,
the things I do are done for a reason.
The best warriors
do not use violence.
The best generals
do not destroy indiscriminately.
The best tacticians
try to avoid confrontation.
The best leaders
become servants of their people.
There are three jewels that I cherish:
compassion, moderation, and humility.
With compassion, you will be able to be brave,

With moderation, you will be able to give to others,
With humility, you will be able to become a great leader.
To abandon compassion while seeking to be brave,
or abandoning moderation while being benevolent,
or abandoning humility while seeking to lead
will only lead to greater trouble.
The compassionate warrior will be the winner,
and if compassion is your defense you will be secure.
Compassion is the protector of Heaven's salvation.
If you want to be the ruler of people,
you must speak to them like you are their servant.
If you want to lead other people,
you must put their interest ahead of your own.
Rivers and seas are rulers
of the streams of hundreds of valleys
because of the power of their low position.
Prevent problems before they arise.
Take action before things get out of hand.
The tallest tree
begins as a tiny sprout.
The tallest building
starts with one shovel of dirt.
A journey of a thousand miles
starts with a single footstep.
Act by not acting;
do by not doing.
Enjoy the plain and simple.
Find that greatness in the small.
Take care of difficult problems
while they are still easy;
Do easy things before they become too hard.
The Tao is the tabernacle of creation,

it is a treasure for those who are good,
and a place of refuge for those who are not.
Large countries should desire to protect and help the people,
and small countries should desire to serve others.
Both large and small countries benefit greatly from humility.
Stop talking,
meditate in silence,
blunt your sharpness,
release your worries,
harmonize your inner light,
and become one with the dust.
Doing this is the called the dark and mysterious identity.
Those who have achieved the mysterious identity
cannot be approached, and they cannot be alienated.
They cannot be benefited nor harmed.
They cannot be made noble nor to suffer disgrace.
This makes them the most noble of all under the heavens.
Those who know do not talk.
Those who talk do not know.
To understand harmony is to understand the Constant.
To know the Constant is to be called 'enlightened'.
To unnaturally try to extend life is not appropriate.
To try and alter the life-breath is unnatural.
The master understands that when something reaches its prime
it will soon begin to decline.
Changing the natural is against the way of the Tao.
Those who do it will come to an early end.
One who is filled with the Tao
is like a newborn child.
That which is well built
will never be torn down.
That which is well latched

cannot slip away.
Those who do things well
will be honored from generation to generation.
Keep your mouth closed
and embrace a simple life,
and you will live care-free until the end of your days.
If you try to talk your way into a better life
there will be no end to your trouble.
To understand the small is called clarity.
Knowing how to yield is called strength.
To use your inner light for understanding
regardless of the danger
is called depending on the Constant.
The world had a beginning
which we call the Great Mother.
Once we have found the Mother,
we begin to know what Her children should be.
When we know we are the Mother's child,
we begin to guard the qualities of the Mother in us.
She will protect us from all danger
even if we lose our life.
The Tao gives birth to all of creation.
The virtue of Tao in nature nurtures them,
and their families give them their form.
Their environment then shapes them into completion.
That is why every creature honors the Tao and its virtue.
No one tells them to honor the Tao and its virtue,
it happens all by itself.
So the Tao gives them birth,
and its virtue cultivates them,
cares for them,
nurtures them,

gives them a place of refuge and peace,
helps them to grow and shelters them.
It gives them life without wanting to posses them,
and cares for them expecting nothing in return.
It is their master, but it does not seek to dominate them.
This is called the dark and mysterious virtue.
Mastery of the world is achieved
by letting things take their natural course.
You cannot master the world by changing the natural way.
One who seeks knowledge learns something new every day.
One who seeks the Tao unlearns something new every day.
Less and less remains until you arrive at non-action.
When you arrive at non-action,
nothing will be left undone.
Without opening your door,
you can know the whole world.
Without looking out your window,
you can understand the way of the Tao.
The more knowledge you seek,
the less you will understand.
The Master understands without leaving,
sees clearly without looking,
accomplishes much without doing anything.
That which is pure and still is the universal ideal.
That which offers no resistance,
overcomes the hardest substances.
That which offers no resistance
can enter where there is no space.
Few in the world can comprehend
the teaching without words,
or understand the value of non-action.
The Tao gave birth to One.

The One gave birth to Two.
The Two gave birth to Three.
The Three gave birth to all of creation.
All things carry Yin
yet embrace Yang.
They blend their life breaths
in order to produce harmony.
People despise being orphaned, widowed and poor.
But the noble ones take these as their titles.
In losing, much is gained,
and in gaining, much is lost.
What others teach I too will teach:
"The strong and violent will not die a natural death."
Thus it is said:
The brightness of the Tao seems like darkness,
the advancement of the Tao seems like retreat,
the level path seems rough,
the superior path seem empty,
the pure seems to be tarnished,
and true virtue doesn't seem to be enough.
The virtue of caution seems like cowardice,
the pure seems to be polluted,
the true square seems to have no corners,
the best vessels take the most time to finish,
the greatest sounds cannot be heard,
and the greatest image has no form.
The Tao hides in the unnamed,
Yet it alone nourishes and completes all things.
All of creation is born from substance.
Substance is born of nothing-ness.
The highest good is not to seek to do good,
but to allow yourself to become it.

The great Tao flows unobstructed in every direction.
All things rely on it to conceive and be born,
and it does not deny even the smallest of creation.
When it has accomplished great wonders,
it does not claim them for itself.
It nourishes infinite worlds,
yet it doesn't seek to master the smallest creature.
Since it is without wants and desires,
it can be considered humble.
All of creation seeks it for refuge
yet it does not seek to master or control.
Because it does not seek greatness;
it is able to accomplish truly great things.
Those who know others are intelligent;
those who know themselves are truly wise.
Those who master others are strong;
those who master themselves have true power.
Those who know they have enough are truly wealthy.
Those who persist will reach their goal.
All things end in the Tao
just as the small streams and the largest rivers
flow through valleys to the sea.
The Tao is nameless and unchanging.
Although it appears insignificant,
nothing in the world can contain it.
If you open yourself to the Tao,
you and Tao become one.
If you open yourself to Virtue,
then you can become virtuous.
If you open yourself to the Tao,
the Tao will eagerly welcome you.
If you open yourself to virtue,

virtue will become a part of you.
The greatest virtue you can have
comes from following only the Tao;
which takes a form that is intangible and evasive.
Even though the Tao is intangible and evasive,
we are able to know it exists.
Intangible and evasive, yet it has a manifestation.
Secluded and dark, yet there is vitality within it.
Its vitality is very genuine.
Within it we can find order.
Since the beginning of time, the Tao has always existed.
It is beyond *Existing* ***and*** *not existing*.
How do I know where creation comes from?
I look inside myself and see it.
If you can empty your mind of all thoughts
your heart will embrace the tranquility of peace.
Watch the workings of all of creation,
but contemplate their return to the source.
All creatures in the universe
return to the point where they began.
Returning to the source is tranquility
because we submit to Heaven's mandate.
Who can be still
until their mud settles
and the water is cleared by itself?
Can you remain tranquil until right action occurs by itself?
Look for it, and it can't be seen.
Listen for it, and it can't be heard.
Grasp for it, and it can't be caught.
These three cannot be further described,
so we treat them as The One.
Its highest is not bright.

Its depths are not dark.
Unending, unnameable, it returns to nothingness.
Formless forms, and imageless images,
subtle, beyond all understanding.
Approach it and you will not see a beginning;
follow it and there will be no end.
When we grasp the Tao of the ancient ones,
we can use it to direct our life today.
To know the ancient origin of Tao:
this is the beginning of wisdom.
Love the whole world as if it were your self;
then you will truly care for all things.
We mold clay into a pot,
but it is the emptiness inside
that makes the vessel useful.
We fashion wood for a house,
but it is the emptiness inside
that makes it livable.
We work with the substantial,
but the emptiness is what we use.
Nurture the darkness of your soul
until you become whole.
Can you do this and not fail?
Can you focus your life-breath until you become
supple as a newborn child?
While you cleanse your inner vision
will you be found without fault?
Can you love people and lead them
without forcing your will on them?
When Heaven gives and takes away
can you be content with the outcome?
When you understand all things

can you step back from your own understanding?
Giving birth and nourishing,
making without possessing,
expecting nothing in return.
To grow, yet not to control:
This is the mysterious virtue.
It is easier to carry an empty cup
than one that is filled to the brim.
When you have accomplished your goal
simply walk away.
This is the path way to Heaven.
The supreme good is like water,
which benefits all of creation
without trying to compete with it.
It gathers in unpopular places.
Thus it is like the Tao.
The Tao of Heaven is eternal,
and the earth is long enduring.
Why are they long enduring?
They do not live for themselves;
thus they are present for all beings.
The spirit of emptiness is immortal.
It is called the Great Mother
because it gives birth to Heaven and Earth.
It is like a vapor,
barely seen but always present.
Use it effortlessly.
The space between Heaven and Earth is like a bellows;
it is empty, yet has not lost its power.
The more it is used, the more it produces;
the more you talk of it, the less you comprehend.
It is better not to speak of things you do not understand.

The Tao is like an empty container:
it can never be emptied and can never be filled.
Infinitely deep, it is the source of all things.
It dulls the sharp, unties the knotted,
shades the lighted, and unites all of creation with dust.
It is hidden but always present.
I don't know who gave birth to it.
It is older than the concept of God.
For those who practice not-doing,
everything will fall into place.
The tao that can be described
is not the eternal Tao.
The name that can be spoken
is not the eternal Name.
The nameless is the boundary of Heaven and Earth.
The named is the mother of creation.
Freed from desire, you can see the hidden mystery.
By having desire, you can only see what is visibly real.
Yet mystery and reality
emerge from the same source.
This source is called darkness.
Darkness born from darkness.
The beginning of all understanding."

Tao Te Ching, by Lao-Tzu, Translation for the public domain by J.H. McDonald, 1996

Confucius: He was a great Chinese Philosopher who was born in 551 BC in the Lu state of China (near present-day Qufu) and died in 479 BC. To Confucius, the main objective of being an educator was to teach people to live with integrity. Today he is widely considered to be one of the most influential teachers in Chinese history.

Teachings of Confucius:

"With coarse rice to eat, with water to drink, and my crooked arm for a pillow - Is not joy to be found therein? Riches and honors acquired through unrighteousness are to me as the floating clouds.

Wisdom, compassion, and courage are the three universally recognized moral qualities of men.

Our greatest glory is not in ever falling, but in rising every time we fall.

The strength of a nation derives from the integrity of the home.

If I am walking with two other men, each of them will serve as my teacher. I will pick out the good points of the one and imitate them, and the bad points of the other and correct them in myself.

In a country well governed, poverty is something to be ashamed of. In a country badly governed, wealth is something to be ashamed of.

You cannot open a book without learning something.

To know what you know and what you do not know, that is true knowledge.

Real knowledge is to know the extent of one's ignorance.

Only the wisest and stupidest of men never change.

Silence is a true friend who never betrays.

Success depends upon previous preparation, and without such preparation there is sure to be failure.

When it is obvious that the goals cannot be reached, don't adjust the goals, adjust the action steps.

By three methods we may learn wisdom: First, by reflection, which is noblest; Second, by imitation, which is easiest; and third by experience, which is the bitterest.

I hear and I forget. I see and I remember. I do and I understand.

Wherever you go, go with all your heart.

Choose a job you love, and you will never have to work a day in your life.

Everything has beauty, but not everyone sees it.

It does not matter how slowly you go as long as you do not stop.

The will to win, the desire to succeed, the urge to reach your full potential... these are the keys that will unlock the door to personal excellence.

When anger rises, think of the consequences.

If you think in terms of a year, plant a seed; if in terms of ten years, plant trees; if in terms of 100 years, teach the people.

Life is really simple, but we insist on making it complicated."– Sayings of the great Chinese Master **Confucius** (551 BC - 479 BC)

Mahatma Gandhi was one of the greatest persons to have graced this earth. After becoming a lawyer, educated in England, he left everything to practise the Truth. He stripped himself of his legal suits to walk dressed only in a dhoti and lead the people of India in the most inspiring non-violent transformations that this world has ever seen. His moral and spiritual influence is keenly felt even today. The famous scientist Albert Einstein said the following about Mahatma Gandhi. "Generations to come will scarce believe that such a one as this, ever in flesh and blood walked upon this Earth." Einstein also said "I believe that Gandhi's views were the most enlightened of all the political men in our time." The 1982 film Gandhi based on the Mahatma's life and starring Sir Ben Kingsley as Mohandas Gandhi, won 8 Oscars.

"Earth provides enough to satisfy every man's need, but not every man's greed.

"You must be the change you wish to see in the world.

The fragrance always remains on the hand that gives the rose." - **Mahatma Gandhi**

"Be the peace you wish for the world.

Like the bee gathering honey from the different flowers, the wise person accepts the essence of the different scriptures and sees only the good in all religions." - **Mahatma Gandhi**

Zoroaster, the prophet of the Parsis: Prophet Zoroaster lived more than 3,500 years ago. Zoroaster was filled from his infancy with profound philosophical and religious thoughts for the welfare and well-being of mankind. This ancient prophet of Persia derived his holy inspiration after thirty years of divine meditation on a secluded and inaccessible mountain-top of Ushidarena.

Zoroaster taught "He, to whom no form, shape, or colour is attributed, stands alone, Omni Unique, the Nature of Infinite Perfection. It is not given to mortals of finite mind to define Him, the most just, the most benevolent, the most merciful. He is One, who dwells in boundless space, clothed in the most resplendent and illumined glory of inscrutable Nature." In Khordah-Avesta, the prayer-book of the Parsis, God describes all His attributes, in the following words:

"I am the Keeper; I am the Creator and the Maintainer; I am the Discerner; I am the Most Beneficent Spirit. "My name is the Bestower of Health; the Priest; Ahura [the Lord]; Mazda [the All-knowing]; the Holy; the Glorious; the Farseeing; the Protector; the Well-wisher; the Creator; the Producer of Prosperity; the King who rules at His Will; One who does not deceive; He who is not deceived; He who destroys malice; He who conquers everything; He who has shaped everything; All Weal; Full Weal; Master of Weal; He who can benefit at His wish; the Beneficent One; the Energetic One; Holiness; the Great One; the Best of Sovereigns; the Wise One."

"He is the Light and Source of Light; He is the Wisdom and Intellect. He is in possession of all good things, spiritual and worldly, such as good mind [vohumano], immortality [ameretad], health [haurvatad], the best truth [asha vahista], devotion and piety [armaiti], and abundance of every earthly good [Khshathra vairya]. All these gifts He grants to the righteous man who is upright in thoughts, words, and deeds. As the ruler of the whole universe, He not only rewards the good, but He is a punisher of the wicked at the same time."

In the Zoroastrian Liturgy (Yaçna I.), Zarathustra describes God as

(1) "The Creator Ahura-Mazda, the Brilliant, Majestic, Greatest, Best, Most Beautiful... (4) "Who created us, who formed us, who keeps us, the Holiest among the heavenly." As ancient as the Zoroastrian religion is, no more comprehensive, lucid, and intelligible definition of the Great Creative Cause can be found in any religious books of the modern religions. It is worthy of note that John Milton, (in his great Epic, Paradise Lost, Book 5), who wrote nearly 2,500 years after Zoroaster, had grasped the true spirit of the Zoroastrian ideal of God.

"These are thy glorious works, Parent of Good,

Almighty, thine this universal frame,

Thus wondrous frame: thyself how wondrous then!

Unspeakable who sit'st above these heavens,

To us invisible or dimly seen

In these Thy lowest works, yet these declare

Thy goodness beyond thought, and power divine." – John Milton (1667)

Sant Tukaram: Sant Tukaram (1608–1649) was a prominent Maharashtrian saint and religious poet. He was born and lived most of his life in Dehu, a town near Pune.

Teachings of Tukaram:

'An individual should make God the center of his universe.

Serving others and loving others is the best way through which we can find Him.

Utmost Faith is most essential for attainment of Sadhana (meditation).

For the attainment of sadhana (meditation), an individual needs to have faith in his/her destiny.

It is not necessary to renounce the world and lead the life of an ascetic in order to be one with God. Spirituality does not require elaborate rituals.

Nama Japa (reciting the name of Lord) is the most important privilege of being a devotee.

Siddhis serve as impediments in the attainment of genuine sadhana (meditation).

Traditions prevent an individual from budding in the love of God. One has to sidestep the usual customs to achieve the same.'

'No human being would ever attain happiness in life till there was a place for God in it. No happiness would be possible till mortals made God a part of their life.'

'Look at my experience. I made God my own and He gave the answers to my questions whenever and wherever I put those to Him.'

'Never keep the company of bad people, strive always to be in the company of saints.

'Uplift of the downtrodden is the greatness of saints, therefore, abjure the bad and hanker after the saints.

Make money through honest means only and amass it with a detached mind.' Tukaram

Shirdi Sai Baba: Shri Sai Baba of Shirdi was an Indian saint who lived between 1838 and 1918. His life and teachings transcended the barriers of religions. No one knows his real name, birthplace or date of birth. Sai Baba of Shirdi is regarded with great reverence by both Hindu and Muslim followers. He lived in a mosque and after death his body was cremated in a temple.

He taught about 'Shraddha' meaning Faith with love and reverence and 'Saburi' meaning Patience and perseverance. According to him Shraddha (faith with love and reverence) and Saburi (patience and perseverance) were the supreme attributes to reach the state of godliness. It is said that when he was just 16 years old, Shri Sai Baba arrived at the village of Shirdi in Ahmednagar district of Maharashtra and remained their till his death.

He lived an extremely simple and austere life, sleeping on the floor of temple and later taking a crumbling mosque as his shelter. Many miracles are attributed to Shri Sai Baba of Shirdi.

As of today, Shri Sai Baba has millions of followers both in India and abroad. Shirdi, the obscure village in Maharashtra has become a pilgrimage destination. Over 25,000 pilgrims throng Shirdi each day and the number of pilgrims climb to over a hundred thousand on holidays and festival days. You will find over 2,000 major Sai temples in different parts of India and 150 temples abroad in places as far-flung as Canada and Kenya, Singapore and England.

Teachings of Shirdi Sai Baba:

"Why fear when I am here?

I am formless and everywhere

I am in everything and beyond. I fill all space.

All that you see taken together is Myself.

I do not shake or move.

If one devotes their entire time to me and rests in me, they need fear nothing for body and soul.

If one sees me and me alone and listens to my Leelas and is devoted to me alone, they will reach God.

My business is to give blessings.

I get angry with none. Will a mother get angry with her children? Will the ocean send back the waters to the several rivers?

I will take you to the end.

Surrender completely to God.

If you make me the sole object of your thoughts and aims, you will gain the supreme goal.

Trust in the Guru fully. That is the only sadhana (meditations).

I am the slave of my devotee.

Stay by me and keep quiet. I will do the rest.

What is our duty? To behave properly. That is enough.

My eye is ever on those who love me.

Whatever you do, wherever you may be, always bear this in mind: I am always aware of everything you do.

I will not allow my devotees to come to harm.

If a devotee is about to fall, I stretch out my hands to support him or her.

I think of my people day and night. I say their names over and over.

My treasury is open but no one brings carts to take from it. I say, "Dig!" but no one bothers.

My people do not come to me of their own accord; it is I who seek and bring them to me.

All that is seen is my form: ant, fly, prince, and pauper.

However distant my people may be, I draw them to me just as we pull a bird to us with a string tied to its foot.

I love devotion.

This body is just my house. My guru has long ago taken me away from it.

Those who think that Baba is only in Shirdi have totally failed to know me.

Without my grace, not even a leaf can move.

I look on all with an equal eye.

I cannot do anything without God's permission.

God has agents everywhere and their powers are vast.

I have to take care of my children day and night and give an account to God of every paisa.

The wise are cheerful and content with their lot in life.

If you are wealthy, be humble. Plants bend when they bear fruit.

Spend money in charity; be generous and munificent but not extravagant.

Get on with your worldly activities cheerfully, but do not forget God.

Do not kick against the pricks of life.

Whatever creature comes to you, human or otherwise, treat it with consideration.

Do not be obsessed by the importance of wealth.

See the divine in the human being.

Do not bark at people and don't be aggressive, but put up with others' complaints.

There is a wall of separation between oneself and others and between you and me. Destroy this wall!

Give food to the hungry, water to the thirsty, and clothes to the naked. Then God will be pleased.

Saburi (patience) ferries you across to the distant goal.

The four sadhanas and the six Sastras are not necessary. Just have complete trust in your guru: it is enough.

Meditate on me either with form or without form, that is pure bliss.

God is not so far away. He is not in the heavens above, nor in hell below. He is always near you.

If anyone gets angry with another, they wound me to the quick.

If you cannot endure abuse from another, just say a simple word or two, or else leave.

What do we lose by another's good fortune? Let us celebrate with them, or strive to emulate them.

That should be our desire and determination.

I stay by the side of whoever repeats my name.

If formless meditation is difficult, then think of my form just as you see it here. With such meditation, the difference between subject and object is lost and the mind dissolves in unity.

If anyone offends you do not return tit for tat.

I am the slave of those who hunger and thirst after me and treat everything else as unimportant.

Whoever makes me the sole object of their love, merges in me like a river in the ocean.

Look to me and I will look to you.

What God gives is never exhausted, what man gives never lasts.

Be contented and cheerful with what comes.

My devotees see everything as their Guru.

Poverty is the highest of riches and a thousand times superior to a king's wealth.

Put full faith in God's providence.

Whoever withdraws their heart from wife, child, and parents and loves me, is my real lover.

Distinguish right from wrong and be honest, upright and virtuous.

Do not be obsessed by egotism, imagining that you are the cause of action: everything is due to God.

If we see all actions as God's doing, we will be unattached and free from karmic bondage.

Other people's acts will affect just them. It is only your own deeds that will affect you.

Do not be idle: work, utter God's name and read the scriptures.

If you avoid rivalry and dispute, God will protect you.

People abuse their own friends and family, but it is only after performing many meritorious acts that one gets a human birth. Why then come to Shirdi and slander people?

Speak the truth and truth alone.

No one wants to take from me what I give abundantly.

Do not fight with anyone, nor retaliate, nor slander anyone.

Harsh words cannot pierce your body. If anybody speaks ill of you, just continue on unperturbed.

Choose friends who will stick to you till the end, through thick and thin.

Meditate on what you read and think of God.

I give my devotees whatever they ask, until they ask for what I want to give.

You should not stay for even one second at a place where people are speaking disrespectfully of a saint.

If you do not want to part with what you have, do not lie and claim that you have nothing, but decline politely saying that circumstances or your own desires prevent you.

Let us be humble.

Satsang that is associating with the good is good. Dussaya, or associating with evil-minded people, is evil and must be avoided.

What you sow, you reap. What you give, you get.

Recognize the existence of the Moral Law as governing results. Then unswervingly follow this Law.

All gods are one. There is no difference between a Hindu and a Muslim. Mosque and temple are the same.

Fulfill any promises you have made.

Death and life are the manifestations of God's activity. You cannot separate the two. God permeates all.

Mukti is impossible for those addicted to lust.

Gain and loss, birth and death are in the hands of God.

When you see with your inner eye, then you realize that you are God and not different from Him.

Avoid unnecessary disputes.

The giver gives, but really he is sowing the seed for later: the gift of a rich harvest.

Wealth is really a means to work out dharma. If one uses it merely for personal enjoyment, it is vainly spent.

To God be the praise. I am only the slave of God.

God will show His love. He is kind to all.

Whenever you undertake to do something, do it thoroughly or not at all.

Be ashamed of your hatred. Give up hatred and be quiet.

The Moral Law is inexorable, so follow it, observe it, and you will reach your goal: God is the perfection of the Moral Law.

I am your servants' servant.

Always think of God and you will see what He does.

Have faith and patience. Then I will be always with you wherever you are."

"I give people what they want in the hope that they will begin to want what I want to give them (knowledge of the Ultimate)." He then taught values of total surrender to the Almighty Master (ALLAH MALIK EK- The only ONE) and experiences his grace." Shirdi Sai Baba recited both Hindu and Muslim prayers.

Lord Mahavir: He passed on to humanity the ancient Jain religion. He lived over 2500 years ago and died around 527 B.C. Mahavira was born about 599 B.C. in the state of Bihar, India.

Mahavir was a prince. He was named Vardhaman by his parents. As the son of a king, he had many worldly pleasures, comforts, and services at his command. However finding no meaning in his life, at the age of thirty, he left his family and royal household, gave up his worldly possessions, and became a monk. He decided to search for a solution to eliminate pain, sorrow, and sufferings from mankind.

During the next twelve and half years, Mahavir spent in deep silence and meditation. He fought to conquer his desires, feelings, and attachments. He carefully avoided harming or disturbing other living beings including animals, birds, and plants. He also fasted for long periods. Because he was calm and peaceful against all excruciating hardships, he was given the name Mahavir, meaning very brave and courageous. It was during this period that his spiritual powers fully developed and at last he realized perfect perception, knowledge, power, and bliss. This Inner Realization is known as keval jnana or the Perfect Enlightenment.

Mahavir preached the Three Laws - right faith (samyak darshana), right knowledge (samyak jnana), and right conduct (samyak charitra). Together these form the real path to attain the Liberation of one's self.

Right conduct for Jains meant the five great vows:

1. Nonviolence (Ahimsa) To do no harm to any living being
2. Truthfulness (Satya) To speak the harmless truth only
3. Non-stealing (Asetya) Not to take anything not freely given
4. Chastity (Brahmacharya) To abstain and not to indulge in sensual pleasure
5. Non-attachment or Non-possession (Aparigraha) The complete detachment from people, places, and material things

In Jainism, monks and nuns had to follow these vows strictly and totally, but the lay people follow the vows as far as their life styles allow.

Mahavir said that, "A living body is not merely an integration of limbs and flesh but it is the abode of the soul which potentially has perfect perception (Anant darshana), perfect knowledge (Anant jnana), perfect power (Anant virya), and perfect bliss (Anant sukha)."

"One who neglects or disregards the existence of earth, water, fire, air, vegetation and all other lives disregards his own existence which is entwined with them." - Lord Mahavira (599 B.C.–527 B.C.)

Sant Kabir Mystic and Philosopher (1398–1518)

Considered perhaps to be one of the greatest mystics ever born in India, Sant Kabir is unusual in that he is spiritually important to Hindus, Sikhs, and Muslims alike.

The Sikh Sacred Book, the Holy Guru Granth Sahib contains over 500 verses by the great saint, Kabir. The verses of Guru Kabir are still read by people with awe and admiration.

Teachings of Kabir

"If he tries to find himself he finds God and if he tries to find God he finds himself."

"I have made Him My companion Who is beyond pleasure and pain; I will revel with Him, I will merge with Him and never be parted again". - Kabir,

"Let no one go searching for Him, still your mind, meditate
on Him, for He, Ram, fills each particle of the creation".
In Kabir's words "The Divine is absolute and indefinable"
"If I call God one, that he is not, if I call Him two, that would be a lie.
The Lord is what He is. I am who I am".

"Having recognized the Lord within, my thoughts rest only in Him. Now wherever I cast my eyes I see only Him, since realization came, here, there, everywhere I see the Lord alone. Within the body plays the Unfathomable Formless One"

"Why then does no one seek Him their? He is neither less here nor more there, he fills each pot to the brim, do not look for the beloved elsewhere for He is within."

"The Lord is within the body. Between the two eyes is the Master,
The messenger of the Lord. Between the black and the white
moles is the shining star, And within the star dwells
The unknown and unseen Lord."

"The physical eyes open to the outside world and the inner eye which has the ability to see the Supreme Being opens inward into the spiritual world which is unending. "That which is visible is perishable; contemplate on Him who is invisible. When you turn the key to the tenth door you will see the Merciful One". – Kabir (1398-1518)

St. John Bosco: The following is a slightly modified text from the public domain book. The Catholic World - A Monthly Magazine of General Literature and Science published in 1903 by the Paulist Fathers.) **Don Bosco:** "THE NINETEENTH CENTURY APOSTLE OF THE LITTLE ONES" - BY E. UHLRICH

'When one man in his lifetime has cared for, trained, and sent out into the world, as useful and law-abiding citizens, ten million children, then the attention of people may well be drawn to him again and again, for it is the lives of such men that keep the heart of the world from despair.

He who was to have such wonderful sympathy and even more wonderful influence on neglected and unfortunate childhood and youth, began his life as a poor, hardworking boy, even as St. Vincent de Paul did in his day. Giovanni Bosco was his name, and he was the son of humble peasants and herded his father's sheep until he was fifteen years old. Then a kindly priest discovered the boy's unusual gifts of mind and heart, and taught him the elements of Latin and Greek. After that Giovanni was sent to the seminary at Chieri, where he was ordained to the priesthood in 1841. Full of zeal to fit himself for his work as a shepherd of souls, he went to Turin and entered an institute for the training of priests in practical work.

It is notable that his first experience was in visiting prisons. Here his heart and mind were touched by the spectacle of the many youthful criminals he met, and he was constantly thinking how to reclaim them and, even more important, how to prevent them from entering upon criminal ways at all.

It was on the 8th of December, in 1841, that Don Bosco found, in a most humble occurrence, the occasion which showed him the mission for which God had destined him. It was, as so often happens, but a simple thing; but, when we are open to the guidance of the Divine Will, the simplest things may have the greatest import. There was no boy to serve his Mass, and a street-boy, who happened to look into the sacristy, was asked by the sacristan to do so.

"I do not know how," said the boy.

"Never mind," said the sacristan; "I'll show you what to do."

"But I never was at Mass before."

"Stupid creature!" said the sacristan, angry now, "what are you doing here then?" And he boxed the boy's ears so hard that the little fellow went off crying. At this Don Bosco turned around and reproved the astonished sacristan for his crossness.

"But what difference does that make to your reverence?"

"It makes a great deal of difference to me, for that boy is my friend. Call him back at once; I must talk to him."

The sacristan did so and the poor boy came back; Don Bosco asked him kindly if he had never heard Mass before, and he said "No."

"Then," said Don Bosco, "stay for this Mass which I am going to celebrate, and when it is over I shall talk to you a little while, if you will wait."

The boy, whose heart had been won by Don Bosco's kindly manner, gladly agreed to stay.

After Mass, Don Bosco said to him: "What is your name, my little friend?"

"Bartolomeo Garelli."

"Where are you from?"

"Asti."

"Is your father still living?"

"No, he is dead."

"And your mother?"

"She is dead too."

"How old are you?"

"I am fifteen years old."

"Can you read and write?"

"I don't know anything at all."

"Did you make your first Communion?"

"No, not yet."

"Did you ever go to confession?"

"I did when I was very little."

"Why don't you go to Sunday-school?"

"I am ashamed because the other boys are all younger than I am and know so much more, and I always have such old clothes."

"If I were to teach you all by yourself, would you like to come?"

"Oh I would be very glad to come, if no one would box my ears for coming."

"You need not be afraid of any one. You are my friend now; no one else will have anything to say to you. When shall we begin?"

"Whenever it pleases you, father."

"Very well, we will begin at once."

Don Bosco found that the boy did not even know how to make the sign of the cross. Yet this poor, untaught child of the street became the corner-stone, so to say, of Don Bosco's life-work. In a little while Bartolomeo brought friends of his along, and they in turn brought their friends. By the 25th of March, in 1842, there were thirty members of Don Bosco's class. Some of them were apprentices to the different trades, some were street vagabonds, and some of them grown men. The next year there were three hundred of them. Don Bosco had to find a place of meeting larger than his little sacristy; but, alas! No sooner was he well established in his new quarters than notice was given him to move.

People insisted that they did not want him and his noisy, disreputable vagabonds in their own respectable neighborhood. When, at last, there seemed no hope of finding a suitable meeting place in the city for his boys he did not despair. For two months, each Sunday he led them out into the suburbs of Turin, said Mass for them in some church, then taught them under the open sky. Afterwards he let them play games and amuse themselves, and in the evening the whole crowd went back into the city, singing hymns as they went.

In 1844, with the help of some kindly priests, Don Bosco opened the first night schools, teaching reading, writing, and arithmetic. These schools were soon imitated all over Italy.

Don Bosco, however, continued to meet with trials and tribulations in his work, as seems true in every good cause. His plans were so novel and so large that he was even accused of being crazy. A crazy man, however, ought to be out of harm's way, and so it was quietly arranged that Don Bosco should be taken to an insane asylum. Two prominent gentlemen of Turin were to manage his transfer to the asylum. They hired a closed carriage and drove to Don Bosco's house. He received them very kindly, and soon was talking to them enthusiastically about the oratorium and the great church he wanted to build, the schools and the workshops which would be grouped around this centre. He spoke so glowingly that one could have thought he saw the whole thing before his eyes. The gentlemen looked at each other knowingly, as if to say: "It is plain that he is out of his mind."

"A little fresh air will be good for you, Don Bosco," one of them ventured. "We have a carriage outside. You might drive a little way with us."

Don Bosco smiled and went out with the two gentlemen. They stepped back in order to let him enter first, but he begged them to precede him.

They did so and then Don Bosco hastily shut the carriage door and called out to the driver, "Ready."

The driver had been instructed to drive to the asylum as fast as the horses could go, and not to mind any possible protests or resistance. So he started off at a gallop at Don Bosco's word.

When the carriage arrived at the asylum, the gentlemen inside were in such a rage that the superintendent ordered them put into separate cells at once, and, if necessary, in straitjackets. Luckily for them, the chaplain of the asylum knew them, and they were let go about their business. However, they at least were convinced that Don Bosco was saner than some people thought him, and did not wish to be the agents of any more forced cures for him.

Don Bosco's trials now took another form. The police of Turin began to take note of his boys and to suspect in them potential socialists. Indeed, the very existence of the work was threatened, when King Charles Albert, then King of Sardinia, took personal action in behalf of "Don Bosco's young rogues," as he put it, and even sent sixty dollars to help the work along. With that the worst storms were over. Don Bosco organized his Oratorium of St. Francis of Sales, as he called his meeting place, for he had a special devotion to St. Francis. He chose the name "Oratorium" because the earliest meetings were in the chapel in which he met that first, pitifully ignorant street boy.

In the spring of 1846, however, he was homeless once more - put out again for the sake of his boys. Thereupon he leased a piece of enclosed land outside of the city. Here, in the open air, under the free sky, the Sunday meetings were again held undisturbed. Early in the morning Don Bosco was there, seated on a grassy mound and hearing confessions. Some of the boys were kneeling nearby, waiting their turn, others were saying their prayers, and still others, farther away, were quietly playing. At nine o'clock Don Bosco called his boys together. He had no bell, so one of the boys beat on an ancient drum as a signal. Then he separated them into little divisions, and sent each division into a particular church to hear Mass. Later they returned, and there was Sunday school, games, and singing.

After awhile a little shed nearby was rented and arranged for a chapel. In the fall of 1846 he added a few rooms, and thus he began his first school.

To be sure the boys' dormitory was nothing but a hayloft pressed into service, while the housekeeper was Don Bosco's sturdy peasant mother, who had come to the city to help on the work of her beloved son.

In 1851, he was able to build a church dedicated to St. Francis de Sales, and two new houses.

Now there is a magnificent group of buildings on this same land. The church is in the centre; two imposing wings are the "Oratorium," of which Don Bosco had dreamed and talked so enthusiastically that once people even thought him crazy. The dream has more than come true. There is a little town in itself here. All about are buildings representing various kinds of trades and activity. There is a great printing establishment with ten presses, a book bindery, a large locksmith shop, a carpentering shop, a shoe factory, and a tailoring establishment. There are, moreover, libraries, study-rooms, classrooms, dormitories, gardens, and playgrounds. Over one thousand people live here and follow their various employments.

Don Bosco is dead; he died on January 31, 1888. But his work went on under Don Michelle Rua, who was himself an orphan, raised and trained by Don Bosco. Here, in the mother house, are some thirty Salesian priests, as the members of the congregation founded by Don Bosco, at the suggestion of Minister Ratazzi, are called; nearly two hundred Salesian brothers, who are the master workmen, and four hundred students. In addition to the resident pupils that are being trained and cared for, about five hundred boys and apprentices spend their Sundays and recreation hours at the institution, something in the way in which children in this country go to the Settlements that have been established here and there in the large cities.

More than one hundred and fifty of these institutions were founded by Don Bosco in Italy, France, Spain, the Tyrol, and England. He also founded a sisterhood, so as to be able to take care of young girls as well as of boys, and to help in the missions which he established in South America, especially in Patagonia, where fourteen thousand tribals were baptized by his missionaries before Don Bosco's death. Latterly the sisterhood he founded has been working among the neglected Italians in this country too, especially in New Orleans, and there are Salesian Fathers of Don Bosco in New York City. This special missionary work, however, was not counted in the general estimate of the ten million children saved by Don Bosco.

Every year eighteen thousand apprentices leave his institutions and go out to work, trained in body and mind for contact with the world.

As a means of maintaining his work, Don Bosco founded a third society to which men and women, lay or clerical, can belong, their object being to help provide means for this great work, and the Holy Father himself belongs to this third society.

In appearance Don Bosco, the simple country boy, who was destined to do this great work in this day and age, and to show the world one true way of helping to solve the problems of labor and capital and government that disturb the nations of the earth so much now, was a tall man of very pleasing features and manner. He was not very eloquent as a talker, but his heart was filled with a heavenly love for poor and unhappy childhood. Few of us are so limited in means, or in opportunity, but we can follow him a little way. Even the young children who go to Sunday-school often know, or could easily learn, of some neglected child that has perhaps no parents, or has parents who have no faith, and which therefore hears nothing of religion and of right. Like Garelli, Don Bosco's first pupil and follower, regular Sunday-school children could take such a child to their own Sunday-school. The children of the Paulist Sunday-school in New York City, for instance, are constantly encouraged to bring with them any child they know who does not go to Sunday-school in any other place. If, in addition to its spiritual neglect, the child is in bodily want, bringing it to Sunday-school attracts the attention of older people who are able, on occasion, to give it material as well as spiritual help.

To those of us who are older, surely there can be no greater appeal than that of childhood for love and instruction. To withhold these is a more bitter injustice even than to withhold food and clothing. The one causes the body to suffer, but the other may mean the death of the soul, and delivers the body to the lawlessness and to the excesses that lead to untimely death in one generation and help on that lamentable degeneration - physically, morally, and mentally - in the succeeding generations which is, today, one of the most discouraging questions in the dark problems of the great cities.

And it must always be remembered that among the poor and the unfortunate the inspiration for better things must come from those who have more than they of means, of time, of intelligence, and, above all, of devotion.

In every age God seems to have raised up men with a genius for holiness, to speak to the people according to the needs of their day. And thus, in a century in which the powers of darkness were directed towards destroying childhood and youth by godless teaching, and by lack of any teaching at all, either sacred or profane, the providence of Divine Love raised up the humble peasant priest of Turin as an apostle to youth and a bulwark against its enemies..."

Uplifting Poems 16

Reeds of Innocence by William Blake (28 November 1757 – 12 August 1827), considered one of the most loved of English poets.

'PIPING down the valleys wild
Piping songs of pleasant glee
On a cloud I saw a child
And he laughing said to me:
'Pipe a song about a Lamb!'
So I piped with merry cheer.
'Piper pipe that song again;'
So I piped: he wept to hear.
'Drop thy pipe thy happy pipe;
Sing thy songs of happy cheer!'
So I sung the same again
While he wept with joy to hear.
'Piper sit thee down and write
In a book that all may read.
So he vanish'd from my sight;
And I pluck'd a hollow reed
And I made a rural pen
And I stain'd the water clear
And I wrote my happy songs
Every child may joy to hear.' – William Blake

'Light Shining Out Of Darkness' - ***By* William Cowper** (1731 – 1800)

"God moves in a mysterious way

His wonders to perform;
He plants his footsteps in the sea,
And rides upon the storm.
Deep in unfathomable mines
Of never-failing skill,
He treasures up his bright designs,
And works his sovereign will.
Ye fearful saints, fresh courage take,
The clouds ye so much dread
Are big with mercy, and shall break
In blessings on your head.
Judge not the Lord by feeble sense,
But trust him for his grace:
Behind a frowning providence
He hides a smiling face.
His purposes will ripen fast,
Unfolding every hour;
The bud may have a bitter taste,
But sweet will be the flower.
Blind unbelief is sure to err,
And scan his work in vain:
God is his own interpreter,
And he will make it plain." - William Cowper, great English poet (1731 – 1800)

Ode on Solitude - Written by **Alexander Pope** (21 May 1688 – 30 May 1744)

I.

How happy he, who free from care
The rage of courts, and noise of towns;
Contented breathes his native air,
In his own grounds.

II.

Whose herds with milk, whose fields with bread,
Whose flocks supply him with attire,
Whose trees in summer yield him shade,
In winter fire.

III.

Blest! Who can unconcern'dly find
Hours, days, and years slide swift away,
In health of body, peace of mind,
Quiet by day,

IV.

Sound sleep by night; study and ease
Together mix'd; sweet recreation,
And innocence, which most does please,
With meditation.

V.

Thus let me live, unheard, unknown;
Thus unlamented let me die;
Steal from the world, and not a stone
Tell where I lie.' – Alexander Pope (1688 – 1744)

To a Skylark - Written by Percy Bysshe Shelley (4 August 1792 – 8 July 1822)

'HAIL to thee, blithe spirit!
Bird thou never wert,
That from heaven, or near it,
Pourest thy full heart
In profuse strains of unpremeditated art.
Higher still and higher
From the earth thou springest,
Like a cloud of fire
The blue deep thou wingest,
And singing still dost soar, and soaring ever singest.

In the golden lightning
Of the sunken sun,
O'er which clouds are bright'ning,
Thou dost float and run,
Like an unbodied joy whose race is just begun.
The pale purple even
Melts around thy flight;
Like a star of heaven
In the broad daylight,
Thou art unseen, but yet I hear thy shrill delight¡
Keen as are the arrows
Of that silver sphere,
Whose intense lamp narrows
In the white dawn clear
Until we hardly see, we feel that it is there.
All the earth and air
With thy voice is loud¡
As, when night is bare,
From one lonely cloud
The moon rains out her beams, and heaven is overflow'd.
What thou art we know not;
What is most like thee?
From rainbow clouds there flow not
Drops so bright to see
As from thy presence showers a rain of melody:
Like a poet hidden
In the light of thought,
Singing hymns unbidden,
Till the world is wrought
To sympathy with hopes and fears it heeded not:
Like a high-born maiden
In a palace tower,

Soothing her love-laden
Soul in secret hour
With music sweet as love, which overflows her bower:
Like a glow-worm golden
In a dell of dew,
Scattering unbeholden
Its aerial hue
Among the flowers and grass, which screen it from the view:
Like a rose embower'd
In its own green leaves,
By warm winds deflower'd,
Till the scent it gives
Makes faint with too much sweet these heavy-winged thieves.
Sound of vernal showers
On the twinkling grass,
Rain-awaken'd flowers;
All that ever was
Joyous, and clear, and fresh, thy music doth surpass.
Teach us, sprite or bird,
What sweet thoughts are thine:
I have never heard
Praise of love or wine
That panted forth a flood of rapture so divine.
Chorus hymeneal,
Or triumphal chaunt,
Match'd with thine, would be all
But an empty vaunt;
A thing wherein we feel there is some hidden want.
What objects are the fountains
Of thy happy strain?
What fields, or waves, or mountains?
What shapes of sky or plain?

What love of thine own kind? what ignorance of pain?
With thy clear keen joyance
Languor cannot be;
Shadow of annoyance
Never came near thee:
Thou lovest; but ne'er knew love's sad satiety.
Waking or asleep,
Thou of death must deem
Things more true and deep
Than we mortals dream,
Or how could thy notes flow in such a crystal stream?
We look before and after,
And pine for what is not:
Our sincerest laughter
With some pain is fraught;
Our sweetest songs are those that tell of saddest thought.
Yet if we could scorn
Hate, and pride, and fear;
If we were things born
Not to shed a tear,
I know not how thy joy we ever should come near.
Better than all measures
Of delightful sound,
Better than all treasures
That in books are found,
Thy skill to poet were, thou scorner of the ground!
Teach me half the gladness
That thy brain must know;
Such harmonious madness
From my lips would flow,
The world should listen then, as I am listening now!' - Percy Bysshe Shelley (1792 – 1822)

The following is a wonderful inspirational poem by Henry Wadsworth Longfellow (February 27, 1807 – March 24, 1882), who was a towering figure in nineteenth-century America.

"Tell me not, in mournful numbers,
Life is but an empty dream!
For the soul is dead that slumbers,
And things are not what they seem.
Life is real! Life is earnest!
And the grave is not its goal;
Dust thou art, to dust returnest,
Was not spoken of the soul.
Not enjoyment, and not sorrow,
Is our destined end or way;
But to act, that each to-morrow
Find us farther than to-day.
Art is long, and Time is fleeting,
Our hearts, though stout and brave,
Still, like muffled drums, are beating
Funeral marches to the grave.
In the world's broad field of battle,
In the bivouac of Life,
Be not like dumb, driven cattle!
Be a hero in the strife!
Trust no Future, however pleasant!
Let the dead Past bury its dead!
Act, — act in the living Present!
Heart within, and God overhead!
Lives of great men all remind us
We can make our lives sublime,
And, departing, leave behind us
Footprints on the sands of time;
Footprints, that perhaps another,

Sailing over life's solemn main,
A forlorn and shipwrecked brother,
Seeing, shall take heart again.
Let us, then, be up and doing,
With a heart for any fate;
Still achieving, still pursuing,
Learn to labor and to wait."
- Henry Wadsworth Longfellow, a great American poet (1807 – 1882)
All The Hemispheres – by the poet Hafez (1315 – 1390)
'Leave the familiar for a while.
Let your senses and bodies stretch out
Like a welcomed season
Onto the meadows and shores and hills.
Open up to the Roof.
Make a new water-mark on your excitement
And love.
Like a blooming night flower,
Bestow your vital fragrance of Happiness and giving
Upon our intimate assembly.
Change rooms in your mind for a day.
All the hemispheres in existence
Lie beside an equator
In your heart.
Greet yourself
In your thousand other forms
As you mount the hidden tide and travel
Back home.
All the hemispheres in heaven
Are sitting around a fire
Chatting
While stitching themselves together
Into the Great Circle inside of

You.' - Hafez (1315 – 1390) though some think he lived (1325 - 1389) was a 14th century Sufi Persian poet. His poetic and inspirational lyrics have resonated with people worldwide all through time.

Jalal Uddin Rumi (1207 – 1273)

'Listen my love, illumination is eternal.

Now is always evolving.

As there are billions of stars, there are billions of steps.

As there are billions of souls, there are billions of ways to grow.

Respond to every call that excites your Spirit.

The soul has been given its own ears to hear things

that the mind does not understand.

Wherever you stand, Be the Soul of that place.' – Rumi (1207 – 1273)

If - by **Rudyard Kipling**. He was an English poet who lived from 1865-1936. He also wrote many children's stories. The poem was written in 1895 and published in 1910. The words from this poem:-

"If you can meet with Triumph and Disaster and treat those two impostors just the same" is written on the wall of the player's entrance at the Wimbledon tennis courts in England.

"If you can keep your head when all about you

Are losing theirs and blaming it on you;

If you can trust yourself when all men doubt you,

But make allowance for their doubting too:

If you can wait and not be tired by waiting,

Or, being lied about, don't deal in lies,

Or being hated don't give way to hating,

And yet don't look too good, nor talk too wise;

If you can dream - and not make dreams your master;

If you can think - and not make thoughts your aim,

If you can meet with Triumph and Disaster

And treat those two impostors just the same:.

If you can bear to hear the truth you've spoken

Twisted by knaves to make a trap for fools,

Or watch the things you gave your life to, broken,
And stoop and build'em up with worn-out tools;
If you can make one heap of all your winnings
And risk it on one turn of pitch-and-toss,
And lose, and start again at your beginnings,
And never breathe a word about your loss:
If you can force your heart and nerve and sinew
To serve your turn long after they are gone,
And so hold on when there is nothing in you
Except the Will which says to them: "Hold on!"
If you can talk with crowds and keep your virtue,
Or walk with Kings - nor lose the common touch,
If neither foes nor loving friends can hurt you,
If all men count with you, but none too much:
If you can fill the unforgiving minute
With sixty seconds' worth of distance run,
Yours is the Earth and everything that's in it,
And - which is more - you'll be a Man, my son!" – R. Kipling (1865-1936)

Here is a wonderful poem by Ella Wheeler Wilcox (November 5, 1850 – October 30, 1919). She was an American author and poet.

Solitude

'Laugh, and the world laughs with you;
Weep, and you weep alone.
For the sad old earth must borrow its mirth,
But has trouble enough of its own.
Sing, and the hills will answer;
Sigh, it is lost on the air.
The echoes bound to a joyful sound,
But shrink from voicing care.
Rejoice, and men will seek you;

Grieve, and they turn and go.
They want full measure of all your pleasure,
But they do not need your woe.
Be glad, and your friends are many;
Be sad, and you lose them all.
There are none to decline your nectared wine,
But alone you must drink life's gall.
Feast, and your halls are crowded;
Fast, and the world goes by.
Succeed and give, and it helps you live,
But no man can help you die.
There is room in the halls of pleasure
For a long and lordly train,
But one by one we must all file on
Through the narrow aisles of pain.' - Ella Wheeler Wilcox

"Only a person at peace with himself can calm others."

- Lao Tzu

"The earth is but one country, and mankind its citizens."

- Baha'u'llah, founder of Bahá'***í Faith (12 November 1817 – 29 May 1892)***

"The gift of God to this enlightened age is the knowledge of the oneness of mankind and of the fundamental oneness of religion. War shall cease between nations, and by the will of God the Most Great Peace shall come; the world will be seen as a new world, and all men will live as brothers." - Abdu'l-Baha, son of founder of Bahá'***í Faith (1844 – 1921)***

"The best time to plant a tree is 20 years ago. The second best time is now."

- Old Chinese Proverb

"The rose has thorns only for those who would gather it." - Chinese Proverb

"All mankind is from Adam and Eve, an Arab has no superiority over a non-Arab nor a non-Arab has any superiority over an Arab; Learn that every Muslim is a brother to every Muslim and that the Muslims constitute one brotherhood. Nothing shall be legitimate to a Muslim which belongs to a fellow Muslim unless it was given freely and willingly. Do not, therefore, do injustice to yourselves..." — ***Prophet Muhammad***'s Last Sermon.

The Prophet Muhammad said: "Anybody who believes in Allah and the Last Day should not harm his neighbor, and anybody who believes in Allah and the Last Day should entertain his guest generously, and anybody who believes in Allah and the Last Day should talk what is good or keep quiet (i.e. abstain from all kinds of evil and dirty talk)."

— Narrated by Abu Hurayrah, Sahih Al Bukhari, Vol: 8 Hadith 47.

The Prophet Muhammad said: "Allah will not be merciful to those who are not merciful to people." — Sahih al-Bukhari, Vol. 9, #473. (Written in 854 AD)

17 Essential Questions and Answers

Qs 1: Can everyone find self- realization?

Ans: Yes. God calls everyone to be happy. You will find permanent joy and happiness only after self-realisation. Till then you will experience ups and downs, sorrows, moments of sadness and depression. Once you uncover your Real Self within, all that pain and suffering goes forever. You become calm and tranquil, full of peace and joy. Nothing disturbs you. You become the tree, not just the leaf. You become the Real and not just the duplicate. You become the Universe, not just a comet.

Qs 2: How does one achieve self-realization?

Ans: First you must desire true happiness with all your heart and mind. Then ask for it and pray for it constantly. Read lots of spiritual books. Have an open mind and study the original teachings of all the masters, prophets and teachers. When the time is ripe, God will then grant this greatest of gifts to you. Your good parents gave you life. God gives you Eternal Life. The life that your mother gave you will one day end, but the Life that God will give you will never end. It lasts forever.

Qs 3: What type of books should I read?

Ans: You can read all types of spiritual books. However, I avoid those books where the authors speak against other faiths. Love is the essence of God. Anything short of complete love is not the greatest teaching. It is incomplete teaching. Remember, if there is anger or intolerance, there is impurity hidden inside. Anger or dislike for others stems from lust and impurity. That teacher who is still intolerant of other faiths had better be silent until he deepens his Being in the Kingdom of God. You will discover that he has become the mighty ocean and not just a small river when he embraces everyone with the eternal love of God. Till then, take such teaching with a pinch of salt. Question and study yourself until you find out the truth. Once you have uncovered your Real Self, there will come a time when you will go beyond books and beyond teachers. All you have to do then, is to be the Void. Be Nothingness. Into Nothingness, flows Everything. So be empty.

Qs 4: Have you uncovered your real self?

Ans: Yes, many, many years ago. The exact time does not matter. God is beyond time and space. He is eternal. I am eternally grateful for this precious gift. I have largely kept silent about it till now.

Qs 5: What did you experience after that?

Ans: Intense joy and happiness. The feeling is indescribable - beyond words. You don't experience anymore ups and downs or any sorrow. Nothing affects you. You just remain calm all the time. People around you will remark that you have suddenly began smiling all the time. In fact, some will even ask you 'Why are you always smiling and laughing?' There is no answer. You just cannot help it. It comes naturally after self realisation. Gone are all the doubts. In its place is absolute certainty. As I began to empty my mind more and more, eternal wisdom flooded in. Love for all humanity flooded in. My heart started to open up and embrace all peoples, all nations and all continents. One began to have a deep sense of appreciation for all creation in the Universe. Over time weaknesses and faults disappear without any effort from your side. It is as if someone is washing you clean without you being even conscious of it. It is the best feeling in the world. And best of all, it does not end. Everyday gets better.

Qs 6: What should one do after self-realisation?

Ans: The most important thing is to keep silent. Achieving self-realisation is like beginning school. You have only started sitting in class. There are so many subjects you know nothing about. The more one remains empty, the more Knowledge and Wisdom will enter. This may take 10 years, 20 years or more.

Qs 7: Does sin and wrongdoing go away completely from a realised soul?

Ans: Only after one sees a bright white light constantly. Sin has no place if one is constantly Aware and Conscious every moment of time about one's True Being. In the beginning it is difficult for even a realised soul to constantly be aware every second of the day. Which is why, they have to be careful. That is why it is crucial to remain initially silent and still, to practise solitude and meditation. It is easy to slide back into sin. That is why it is important not to be a teacher unless one has become white as snow permanently. Otherwise it may lead your followers to be disappointed and lose faith when they see that the teacher is not absolutely clean. This state of constant awareness takes many years to acquire and develop. You'll find in history that most teachers, masters and prophets spend years in silence, solitude and meditation before they reach the stage of complete Awareness and total Light. Teaching before that stage is reached may indicate spiritual pride and arrogance which is dangerous. Joy, Happiness, a constant Smile, Radiance, Outer and Inner Glow, Silence, Stillness, Love, Purity, Calm, Tranquility, Kindness, Compassion, Forgiveness and Humility are the hallmarks of a great Master.

Qs 8: Why is Self-realisation important?

Ans: Believe me, this is the most important purpose in life. Nothing else matters but this. Everything will one day end. Your self-realisation is like finding the Kingdom of God within you. That Kingdom will never end. If you are a student, your studies will one day end. If you are working, your job will one day end. If you are a sportsman, your sporting career will gradually finish once you cross 30 years old. Your money and wealth will also end. Even if you have billions, you can carry nothing to your grave. You go alone to face the Eternal. However, the moral and spiritual values which you store up in your life, go with you. They remain like sweet and treasured memories on this earth's history. No one can recall much about the men and women who lived at the same time as Lord Ram, Lord Krishna, Lord Jesus, Lord Buddha, Sant Kabir, Zoroaster, Prophet Muhammad, Lord Mahavira, Guru Nanak and all the other great Masters and Teachers. But these names shine brightly forever through the pages of history. This joy and happiness which comes with inner realization, will never end. It only gets better and better and better. Words cannot describe this state. It is sheer bliss. I invite you to experience it yourself.

Qs 9: What happens when I empty my mind?

Ans: After you empty your mind, you need not do anything. God takes over. He will do the rest. When your mind is empty, God will fill it with supreme knowledge, wisdom, joy, happiness, confidence, purity, love and power. When your mind is blank and empty, you will experience great joy and happiness. A smile will break out on your face even without you desiring it. You will also begin to breathe deeply and naturally without the slightest effort on your part.

Qs 10: After practising meditation, how long does it take to achieve self-realisation?

Ans: It varies from person to person. It may take 5 years, 10 years, 20 years or it could happen in just a moment. However, once you achieve it, keep silent about it until you are sure, you are totally free from sin. Even then, the preferred option is silence. Remember, God is silent. He speaks through nature, he speaks through Special Ones, whom he sends down time and again. But he himself is silent. Silence requires great humility. There is no ego or pride in silence. It is the eternal language of God. Human languages come and go. Some languages have gone extinct. Latin was the language of the mighty Roman Empire. It was once spoken across the Roman world. Where is it now? It is spoken by just a few people. It is the same with the Sanskrit Language. However, Silence, because it is God's language, will never die.

So, if you are absolutely sure that you are directed by your inner voice, then teach. If not, remain silent.

Qs 11: How does one benefit the world if one maintains silence after achieving self-realisation?

Ans: God has remained silent. And yet He created all that we see around us. He speaks without speaking. He acts without moving. He does without doing. Think deeply about what I just said. Look at the tree. The tree is silent and does not move. Yet, look at how much it accomplishes. It shelters birds. Birds often have their nests in the trees. Trees provide fruits which feed our human species as well as animals. Trees give shelter from the Sun. They absorb CO_2 and provide oxygen. Trees also heal us. Look at the majestic Himalayan Mountains, the grand Alps or the beautiful Andes mountains. They do not speak, nor do they move. They are silent and still. Yet they are so beautiful. People are naturally drawn to the mountains. Humans derive inspiration from them. It is up to each one to decide with his Eternal Maker whether he or she wants to teach or be silent. All I can say is that the Eternal who knows everything and is the Source of all Wisdom, keeps silent. Yes, he sends his messengers from time to time but He himself maintains silence. So that is the Highest spiritual state. That is the ideal state for all. There is no other state higher than that. The state of emptiness, silence and stillness. The absolute Void or State of Nothingness. It is the eternal state of God. And who bigger than Him. It is the supreme state of perpetual Happiness. And yet as I keep repeating, no one, yes, no one has created or done as much as God has. No one lives longer than God does. No one is happier than Him. No one is kinder or more compassionate. No one loves us all as much as Him.

Qs. 12: Why is the Empty Mind so important to God?

Ans: It is so valued to God because the essence of the Eternal is Love. When your mind is empty, it does not sin against anybody. The mind is free of bad or evil thoughts when it is empty. When a person is empty and still he cannot act or do harm to anyone.

When a person is silent, he does not speak ill against anyone. So emptiness, silence and stillness makes a person just a pure being.

Qs 13: Is Self-realisation meant only for those who renounce everything?

Ans: No. Uncovering one's true self or finding the Kingdom of God is for everyone. Living a stress free and peaceful life is beneficial to all. It does not matter what your occupation is. You may be a student, working woman, mother, household wife, farmer, factory worker, salesperson, industrialist, businessman, soldier, government servant, executive, doctor, lawyer, school teacher, nurse, professor, shopkeeper, retired person or holding any other post and position in your life. Being happy and calm always helps you in whatever career you are.

Qs. 14: What about prayers? Are prayers answered? Sometimes I feel that my prayers are not answered.

Ans: All prayers are answered. I repeat, all prayers are answered. With three conditions. First, they have to be genuine and true. Second, they should not hurt anyone. Third, you should be persistent and not give up. If you fulfil these three conditions, all prayers are answered. Yes, those who have more faith, will have their prayers answered more quickly. Those who have less faith, will be answered in due time. A master, like Jesus or a Saint, like Don Bosco had their prayers answered immediately. However, for most people their prayers will be answered after some time. God is not only spiritual but highly scientific as well. The Universe He created is all science. When your laptop has a problem, you write to the company and ask them to help you. If you persist, the company will do so. They will try to rectify your problem. So when you have difficulty in your life, send an 'email' or 'letter' to God's company. Lucky for us, we don't need to open our laptops or take a pen or paper to inform God. All we need to do is close our eyes, be still, and say a prayer out loud or silently either alone or preferably with other loved ones. So remember, the greater the problem you have in your life, the more persistent you should be in your prayers. Storm the Heaven with your prayers.

Most of us, after praying, say Amen or Om and then return to whatever we were doing. However, it is more effective if you pause in silence for a few minutes after your prayer. Be very specific about what you are praying. You cannot go to a bank and say give me a loan without being very specific about what type of loan you want. It is the same with prayer. If you are sick, you must mention the exact place where you are sick. If you want a job, you must at least do your homework and specify what types of jobs you want. All prayers are more effective when they are detailed and specific. How can you expect God to show interest to you, if you are not interested in yourself? How can you expect God to answer when you do not know what you want.

Qs. 15: Why are you insisting so much on Being Empty or Being Nothing?

Ans: The Void or Nothingness is like the Internet or the World Wide Web. The moment you are Empty in your mind and completely still, in that very moment you are not only connected with the Supreme but you are in the Divine Presence. And just like the internet, downloading begins. When you are not connected to the internet, you cannot download anything. But the moment you are connected to high speed internet, you can download lots and lots of information. It is the same with The Void. Nothingness is God's super high speed internet connection to you. And when you are in the state of Emptiness, God begins downloading into you bliss, joy, happiness, goodness, compassion, wisdom, knowledge, intense love of God, love for the whole of creation, healing, life, beauty, power, discernment, purity, guidance, clarity, vision and so many untold gifts. And unlike our human internet which can sometimes go off or crash, God's internet connection never goes off unless you get distracted and stop being silent and still. Emptiness never crashes, it can never be hacked. It is the perfect internet connection which is always there. Moreover it is ultra fast. Nothing that we can create can compare with it. From God's side the connection is always there. You have just to be silent, still and empty anytime of the day for the connection with God to come on. You do not need any software or any computer to be connected with God. You yourself are the software, you yourself are the living computer. Switch on your eternal computer by switching yourself off and being Blank to be instantly connected to God. And it's free. You do not have to buy any internet modem or pay pre-paid or post-paid fees. The connection to God is free, it's always there wherever you are and it's awesome. Try it. I have done so. Believe me, it will change your life for the better completely. You will become more joyful, happier, more secure, more content, more fulfilled, more satisfied and your good dreams will come true.

Qs. 16: I am trying to practise what you are teaching but it is so hard to be empty, to be silent and to be still? What do I do? I feel like giving up.

Ans: Never give up. If you are the only person who knows where a gold treasure is, you would try to reach it no matter how far it is. How much more for this eternal treasure that I am showing you? If at the end of it all, you can achieve happiness and joy, peace and calm, kindness and gentleness, love and compassion, knowledge and wisdom, health and eternal wealth, eternal life and oneness with divinity, it is surely worth it. Nothing is ever achieved without a lot of effort. Whether it is studies, sport, business or any other success, you have to work hard for it. This is the greatest treasure of all, the best job of all, the most satisfying life of all, the source of all happiness. I ask you to keep trying. God does not judge you because you get distracted. He loves you all the more when you keep trying. Keep falling but keep rising up. Never give up no matter what. Even if thousands of times you get distracted, well then, try again thousands of times. Your mind wanders naturally so don't worry about it. The main thing is that you should be consistent with your practice of stillness, silence and emptiness. That is all. Over time, even when your mind wanders off, you will find yourself gently drawn back to your innermost core, your Sense of Awareness, your Sense of Consciousness.

Qs. 17: How does practising what you are teaching help solve my everyday problems? I suffer from fear, worries, depression, unemployment, sickness, loneliness, anger, lust and many addictions.

Ans: It is the best answer to all your problems. When your mind is empty, you do not fear. Since your mind is not thinking about anything at that moment, you are not thinking about fear. Fear comes only when you think about it. It is the same with worries. Where is the worry when the mind is blank? You worry only when you allow worry to enter your mind. As long as your mind is empty, there is no worry. The other great thing about being Nothing is that miracles start happening in your life. Unexpected pleasant surprises will keep taking place. Out of nowhere, your problems will be solved when you least expect it. Then fear and worry disappear from your life. Is Prince Charles worried financially? No! Why? Well, because he is the son of Queen Elizabeth. So once you achieve Inner Realization or Nirvana, you enter the Divine Royal family. God and his angels take over all aspects of your life forever. Where is the worry then? Remember that God calls you and everyone else to be part of the Divine Royal Family.

Anger also goes in this way. Depression has a hold on you because you keep thinking about your state of affairs again and again. However once you begin practising the exercise of the Empty Mind, you will find without any effort from your part, that depression gradually goes away from your life. You become more at peace - joyful and cheerful. The moment you become Nothing, you achieve everything. You are no longer lonely. You do not feel lonely anymore. In fact, solitude then becomes fantastic. Why? It is because the entire Universe becomes your friend. The stars become your friend. The galaxies become your friend. The distant planets become your friend. Every animal becomes your friend. The trees become your friend. Fruits and plants become your friend. Mother Earth becomes like your mother. The Source of Everything becomes like your father. The rain, the clouds, the sun, the river, the stream, the wind, the flowers, every insect, the waterfall, the mountains, the glaciers, the seas, the oceans, the seashore – all become your brothers and sisters. You yourself become one with them.

Lust and your many addictions gradually lose their hold of you when you are empty because God takes over the process of cleaning you up. Ignore your addictions. Focus on emptiness, silence and stillness. All your struggles to defeat your addictions have failed. The more you tried, the more you failed. Well stop trying. Let the Eternal take over. You concentrate on being silent, on being empty and on being still as often as you can but at least every day. Watch what happens. All addiction, one by one will gradually leave you. If you don't believe me, make a list of all the things in your life that you wish to give up. Write down the date and time. Stick it on your wall. After one year, you will see that one by one, they are gone from your life. The Eternal is the best de-addiction centre. Empty the pot if you want to cook something delicious. If the pot is dirty with addictions, it can only be washed and cleaned up if you empty it first.

You are unemployed, you want to get a better job and you can't get it. Well, let God find a job for you. Just pray with all your heart, empty your mind, be persistent and then watch what happens. It may take time but you will surely get a job. Not only that. You will even find that your loved ones are being offered jobs out of nowhere. Pleasant surprises take place not only to you but to all those who are near and dear to you. However some of you may be called not to work but to spend every moment with the Supreme. God will then take care of all your needs in a special way far better than you yourself ever could. Your pay check will be issued from Heaven. You need something. Send the cheque upstairs.

Qs. 18: Which is superior, prayer or just being empty?

Ans: Both are important. However, the state of the empty mind is far superior. When you are empty, you are one with the Eternal.

God then sees your mind and your needs and fulfills them like any father would, without your even asking for them. Did you have to ask your father or your mother to send you to school? No. They did their duty. Did you ask your parents to feed you or cloth as a child? No. They did it naturally. Well God who is both your father and your mother provides for you more than your own beloved parents could. If you have no father or no mother in your life right now, then it is all the more important to consider God your father and mother. He is there. We only have to call on Him.

Prayer, though important, can sometimes be driven by greed, by desire or by other emotions. That is why, some prayers are unanswered. If the motives for your prayer are not clean, humble or sincere, then God will surely not reply. In an empty mind, however, because you are blank, there are no motives. You will discover a lot of good things happening to you and around you without your even asking or thinking about them. God takes very special care of those who strive for oneness with Him. My advice is do both, but spend more time in silence and stillness. Pray when in urgent need. We are humans and we panic. Prayer helps in those occasions.

Qs. 19: Please describe God. Who is the Supreme One? Can we hear God? Can we see God?

Ans: God is silence. His language is silence. He silently speaks to us through nature. Look at the mountains, the trees, the earth-they are silent. We learn from them about God. God is still. And yet, He does more things than we can do with all our frenetic activity. The mountain which is silent and still, will last many more years than our human life of 70-90 years, filled with talking and running around. It is the same with trees, too. They are silent and still. Yet, they provide a home for many birds, give shelter from the Sun and protect us from pollution. "On average, one tree produces nearly 260 pounds (117.93 kg) of oxygen each year. Two mature trees can provide enough oxygen for a family of four." - Environment Canada, Canada's national environmental agency. What is indisputable is that we cannot survive without trees. We need trees to absorb carbon dioxide and CO2 from the air. We need trees to release oxygen back into the atmosphere for us to breathe. Stillness accomplishes more things than activity.

God is formless. And yet, we see Him in all the magnificent forms that He has created; the Universe, galaxies, stars, planets, asteroids, comets, moons and the entire natural world. After one achieves Realisation, when your mind is empty and you can see nothing because your eyes are closed, that nothingness, that formless void which is in your mind, that is the Eternal. That is the shape and form of the Supreme. It is difficult to understand and comprehend, but true. We are so used to shapes and forms which do not last, because they are unreal, that we cannot imagine the Eternal One as being without form, yet able to assume all forms. There is a 1977 movie 'O God!' where renowned country singer, John Denver acts as an ordinary man, who meets up with God in the shape of an elderly man. Watch that movie. George Burns plays the role of God. Also watch 'Bruce Almighty' where Morgan Freeman plays God and Jim Carrey acts as a TV Reporter.

God is unseen, unheard and invisible. God is unknown and the source of all wisdom and knowledge. We study more about Geography and History than we do about God. Our Geography is limited to this planet. All History will pass away into the mists of time. However, the knowledge of God, his attributes, is endless and eternal. We need to spend more time on that. We don't even know how many galaxies there are up there.

God is pure being. He just IS. He had no yesterday and has no tomorrow. He is total and complete here and now. God is a creator par excellence. He is an inventor and innovator. Look at the mighty Universe that he created; from the smallest insect to biggest star. His creation fills us with awe. God is love, gentleness, kindness and compassion. The love that He put in the hearts of our parents for us is but a tiny reflection of His great affection for us. No one in history can claim that God Himself came down to condemn any of us. Even when we say sorry a million times, He forgives and loves us a million times.

God is present everywhere. He is present here and now as you read this book. He is present in the little flower and in the majestic lion.

God is eternal. He was never born and will never die. Though we were born with a limited physical body, He calls each one of us to share in a life of eternity with Him. God is beyond words. He is beyond description. His attributes are so many that there are not enough books to describe him nor enough words. You will discover Him in the silence of your heart, in the silence of nature, in the silence of the woods. Go beyond my words. Go beyond all teachings. Go to that place beyond all places where you will find the Almighty. Nothing that I tell you can describe God's beauty, grandeur, bliss, magnificence and power. Each one needs to uncover the Supreme by themselves. We are here just to point out the way.

Qs. 20: Are you meeting and teaching people?

Ans: No. As of now, I neither meet nor teach people. I lead a withdrawn life and focus on meditation, prayer, silence and stillness.

Qs. 21: How do I conquer the difficulties I face, like sorrow and depression, bad habits, anger, and other forms of sin?

Ans: Pray often. Inform God about all your problems. Just as you cried for your parents when you ran into difficulties as a child, so too run to God every time you need help. There is nothing to feel shy about prayers. Say them many times a day. Talk to God exactly as you would talk to your friends. After all, He is your best friend. Tell him everything – your joys, your sorrows, your hopes, your dreams, your wishes and your needs. Unlike friends who may gossip about you, God does not chatter because his language is silence. He will never leak out your innermost secrets. So trust Him with everything. He can listen with endless patience. He does not get fed up of listening to you. He can hear you all day. He will never judge you nor ever criticize you.

Learn to say 'No' to temptations, It is natural to be tempted but you can say 'No'. Remind yourself – 'I am joy, I am happiness.

This sadness is not me. It will pass. I am not this depression. I am an ocean of bliss. I am one with the Eternal as the Eternal is one with me. I am the Source of All Things.

Avoid the places or people who cause you temptation. Make a list of them and keep away. Instead make a list of good things which give you joy and pleasure. Get involved in them with gusto. It could be anything – playing sports like tennis, football, cricket, golf, volleyball, running, athletics, badminton, basketball, mountain climbing, watching the news, watching sports, reading, listening to music, visiting places, travelling, meditation, meeting friends, newspapers, gardening, walking, exercise, family and so on. Anything which does not tempt you into sin is good for you.

Qs. 22: How should people of different occupations live their day to day life? Can you advise us?

Ans: Always be kind, gentle and compassionate to all. Forgive generously. Just as you wish others to pardon you, so you should be forgiving towards others. Try to be calm and peaceful at all times. When you find yourself stressed out, withdraw into solitude wherever you are and still your mind. It is perhaps harder to be loving and understanding towards those who live with you – your loved ones. What is the use of talking of love, if you cannot start at home or in your office? If you have a nasty tongue, watch it carefully. It would be better to be silent than to retort to every perceived insult. Be strictly honest. Live straight. Neither left nor right but straight. Be punctual. Don't be late. Your time on earth is limited. Why waste it and the precious time of others by being late. Be on time always. And don't blame traffic for being late. Be perfect. Do your job as perfectly as possible, whatever it is. It does not matter whether you are a farmer, a student, a single woman or an entrepreneur. Has the sun ever failed us? No. It is always there. Be reliable. Be true to people. Do not hurt anyone. Just as you feel sad and disappointed when someone fails you, so do others feel the same when you fail them. Never cheat or steal. If you are a manufacturer, make the highest quality product. If you are an employer, pay your salaries always on time. Be kind to your staff. If you are a teacher, be the best teacher in the world. If you are building a road, build the best road in the world. It makes good business sense too. As your reputation for honesty and quality grows, so will your business. If you are a farmer, grow the best produce and organic if possible. If you are a worker, be sincere and true to your job. Many young people in the world have no jobs. Do not lie nor gossip. When you lie, you will soon have to tell another lie to cover the first lie. Then it never stops. One lie leads to another. In the end, you will get entangled in the web of your own many lies. It is better to be silent or always truthful. Do not gossip. The person who gossips evil about others is one of the worst types of persons. You expect others not to gossip and tell tales behind your back. Then do the same to others. Extend to them the same courtesies that you expect from them. Don't deal in drugs. Have you seen the effect drugs have on people and families? A young boy or girl, who is initially innocent, becomes like a devil under the influence of drugs. A drug addict lies to his friends and family, steals from his friends and family and commits other crimes because he or she craves for that substance. It is so difficult to get out of that addiction. So don't lead young people into temptation by dealing in drugs. Never!! Do not drink. Many young people start with a beer, thinking that nothing will happen to them. Then they slowly move to harder drinks and before you know it, they have become alcoholics. So many promising young lives have been lost and families hurt because of drink and drugs. Say 'No' to drugs and drinks from the very beginning. It could mean life and death to you. You will have a happier life for yourself and a more peaceful life for your family. Corruption is the reason for the world's poverty. So I call on leaders not to be corrupt. It is the worst form of exploitation. Bureaucrats and government servants should remember that there are many young people who have no jobs. They should consider themselves lucky to have a job. Government servants should be totally honest, punctual and hard working.

Qs. 23: Who am I? Can you tell me?

Ans: Deep inside you when you have removed all that is unreal in you, you will realize that you are the Formless One, One with the Eternal as the Eternal is one with you, a branch of the same Vine, that you and the Father are one, never born and never will die, full of unspeakable joy, pure love, endless living being, unending delight, tenderness and compassion, goodness and kindness, spring of true pleasure and foundation of all things. All else is temporary and unreal. Your name was given by your parents and will end at your grave or cremation. Your childhood has faded away and will never return. There will be only faint memories that will remain kept alive by photos and videos. Your school time is also gone, never to come back. Your youth and its follies have disappeared. Your job will end with your retirement. When you peel all that is not true and not real, then all that remains is the Real You. Empty your mind of all that is not really you, embrace the Void and Nothingness and you will go back to your true Source - that which will live forever, the Supreme Power. Be quiet. Be motionless, Be Empty. That is all that matters. Let the Power that created the Universe take over and remould your life, your thinking, your being and you will have found all Happiness.

Qs. 24: The world is such a busy place, full of all types of sounds. Why do you teach me to be silent and still? I wish to live a good, long life on this earth. How shall I do so if I am mostly still?

Ans: I will tell you a story. A talkative man went up to a big tree. He said "Brother tree, why are you silent all the time? Why don't you speak to me? I would like to talk to you." The tree kept silence and said nothing. After half an hour of talking to the tree, the man grew tired and became silent.

Then in the innermost part of his heart, a tiny whisper said "Brother Man, please don't think that I do not speak. I do speak.

My language is silence; it is the language of God who created both you and me. Silence is a language that unites. On the other hand, the human language divides.

Silence is a universal language which is spoken by everybody. It is understood by everyone. Your human language is spoken by only a few. Other people in the world do not understand your language.

Silence never hurts. But the human language can hurt deeply.

The language of silence lasts forever. Human languages can and have gone extinct."

The talkative man then addressed the tree, "Brother Tree, okay, I have understood the value of silence. However, why do you not work? Why are you not active? Instead of standing here the whole day, you could move around and do some work." Again, after talking for some time, the man grew tired and became silent. Again a tiny whisper in his heart talked to him, "Brother man, I do work really hard and so do all my brother trees. Do you not see that we shelter millions of birds in our forests? If you look closely at me, you will also see many insects that I provide food to. Brother man, if we trees were not here, how would you breathe? Did you not know that I absorb carbon dioxide from the air? Carbon dioxide is poisonous for you. Instead I release oxygen into the atmosphere. Without fresh oxygen, you and your family would not be living. In any case brother man, with all your movement and activity, you will live a life far shorter than mine. I will live many more years than you. So which is better, brother man, my standing still and living longer or your tremendous activity but living shorter?"

The talkative man then understood and became enlightened.

Qs. 25: What according to you are the urgent problems of the earth?

Ans: There are many issues which trouble our earth. I will list just a few of them. They are the following:- corruption, deforestation, poverty, greed, hunger, lack of education for the poorest, women's education, women's security, drugs, alcoholism, violence, selfishness, lack of housing, bad governance, inequality, over-extraction of minerals without thinking of future generation, uncaring attitude towards other species, no landscape protection, which means hills and mountains are being flattened, endangering the Arctic and Antarctic regions by drilling for oil (These are like our air-conditioners. We tamper with them at our own peril), crime and others. You may have other pressing problems which you may wish to add to this list. Feel free to do so.

Qs. 26: What happens if I fail not once, not twice but many times? What do I do then? What is your advice?

Ans: If you fall down in sin, get up, say 'Sorry' and start again. Even if you fail many times, keep getting up. This is like a World Championship in boxing. Do not let evil win. You may be knocked down umpteen times. Get up every time and take fresh guard. Be determined to win the fight of your life. You will knock evil out of the ring. Ultimately, even if it is after a million times, you will prevail. You will be the world champion for God. Never give up. Evil cannot win if you keep getting up and saying 'Sorry'. This is the greatest of gold medals. This is the grandest Olympic event. I know that you will win. Do not be discouraged.

Have you heard of John Newton (1725-1807)? He was an Englishman born in London. He was a deserter from his ship, a hopeless sinner, who plumbed the depths of depravity and **a slave trader** who captained his own slave trading ship. He tried to commit suicide. He planned to murder his captain. He composed obscene songs and ditties. He traded in slaves. Then on a voyage, when his ship was about to sink, John begged for Divine help and gave his life to God. His ship did not sink and he was saved. Newton totally reformed himself, became an Anglican priest and wrote one of the most beloved hymns in history, 'Amazing Grace'. From a slave trading captain of a ship, to an Anglican priest, that is the change which took place in John Newton. He was truly a wretch who was saved by God's grace. If God can forgive John Newton, God can forgive and rescue us.

Qs. 27 I do not agree with you on some of the issues. Is it okay?

Ans: Yes. It is natural if you do not agree with me. I respect you for that. However, do not throw away this book. Keep it. You may reread it after some time. Why do I say this? It is because what I am sharing with you is my true, personal experience. I have bared my heart out in this book. I have found lasting Happiness. I have found my Father's Home. I have uncovered the Kingdom of Heaven within. I have found the Eternal Spring of Joy. It is a spring which does not run out. It is a spring which is eternally full. There are no depressions. There is no sadness. There is just joy and bliss – undiluted and ever fresh. I have found the secret treasure of happiness which every human being longs for. I AM LIVING HEAVEN HERE ON EARTH. May you, my friends uncover the same. Do not depend on me. I am just the footpath for you to travel on. Go on beyond me, till you reach your destination. You need not go anywhere far to search. It lies within you. It is already inside you. It is you itself, if only you would discard what is not you. It is the 'Amen', it is the 'Om', it is the 'I AM' within you.

Even if you do not agree with me, I humbly request you to do four things:-

1. Pray often for true happiness. Focus on what you are saying in prayer.
2. Be silent. It is the language of God. It is the greatest language of all. It is the only language which will never die. It is the language which will live forever. Practise meditation daily.
3. Be still. When you are completely still, you are transported in that instant to the presence of God.
4. Have an Empty Mind. Be the Void. It is that Supreme state which existed before darkness and light. It is the Formless nature which existed before all creation. It is the Source of everything. Practise being in that Supreme state of Emptiness and your life will gradually be changed forever, without your needing to do anything.

Think carefully about what I have said. All else in life does not matter, if you have not discovered lasting happiness. Find the truth, find real happiness and you would have found everything.

May the Joy of Heaven be your joy.

Some Humble Suggestions 18

Transparency

If you are a bureaucrat or a politician, be honest. Do not compromise or cut corners. Lots of people depend on you. They have given you their sacred trust. They have voted for you. Serve everyone sincerely even those who did not vote for you. Be humble enough to say sorry when you make mistakes. If you make many mistakes, say sorry many times. You do not go down in people's estimation of you. Rather they respect you all the more for having the courage to admit you went wrong. The higher the post you hold, the more humble you should be. Bureaucrats should remember that they get their salaries from the taxes of the public. They owe it to the public to be scrupulously honest, sincere, hardworking and punctual. Every government should make a list of the most upright and efficient of bureaucrats. These should be appointed to the most important positions of the country. The rest who have a whiff of corruption about them should be sacked. The people cannot afford to pay for the corruption of such officers. Every politician should study the life of the late Lee Kuan Yew, former Prime Minister of Singapore and the father of the present Prime Minister Lee Hsien Loong. Did you know that in 1951, Singapore was a swampy island, full of crime and corruption? Prime Minister Lee turned a third world country into a first class nation. Singapore is a tiny island, slightly smaller than New York City. It has no land and no minerals. Yet today it has trillions in assets and is considered one of the finest financial centres of the world. The secret of Lee Kuan Yew's good governance were:-

1. Stringent zero tolerance for corruption. He was very strict about this. No corruption was allowed. No giving and no taking of bribes. He handpicked the most honest police officers and empowered the anti-corruption vigilance bureau. Even ministers, bureaucrats and police went to jail if found cheating and stealing from the public. There were harsh jail sentences for corruption offenders. This had a restraining effect. All countries especially the poorest ones should adopt Lee Kuan Yew's standards of honesty and integrity.
2. He raised the salaries of all politicians and government servants to world class standards in order to remove temptation and prevent stealing. It worked. From being one of the most corrupt countries in the world, Lee changed it into the most transparent on planet earth. Singapore regularly ranks among the top ten most transparent nations and least corrupt. Lee felt that good salaries not only minimized corruption, it attracted the best individuals. He thought that it is far better to have a competent man with top integrity than a morally corrupt politician, bureaucrat or police officer who makes up for a low salary with huge bribes.
3. Sincerity and Hard work
4. Highest Quality. Lee got the whole nation to aim to be the best in the world in everything that they did. In just one lifetime, he transformed this backward, sleepy nation into one of the most developed in the world.
5. Ensuring a hard, strong and stable currency. Today 1USD = 1.37 Singapore dollar.
6. Nurturing the environment. Lee transformed Singapore into one of the greenest city states of the world with his tree planting programs.
7. Communal and religious harmony. Lee did not allow anyone to say a word against other communities or other religions. If you did so, you faced the law. He refused to put up with any discrimination based on language, race, religion or culture.
8. He successfully fostered and encouraged co-operation, discipline and austerity among all Singaporeans.

As a result of his good governance, he remained undefeated as a Prime Minister for 31 years, from 1959 till 1990 when he voluntarily resigned. By that time, he had become the world's longest serving Prime Minister.

Full Convertibility of your national currency is one way to ensure transparency and dramatically reduce corruption. I have spoken about maintaining the strength of the Singapore dollar as one of the reasons for Singapore's success. Contrast that with the Indian rupee which is not currently a hard currency and is not fully convertible. The rupee has been devalued over time from 1USD = 1Rupee at Independence in 1947 to around 1USD = Rs. 63.51 today. You can exchange the Singaporean dollar anywhere in the world but you cannot freely exchange the Indian rupee. What is legal in all developed and transparent countries, is unjustly considered illegal in India. Had he been alive, Mahatma Gandhi would have led another Salt March like movement to give freedom to the Rupee. We got political independence in 1947, but we will truly get economic independence when the Rupee is free. Just in 2007, one USD = Rs.39 whereas now it is Rs. 63.51 for just one dollar. Consider this. From 1990 to 2012, the Rupee has fallen by over 300 per cent. From 2007 till 2015 alone, it has fallen by about 63.50 per cent. Most staggering of all, from 1947 till now, the Rupee has fallen by 6351 per cent!! The poorest people of India, groaning under grinding and unbearable poverty have lost out. Because of the weak currency, most Indians could not go abroad nor travel. They could not afford to send their kids to the best educational institutions of the world. Only politicians, bureaucrats and the rich could do so. They thought it was normal to give bribes to get things done. Had they travelled to South East Asia, to Europe, to USA, UK, Canada and the rest of the developed world, maybe they would have demanded change. We should have been by now one of the most advanced and developed nations in the world. In 1991, the Indian economy was liberated from the corrupt License Raj, but the Rupee is yet to be made a transparent, free and fully convertible currency. It is not only in India. Many poor nations across the world especially in South Asia, Asia, Africa, Middle East, South America and Eastern Europe suffer from the horrible consequences of corruption. Forgive me if I have been too harsh on this subject. It is just that I feel so passionately about the rupee when I see the utter and hopeless poverty in the villages.

Consensus:

My own humble suggestion is that perhaps it is time for nations to move on to governing by consensus. One of the reasons why Sir Winston Churchill prevailed in the Second World War was that he insisted on forming an All-Party Government comprised mainly of Conservative and Labour. Winston Churchill from the Conservative party became Prime Minister while Clement Atlee, Labour party leader became Deputy Prime Minister. When you are united at home, you win abroad. The Swiss too have achieved so much for so long because of their "magic formula" (German: Zauberformel, French: formule magique, Italian: formula magica) – a system of perpetual coalition which is a sort of an all-party, consensus government. It is unthinkable now to recall that the Swiss were once the poorest nation of Europe wracked with crime, violence and corruption. It was such a poor country with such massive unemployment that they were sending mercenary soldiers to the service of foreign armies. Soldiers were their only export goods. Then the main parties decided to come together to form a perpetual coalition. It was a magical formula and has proved a grand success. Originally in 1959, when the 'magic formula' started, there were all the four main Swiss political parties in Government. They are the Free Democratic Party, Social Democratic Party, Christian Democratic People's Party and Swiss People's Party. That has recently expanded to five political parties with the addition of the Conservative Democratic Party of Switzerland. Counted together, they won around 76% of the popular vote in the last Swiss elections in 2011. Today all the five main Swiss political parties are present in their "magical perpetual coalition". The five parties represented in the Federal Council are generally called the government parties. They are the Free Democratic Party, Social Democratic Party, Christian Democratic People's Party, Swiss People's Party, and Conservative Democratic Party of Switzerland. The results of consensus government speak for themselves. Since then, they have consistently ranked as one of the richest nations on earth with the best and highest living standards. Other nations can only admire them. The last armed conflict on Swiss territory took place in 1847. Despite tremendous pressure, they avoided both the First World War and the Second World War. It requires leadership for people and parties to come together and unite rather than fight each other all the time. The great Indian reformer Anna Hazare too suggests changing from a party system to a Gandhian style of Parliament filled with individual independent MPs of merit rather than being filled with political party MPs who are mostly party minded. Imagine what heights the US could scale if Democrats and Republicans came together to form a National Unity Government. All the energy spent on fighting each other would go to solving the most pressing problems of the US and humanity. The intractable Northern Ireland troubles were largely resolved by forming an all-party government between the two main enemies, the Unionists and the Nationalists. Peter David Robinson, MLA, leader of the Democratic Unionist Party (DUP) has been the First Minister of Northern Ireland since 2008 and Martin McGuinness, MLA from Sinn Féin is the Deputy First Minister since 2007. **Consensus governments or a Parliament of meritorious independents dramatically reduces corruption, crime and violence to almost zero.** Transparency, integrity, quality and standards of living go up. Unless led by men or women of exceptional moral and spiritual fibre, political parties tend to serve themselves first and the nation last. They will do anything just to win elections. An independent however is limited by how much harm he or she can do.

My own legislative experience: I have been both a state legislator at the state level and a parliamentarian at the national level. In the early nineties, when I contested for the first time to be a Member of the Legislative Assembly (MLA), I had promised the electorate that I would always be guided by my conscience. However, within a month or so after being elected, I had broken that promise. On that fateful day, as I was about to enter the Legislative Assembly of the Indian state of Meghalaya, my then political bosses asked me to move a motion of No-Confidence against the then Deputy Speaker. Without a second thought, I complied. I moved the motion of No-Confidence against the Deputy Speaker just because he belonged to the Congress party which was then in opposition while we were on the ruling benches. My speech was not truthful. I remember the speeches from the Opposition. They taunted me. One by one from the opposition benches, they asked how could a young, newly elected legislator, who had promised to stand by his conscience, now lie in the House about a Deputy Speaker, whom he had not even seen functioning. That hit me hard. It felt like arrows piercing my heart. Off course, we succeeded in winning the No-Confidence vote and removing the Deputy Speaker. We did it just because he was from the opposing party. There was no other reason. He is a very good man.

Later that evening, when I sat and consulted my Inner Voice, questions arose in my mind. How can I ever hope to be an example in India, if I betray my conscience? How can I ever hope to be a guiding light for others, if I did not have the courage to say 'Sorry'? That evening, writing an apology was like writing in blood. It was very difficult. The next day, I got up in the Meghalaya Legislative Assembly and said 'Sorry' to the ousted Deputy Speaker and to the whole House for lying. The whole House heard me in stunned silence. I cannot explain to you how hard it was to say 'Sorry' in front of my colleagues and in front of the media. I then realized how accurate the English Lord John Dalberg-Acton (Born: January 10, 1834, Naples, Italy - Died: June 19, 1902, Tegernsee, Miesbach, Germany) was, when he said "Power tends to corrupt and absolute power corrupts absolutely." I promised during that speech in the Assembly, that I will devote much time to study why it is that good men change when they enter office. After more than 20 years in politics, I can firmly say that party politics is not the best democracy. The best legislature or parliament or senate or house is one where all the members would be independents. Each one would then speak according to merits. Each MP or Senator would then be both ruling and opposition. Where he supports an issue, he would be on the governing side. Where he opposes an issue, he would be on the opposing side. All members of the House would sit around in a circle rather than be divided as it is now into Ruling benches and Opposition benches. Right now, if you are on the ruling side, you support Government policies regardless of whether you agree with them or not. And if you are on the opposition side, you oppose everything just for the sake of opposing without genuinely considering the merits of the case. When a party is corrupt, it can loot in billions and trillions. When an independent MP is corrupt, the damages to the nation are far less. A party thinks first for itself and last about the people or nation. The only concern for a party is how to get back to power. They are prepared to lie to the electorate just to win back power. The whole time of the party is spent in demeaning and attacking the other side. Very little effort or time is put into thinking about genuine public issues and how to resolve them. Democracy has evolved a lot through time and history. It is time to transform and evolve once again. I call upon budding young leaders all across the world, in all continents to take this up.

Right to Information Act (RTI): In June 2005, the United Progressive Alliance (UPA) Government in India, under pressure from social activists and reformers like Anna Hazare had enacted the Right to Information Act (RTI). This Act was a powerful tool in the hands of ordinary citizens to find out what the Government was doing in various departments. It was hoped that this would usher in greater transparency and reduce corruption. However, in 2006, the same Government wanted to amend the law so that file notings of Ministers and senior officers were exempted from being revealed to the public. In other words, if there was massive corruption, the junior officers would be caught while the Ministers and senior officers would get away scot free. When I learnt that noted Gandhian, Anna Hazare had started his hunger fast in Pune, to protest against attempts by the Government to weaken the RTI by amending the law, I consulted my Inner Voice on what to do. I then rang up my good friend Dinesh Trivedi, Trinamool Congress MP in the Upper House, Rajya Sabha, (later Railway Minister of India), and together we went to Jantar Mantar in New Delhi where other supporters of Anna Hazare were fasting. NDTV reported then 'Supreme Court Justices, students, ordinary Indians, and even Members of Parliament came out against the government's decision to amend the Right to Information act on Wednesday. As the movement to put pressure on the government to withdraw the proposed amendments, the MPs say that on Thursday they will kick-start a signature campaign to put pressure on the government.

Robert Kharshiing joined thousands of Indians determined to block attempts by the government to get Parliament to amend the RTI act which has been hailed for combating corruption. Ironically Kharshiing is also the chief Whip of the NCP in Rajya Sabha. His party is part of the UPA alliance, the same government which now wants to amend the law. Kharshiing says that he will vote with his conscience if the amendments are brought in Parliament. "I feel that this amendment is wrong as in my state, the north east and in India where there is corruption, this has come as a breath of fresh air. Bureaucrats and politicians have started to feel the pressure," he said.

Kharshiing was joined by Trinamool MP Dinesh Trivedi. Both MPs now plan to rally other MPs on board. "We will start a signature campaign and go to MPs across party lines to get them to go against the amendment and make sure that it does not come to Parliament," said Trivedi.'

This is what Trivedi and I did. Over the next few days we actively lobbied MPs from all parties and the signature campaign against the Government amendment gathered steam. I was spoken to by my party leaders and asked to desist. But I stuck to my conscience and redoubled my efforts. In the end, hundreds of MPs signed up and the Government facing defeat in Parliament was forced to withdraw the amendment. The Right to Information Act (RTI) was saved and would remain intact. It was Anna Hazare and all the activists who inspired every Indian to stand up for transparency.

Consensus Government: I always believed in consensus government. I fervently advocated an All-Party, National Government as the best way to govern a huge and diverse nation such as India. To test the waters, in 2007, I drafted and circulated an open letter calling for the formation of a National Government during the time when the UPA, led by the Congress party was ruling. Requesting for support to the suggestion, originally floated by former President R. Venkataraman, for an all-party national government, the letter appealed to Parliamentarians "to rise above party lines (like we do so admirably in Parliamentary Committees), to place the nation before self and party and to think for the poorest in this country of ours." The letter went on to say "Let us make history and take our governance to the greatest heights where we govern by consensus and not by confrontation." I was then the Chief Whip of one of the partners in the Ruling Coalition. A fellow MP had jokingly said that not even one MP would sign up for an All-Party National Government. Though it was just a trial, to see how many would sign up, the brief experiment succeeded. In just half an hour, 12 MPs from various political parties of India put their signatures on the document. It proved that even today if there was the will in the major parties to unite for the sake of the people and rise above petty party politics, an All-Party Government for India could be formed.

This would avoid the intense blame game, antipathy, party mindedness and divisiveness which afflict party politics.

Afforestation:

I call on students and young people to approach their respective City Mayors and Speakers of Assemblies, Legislatures or Parliaments with signatures requesting the City Mayors and Honourable Speakers to arrange for all Legislatures and Parliamentarians to plant trees every Saturday involving the whole community. We need to reforest our planet before we drive ourselves extinct. Already many species have died out due to dwindling forest cover. There are millions of species known to exist on this earth created by God. We created none of them. We have only managed to specifically study 44,838 species out of the millions there. The sad news is that of those we have examined 905 are extinct and 16,928 are listed as being threatened with extinction. We do not know the status of millions of other species that have still to be studied. Therefore, the number of extinct and threatened species is certainly much higher than our current estimates.

At least five precious animals have been lost in the last 50 years.

1. The Western Black Rhinoceros which once populated much of the savannas of Africa.
2. The Pyrenean Ibex common to the Iberian Peninsula in Europe. This beautiful animal went extinct in 2000.
3. The Golden Toad, native to Costa Rica.
4. The majestic Javan Tiger found only on the island of Java in Indonesia.
5. The Baiji River Dolphin, a species of the Yangtze River in China.

The late Prime Minister of Singapore, Lee Kuan Yew transformed his island city state into a green one by requiring all his parliamentarians to plant trees every Saturday. The matter is so urgent that it is not enough to celebrate world Environment Day once a year. We need to plant trees every week. Young students should also approach their respective First Ministers, Chief Ministers and Governors with the same signature campaign.

I call on Mayors, Chief Ministers and Governors not to approve any new city plans without provision for a sacred forest, a city forest and a commercial forest. The sacred forest in every city will serve as its heartbeat. No trees should be cut from there. Even fallen branches, trees or twigs should not be taken away. Silence should be maintained at all times. This sacred forest shall serve as a spiritual oasis of peace and tranquility. Entry into the Sacred Forest shall be strictly regulated and restricted. The city forest however is for everyone to take a walk in. It will be more of a Forest Park open to all and at all times. The commercial forest will be for the city dwellers to use for wood provided they plant 100 trees for every tree they cut. They can only cut a tree if they have planted and nurtured 100 trees for two years beforehand. This means looking ahead and planning. No one can just cut a tree at any time they want. This means that they should first plant 100 trees, nurture them for two years and then only they can a tree for their personal use. Here's why?

- 50% of the world's forests have already disappeared.
- As of today, in a single year, we lose roughly 13 million hectares of forests. That is the size of 36 football fields per minute gone for good.
- More than 80,000 acres of tropical rainforest are being lost daily.
- These are startling figures and require urgent action. I call upon the youth to take this up.

Pope Francis is doing a marvellous job taking this issue up. We need to support him for the sake of future generations and for the survival of this Planet. This is the only home we have right now.

Population of the Earth:

As of today, 2015, the population of the earth is 7.324 billion people. In 1960, the earth's population was just 3 billion whereas back in 1930 it was 2 billion. We are projected to reach 8 billion people in 2024 and 9 billion by 2050!! Remember the size of the earth does not increase. The forests and natural resources of the earth do not increase. They remain the same. But by increasing our population so much we burden our Mother Earth to the point where it may implode. For example, in the Amazon around 17% of the forest has been lost in the last 50 years.

Instead, we should be pooling our resources to explore other habitable planets and sending people there to live. The circumference of Earth at the equator is about 24,902 miles (40,075 km), but from pole-to-pole — the meridional circumference — Earth is only 24,860 miles (40,008 km) around. This shape, caused by the flattening at the poles, is called an oblate spheroid. Mind you, not all of the earth is currently livable. Of this about 70.8 % of the earth's surface is covered with water, meaning that we humans have to manage to live on 29.2 per cent of the earth. The remaining 29.2% (148.94 million km2, or 57.51 million sq mi) not covered by water consists of mountains, deserts, plains, plateaus, and other land forms.

India's estimated population for 2015 stands at 1.25 billion. India alone adds 15.5 million people every year. Its size is 3,287,590 km. At this same size of land surface, India's population in 1950 was about 350 million and in 1970, it was 539 million. Our Mother India is groaning with the weight. How long can she sustain this? Shall we not have mercy on the melting glaciers, the holy rivers which sustain so much life, the forests, the precious God-given wild life, the land which bears us? The US is three times bigger in size at 9,857,306 km^2 but it has a population of about 321 million. Other nations too, who are growing faster than India, need to control their populations. There is a false pride in having a population bigger than others. What matters is having the highest quality of life, morally, spiritually and economically.

We must aim to have the best living standards for all people and all species. Shall we not save the bees that are dying in the millions? Shall we not save the tigers that number just 3200 in the wild now? Shall we not save the magnificent polar bears? Shall we not save the majestic lion, king of the jungle? What about the elephants hunted for their tusks? What about the rhinoceros also hunted for their horns? Shall we not save them? Shall our children, grand children and their descendants only see wildlife in photos, movies, books and cages and not have the privilege of seeing these great animals in their natural habitat just because we did not take care of them? Every bee that dies, we die with it. Every tiger that dies, we die with it. Every elephant that dies, we die with it. We move ever closer to extinction when we fail to ensure the survival of other species.

Health care:

Health ministries, health departments and hospitals should change to being holistic. What do I mean by this? What I mean is that all hospitals especially government hospitals should embrace all forms of healing and not just one system of healing. When a person walks into a hospital, he or she should have a **choice** of allopathic treatment, herbal medicine, Chinese acupuncture, alternative medicines, Tibetan medicine, acupressure, Indian ayurvedic medicine, reflexology, Khasi herbal medicine and so on. Tax payers' money should not be used to propagate and fund just one system of medicine. It is not fair. Let the patients decide which suits them best. Receiving government funding will help other forms of healing to raise their standards and testing methods to world class levels in the way that allopathy alone has benefited. Health care should ideally be free for all. Where will the money come from? I tell you that if there is no corruption and if there are high transparency standards, there will be enough funds for this. It is when corruption sets in that money becomes a problem. Free health care without the highest levels of transparency will not work.

Gold:

Every person should have at least part of their savings in gold. Every nation should have at least part of its currency fixed to gold. Why? Gold is universal. Currencies are not. When Iceland ran into financial problems, its currency, the Icelandic krona collapsed. When Russia was hit by sanctions recently, its Rouble plunged. When Greece faced their worst financial crisis, the Greeks were allowed to withdraw just 60 Euros per day from their banks. In an emergency, nobody would touch the krona or the rouble. But you could easily have sold your gold if you had some. Who gets hurt most when currencies fall? It is the poor, pensioners, single parents, students, farmers, low income groups and the weak. The well to do can ride out the crisis. Gold is the best hedge for the poor even when prices are down as it is now. Let me explain. Take India for example, the country where I live in. This beloved country India is home to more poor people than anywhere else on earth. In 2011, about 179.6 million people lived in India below the poverty line. In 1947 when the Indian people got independence, an ounce of gold was $43. Today as I write this book, it is

$1097 an ounce, an increase of 2551 per cent. The Indian rupee on the other hand fell from being Rs. 1 = one dollar in 1947 to Rs. 63.68 = one dollar today in July 2015, a collapse of 6368 per cent. To recap, in the same period from 1947 to 2015, gold has risen by 2551 per cent whereas the Rupee has fallen by 6368 per cent. This explains why Indians are the largest buyers of gold in the world. In fact, the current low prices of gold are a marvellous buying opportunity for Central Banks and Governments to fix part of their currency to gold.

To summarize, my preferred government would be one which incorporates some of the following policies:-

- Consensus government (preferably a parliament with only independents or to begin with an all-party government)
- Transparency (zero tolerance for corruption)
- A surplus budget with no national debts
- Free education for the poor
- Free health care for the poor
- Fully convertible currency
- Protection of the environment
- Afforestation
- Control over population
- And a return to a partial gold standard

Conclusion - Final Thoughts 19

Besides my beloved Grandparents and Parents, these are the great people who have had a deep spiritual influence on me - St. John Bosco and the Salesians of India, (Watch the movie St. John Bosco – Mission to Love, DVD Movie 2004. Beautifully filmed in Italy, this moving and touching movie depicts the many challenges that Don Bosco had to overcome from his childhood till he founded his religious society), Loreto Nuns, Lord Jesus and Mother Mary, Lord Buddha, Mother Teresa, Mahatma Gandhi, Stanley Nichols Roy, Frank Buchman, Captain John and Jeane Faber, many outstanding friends in Moral Re-Armament which is now called Initiatives of Change, Dr. Vinod Mittal and his family, Nisargadatta Maharaj and Anna Hazare.

The world has seen throughout history great Divine beings, Enlightened Ones, Prophets, Masters, Religious Teachers, Reformers and philosophers from all religions. Some of the names are Lord Buddha, Lord Jesus, Lord Ram, Lord Krishna, Confucius, Lau Tzu, Aristotle, Plato, Prophet Muhammad, Martin Luther, John Wesley, Baha'u'llah, Mahatma Gandhi, Emperor Asoka, Abraham Lincoln, Nelson Mandela, Martin Luther King Jr, William Wilberforce, Zoroaster, Adi Shankaracharya, Haji Ali, Sufi saints, Baba Amte, Guru Nanak, Sant Kabir, Sant Tukaram, Lord Mahavira, John Locke, John Calvin, Fyodor Dostoevsky, Billy Graham, Voltaire, Frank Buchman, Mother Teresa, Nisargadatta Maharaj, Pope John Paul II, Eckhart Tolle, Archbishop Desmond Tutu, Anna Hazare, Dalai Lama, Thich Nhat Hanh, Pope Francis, Sri Sri Ravi Shankar, Franklin Graham, Joel Osteen, Rick Warren, Richard Bach, Malala and Amma. Have an open heart and mind. Read all of them. I tell you again that it is like eating a plate of the most delicious fruits instead of eating just one particular fruit all your life. Remember your ultimate goal and purpose in life is to be happy with God forever here on earth and in heaven. So get to your goal as fast as you can. All else are pointers and signposts for you on the Way. I apologise if inadvertently there are worthy names missing. Trust me; I hold all of them in great respect and reverence. All of them point to the Eternal One.

When we arrive at Heaven or Paradise, there will be those whom we do not know or recognize, sitting next to God. We do not recall them from the pages of history. We will wonder who they are and why they are so extraordinary that they are seated next to the Everlasting One. They will be the special ones who while on earth have intensely studied and understood the true nature of God. While we spent our years studying other things, which in any case would end with our death, they meditated for many years on the unique character of God. Like him, they remained Silent. Like him, they never speak nor write. Like him, they practise stillness, yet everything gets done. Like him, they remained formless living in solitude in the mountains or in the forests or amongst us but unrecognized. Like him, they remained Unknown. Like him, they never hurt anyone. Like him, they are always Happy and Content. Like him, they have all that they need without being attached.

Final Thoughts

The Sure Road to Happiness

To find the Path to Happiness, you must know who you really are
You must find out who you were, before you were born
You were never born, you will never die
You are Formless, You are the Void
Before you spoke and learnt a language
You spoke the language of the Eternal
That language is Silence
It is the only language which will live forever
Relearn that language; it is one of the secrets to Happiness

Fall in love with silence; after all, it is what you spoke when you were in the womb of your mother
Learn the art of being perfectly still; it is the second secret to Happiness
It is amazing to think that stillness is the fastest speed known
We believe that in being still, we go nowhere
And yet the truth is when we are still, we reach the presence of the Creator
Faster than the speed of light or sound is stillness
The moment we are still, we arrive in front of God
The Eternal One is the Creator, the Maker, the Great Spirit
The Collective Mind, the Source of All Things
As long as we are still, we remain in that Divine Presence
It is like being in a royal court or like being with a president
Though trillions of times greater in majesty and splendour
Stillness attracts and draws all to itself
Like the Himalaya mountains
They do not move but thousands go to climb them
Like the Alps
They too do not move, yet, they are so admired and so visited
Like all sea shores that go nowhere
Yet, millions flock to them every year
We learn about the personality of God by looking closely at nature
Nature, in all its beauty and splendour, teaches us about the Creator
Empty your mind and you receive true Wisdom
Empty your mind and unspeakable Joy floods in
Empty your outer self and you gain everything
This is the third secret to Happiness
Become Nothing and you become All
Love means not hurting anyone at all
When we are silent and still and empty, we hurt no one

Not by our thoughts because our mind is empty
Not by our words because we are silent
Not by our actions because we are still
When our mind is blank, we do not entertain anger against others
When we are silent, we do not speak against others nor gossip about them
When we are still, we do no harm to anyone
Laugh and the whole world laughs with you
Smile and you make this earth a better place
Be kind and you are like the Gods
Do not speak when in anger
It is better to keep silent until the anger subsides
If you are often angry about things
Look inside; anger stems from lust
Be pure and you become all peace and calm
Aim to be as white as snow
As you practise meditation, your lust gradually subsides
Until you are free
If you are faithful to meditation, you need not make any effort
The Eternal will cleanse you, without even you realising it
The most powerful meditation is silence, stillness and emptiness
When you are sad, remind yourself that you are the limitless Ocean of Joy
When you are agitated, remember that you are peace and calm
When you are disturbed, recall that you are not the snow but the mountain of tranquility
Reject any negative thoughts about yourself
Just be patient; the bad temptations will go away after some time
Your normal state is bliss
Any other state than that is false, untrue and will pass
Be cheerful, because you are Joy itself

Sadness has no business being in you
Kick it out
When you are facing financial difficulties, evoke your Divine Heritage and claim your right through prayers
If you are truly practising the meditation of silence, stillness and emptiness, you will never be in want
You will have all and more than you need
God is extremely generous to those who are loyal to Him
Set the highest standards for yourself
Be the best in whatever you do
Be honest; Be punctual; Be sincere
Corruption is genocide of the poor
Corruption is the worst human rights violation
Earn your wealth by integrity, by hard work, by the highest quality and by following moral and spiritual principles
If you are rich, create as many jobs as you can
Let others share from your prosperity
Don't take a bribe, you politicians and you government servants
You live off others' suffering when you are crooked
The money you steal belongs to the people
Many villages still have no basic electricity
Many people have no jobs
Many people have no houses
Many cannot feed themselves or their families
They barely survive because of your corruption
Many commit suicide because of your theft
You will carry only yourself to the grave
Nothing else; not your money; not your fancy house; none of your possessions
The cry of the poor reaches the throne of God
It is these poor who will judge you on the other side

You may feel you enjoyed your ill gotten wealth for 80 odd years
Think about your suffering for billions of years after that
Be quick to say sorry when you make mistakes
Make amends and put right your wrongdoing
Humility is the hallmark of greatness
Take care of other species; Take care of all life
Can we create even one magnificent lion? No!
Can we create even one royal tiger? No!
There are just a few tigers left
Who will protect them?
Protect the Creator's architecture and design
It is exquisite; Don't tamper with it
Why do we have to level the hills and mountains?
How long will we keep cutting the trees?
If we mess about with the earth's cooling system
Our planet home will become too hot
The forests keep the earth's temperature cool
But half of the world's forests have vanished
The Antarctica is our air-conditioner
It is melting
The Arctic is our air-conditioner
Dig in it and peril, Oh mankind
The spectacular polar bear is struggling to survive
One by one volcanoes will explode as the core of the earth heats up
When the little bees start dying, then the countdown to mankind's disappearance has begun
We are heading towards extinction if we don't stop our madness
It requires enough of us to begin living the Divinity within us
For mankind to survive
It requires many of us to change
So that future generations can live on

If we want to save the world, we need to uncover our Real Self first
No one can do it for you
You have to begin the search yourself
Start today; Start now; Don't delay
Keep climbing up the mountain of Happiness
Do not stop until you reach the pinnacle
The Highest dwells inside you
So scale the mountain within

Oneness

Complete Oneness is with you here and now. All you need to do is take it. This is the most important goal in life. Nothing else matters. At this very moment and every moment BE AWARE of your Being One with the Eternal. Focus and remain in that Oneness as long as possible. This is the greatest Secret of all, the secret of the Empty Mind. It is like Dark Matter in the Universe which attracts and draws everything into it. All Grace and goodness flows into the Empty Mind. This is the Kingdom of God, Nirvana and Self Realisation.

When you read or research about some of the Masters or Saints mentioned in this book, you will find some wrongs in them which will put you off. But just like you ignore the torn, dirty pages of a good book and focus on the content, so too ignore their mistakes (which could be also due to the period or the times when they lived) and focus on the essence of what they are teaching.

I give my special blessings on all who read this book and practise what is taught therein. May you grow spiritually, ever closer to Oneness with the Eternal. May you and your loved ones be protected physically at all times from all sicknesses, injuries, accidents and harm. May you prosper in life many times over and be successful in whatever you do. May you be always be happy and experience the greatest of joy in this life itself. May you always receive forgiveness when you slip up and do wrong. May you avoid doing harm to yourself and others as you go on in life. And may you uncover the Divinity within you so that you live on for all Eternity.

Be Always Aware of your Divinity - of who you are!!

Eternal One, I pray for complete total oneness with Thee. I wish to be always one with Thee for the rest of my earthly life. This is my deepest and greatest wish.

Note: I have tried my utmost to use material only in the public domain i.e. matter published before 1923. If however, I have inadvertently infringed on some copyright, please let me know so that it can be removed.